Upstart!

Visual Identities for Start-ups and New Businesses

gestalten

Introduction
by Anna Sinofzik

Today's brands are many things. They are start-ups and spin-offs. Storytellers. Prop stylists. Sandwich makers. Pancake artists. They are purveyors of quality drugs pp. 30–37 and initiators of agave cultivation programs pp. 222–231. They are avid promoters of life's little pleasures. Advocates of free-range fantasies. Distributors of letter-pressed loyalty cards. Stamp champs pp. 92–93. Prolific paper cup producers. They are one-man shows and comprehensive, collaborative projects.

Today's brands are creative platforms, poised between playfulness and professionalism, between artisanal jam pp. 216–217 and pink jello pop pp. 212–213. They marry vino with vinyl pp. 234–235 and synthesize wine into sound with the help of self-made machines pp. 126–127. They fly over farms to bring us picturesque photographs of their products' provenance pp. 68–75. They have the hottest chickens on the block pp. 190–193 and some secret ingredients in their style sauce.

Today's brands stir emotions and make mouths water and hearts beat faster. Some are minimalist to the max. Others are opulent, with a touch of irony inherent in their too-muchness. Some take normcore to a decidedly nondescript level in these overdesigned times. Many draw inspiration from practically everything, including old family albums pp. 140–147 and kitschy cats pp. 240–241, and surprise us with a range of references, imagery, and ideas.

Today's brands counter stale style and cookie-cutter commercialism with the idiosyncrasies of imperfection. They offer oddly shaped artisanal cookies and visual identity systems that are flexible enough to let the businesses behind them breathe and develop. Breaking through antiquated corporate culture, they celebrate diversity and provide a blank canvas onto which we can project our own aspirations. While few still presume to pedal perfect dreams or fixed lifestyles, many meet us on eye-level, as suppliers of the products that become part of our lives.

Today's brands are designed to sell (dog biscuits, dairy products, craft beers, haute couture, repair and renovation services, attractive holiday accommodations). But beyond that, they aim to engage and excite. They are inspired by the past, are very present, and forward-looking. Notwithstanding their small size, most are big-picture oriented; and even in minding their own business, they look beyond their backyards, with eyes on the prize.

Instead of targeting trends and consumers, today's brands are designed to speak to the people. Person-to-person. Because, above all, they are the people behind them: seasoned chefs and specialty butchers, creative beer brewers and coffee roasters, builders, bartenders, sommeliers, and mezcaleros. Adventurers and explorers, extended families, single moms, old childhood friends, newlyweds, and kindred spirits. Bon vivants on courier bikes, tried and true traditionalists, office acrobats, and tech nerds.

Today's brands are built by believers, those who remained steadfast in themselves and their missions even when the only other believers were their moms. And though today's believers may be carried forward by a bit of naiveté, they are smart enough not to mistake small for the new big. While staying business-minded, today's brands grow organically, rather than for growth's sake, enabling entrepreneurs to remain true to their original values.

Today's brands are not what they used to be. They do their best to do better.

Hula Del Hawaii

PARÁMETRO updates mid-century style to create a tropical aesthetic for the Hawaiian restaurant in Mexico.

Located in San Pedro Garza Garcia in Mexico, Hula del Hawaii serves sushi, burgers, and tacos with a tropical island vibe. Inspired by the travel culture of mid-century America, Parámetro's branding for the restaurant has a logotype reminiscent of motel signage from the 1950s, and vintage illustrations recycled as modern postcards. The designers also developed the iconography of a hula girl, palm trees and a wave-like pattern, that adds detail to all of their printed collateral, including menus, receipts, coasters, matchbooks, and takeaway bags. A pink and orange color palette with pops of deep blue were chosen to evoke the famous Hawaiian sunset.

Salón Sociedad

COMMUNAL's branding combines illustrations, old photographs, and period-inspired typography to celebrate the historic location of the gathering space.

Established for the employees of drinks corporation FEMSA, Salón Sociedad is a renovated gathering space where staff members and their families can get together in a warm and welcoming atmosphere. Communal developed the interior design and visual identity, which is inspired by the heritage of Sociedad Cuauhtémoc y Famosa, the complex where it is located and that originally served as a space for leisure and recreation. The designers created a series of illustrations and combined them with vintage photographs of the complex to reflect the historic environment. The logo system is inspired by typography popular at the time of the society's founding in 1918, and it is set within an arched frame representing the new and reconstructed hall.

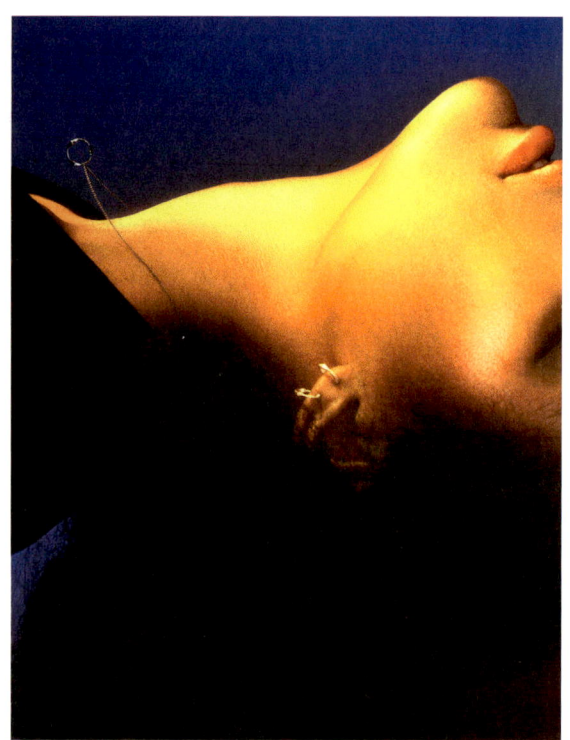
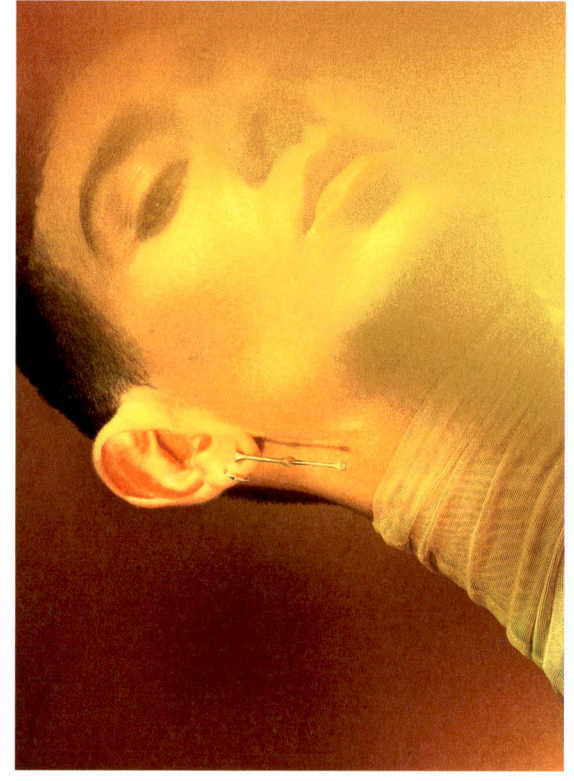

Savoir Joaillerie

PARASOL's tactile brand identity for the Berlin-based jeweler highlights the human aspect of her work to create a connection between product and customer.

Lou Andrea Savoir is a Parisian based in Berlin and the owner of, and maker behind, the jewelry brand Savoir Joaillerie. Savoir describes her work as both refined and sensual, and she is known for her collaborations with other makers and artists. Through these collaborations, her goal is not just to make wearable accessories, but to show the expressive potential of modern jewelry. Parasol helped Savoir distinguish her business by creating a visual identity that celebrates emotion and the importance of human touch. They developed a bespoke typeface for use across all materials, a tactile wooden jewelry box intended to surprise and delight when opened, and notecards upon which a personal note can be handwritten.

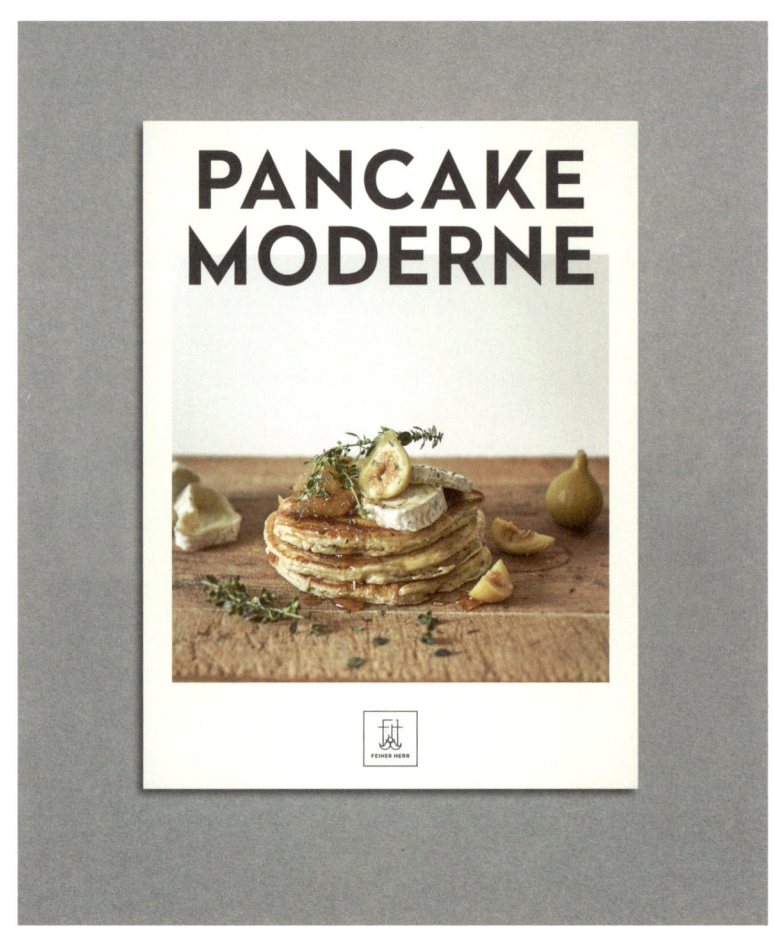

Feiner Herr

SEBASTIAN HAUS and **HOJIN KANG** embrace a contemporary interpretation of art deco graphics for the brand identity of the Berlin food truck.

The Berlin-based food truck Feiner Herr (named for a German phrase that means both gentleman and a gourmet) serves up a modern take on the traditional pancake. To create a branding that resonates with this culinary endeavor, the designers took inspiration from art deco style to design an identity system based on geometric shapes and fine lines. A line-art logo personifies the namesake, and line and spot illustrations create slightly abstracted patterns for use across menus, stationery, and signage. When developing ways of telling the brand story, Haus and Kang use traditional techniques for printed collateral, photography, and digital design to build a social media presence.

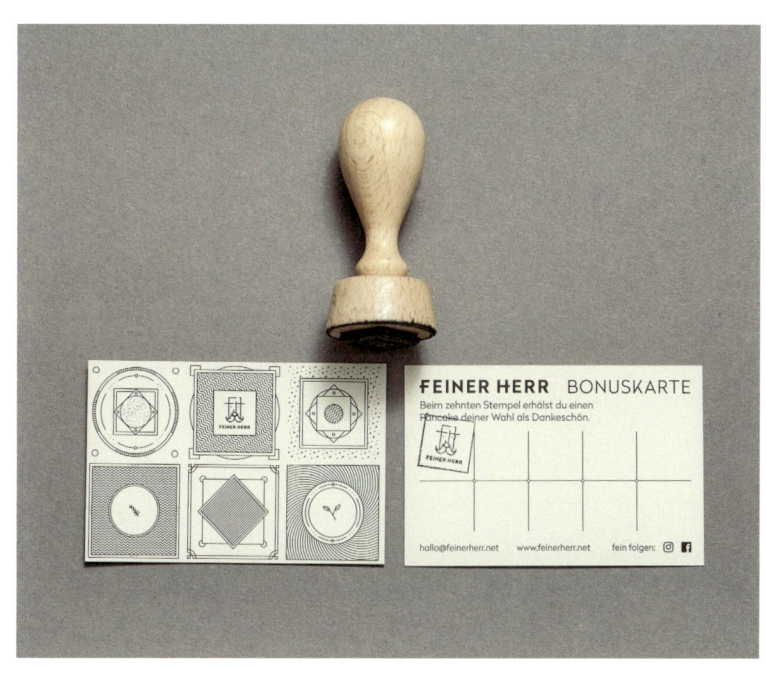

Eolo

ATLAS translates maritime signal flags into symbols and patterns for the Spanish seaside hotel.

Eolo hotel is located in the north of Majorca, on the maritime promenade in Puerto de Pollença. It offers breathtaking views of the bay and the many boats moored in the harbor. With such a strong connection to the sea, Atlas incorporates red and blue maritime signal flags into every aspect of Eolo's identity and design. The hotel owners have also renovated the exterior and interior of the building, allowing Atlas to apply the graphic elements in oversized versions to the facade, floors, walls, signage, and furniture in the guest rooms.

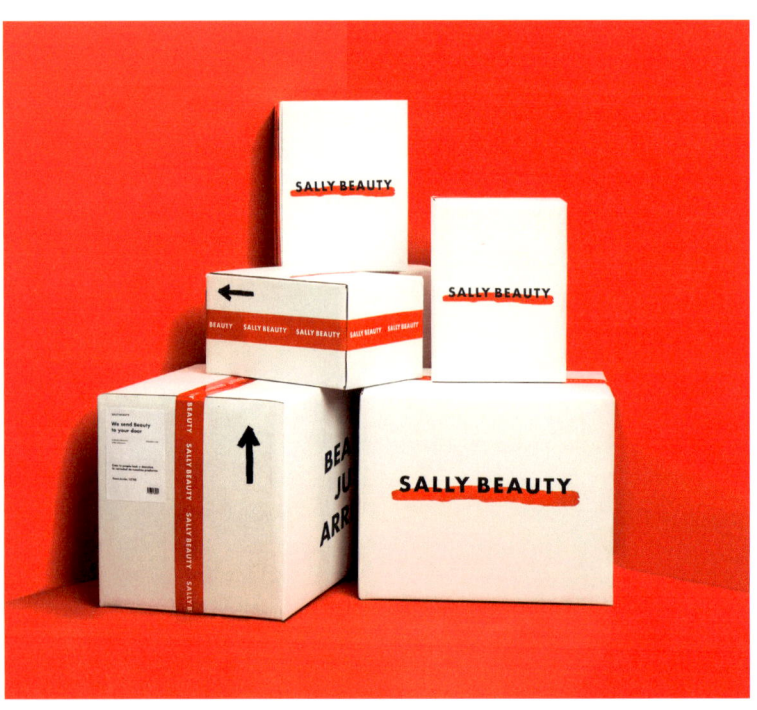

Sally Beauty Supply

While competitors present themselves polished to high-gloss perfection, this beauty giant stands out with a quirky new look designed by ANAGRAMA.

Since its founding in New Orleans in 1964, Sally Beauty Supply, with nearly 3,000 stores across the globe, has grown into the world's largest professional beauty retailer. For its rebrand, Anagrama focused on the company's core role as a trendsetter in skin, hair, and nail products, a position that requires it to evolve with every season. To work with the ever-changing nature of its business, Anagrama developed a logo that is at once neutral and flexible, timeless and ahead of the trends. A single smudge of lipstick produces a recognizable and playful graphic element. Instead of the flashy, perfectly retouched styles typically favored by the beauty industry, Sally Beauty Supply's new aesthetic is clean and simple.

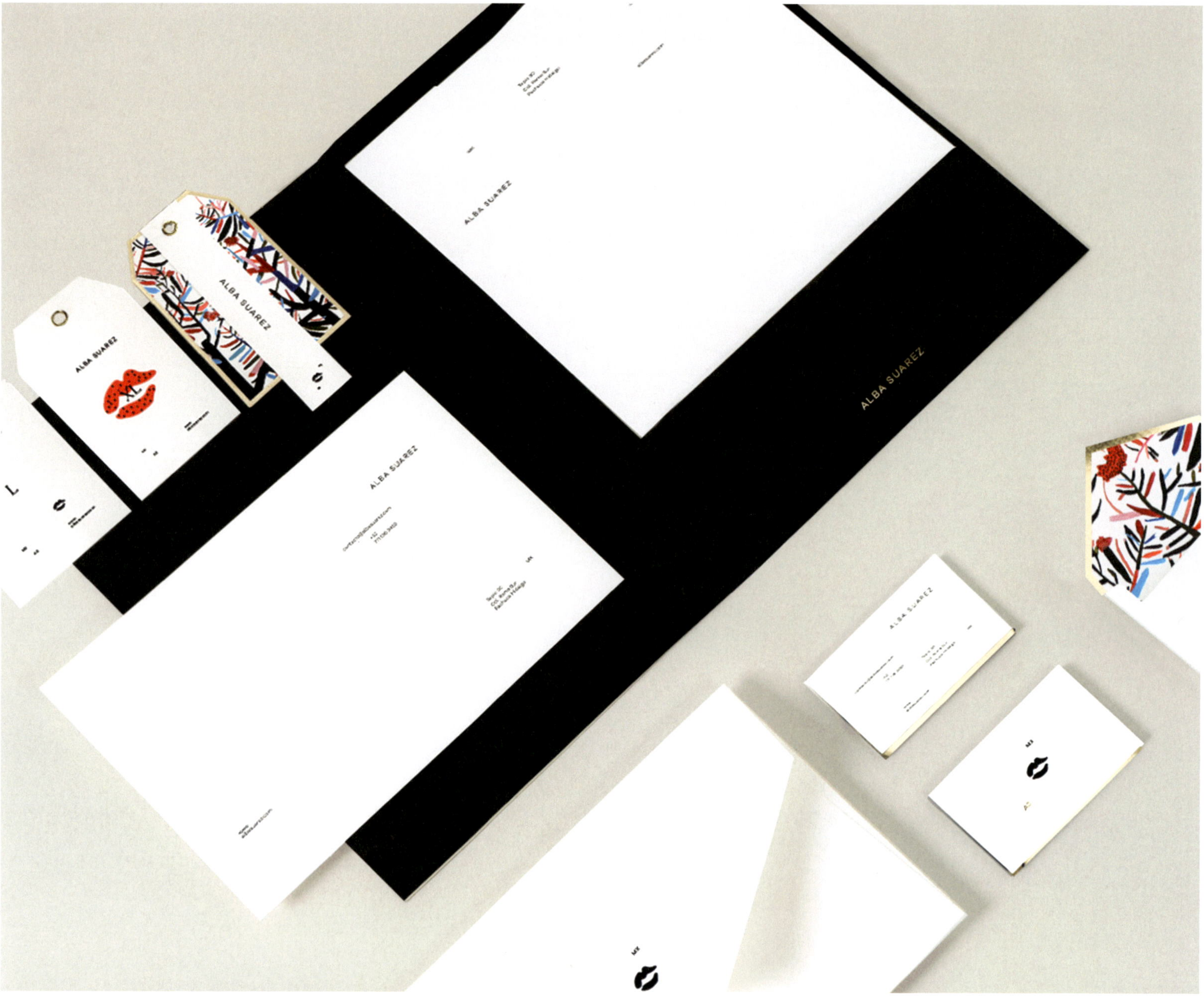

Alba Suarez

KARLA HEREDIA MARTINEZ's vibrantly illustrated identity encapsulates the wide-ranging tastes of the Mexican fashion brand's young clientele.

Alba Suarez is an emerging fashion brand with a focus on a young and diverse customer base. Mexican designer Karla Heredia Martinez developed a visual identity system that uses a hand-painted lips icon and simple typography in conjunction with a colorful and expressive nature-inspired illustration. The solution allows the evolving brand to develop in new directions, while maintaining a consistent message. Martinez designed individual tags for each product that are a variation on the same theme and in keeping with the customization trend.

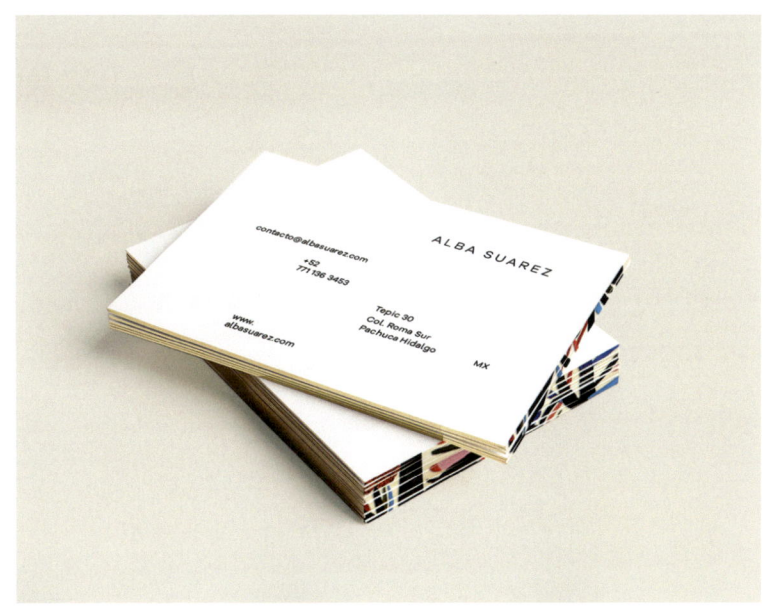

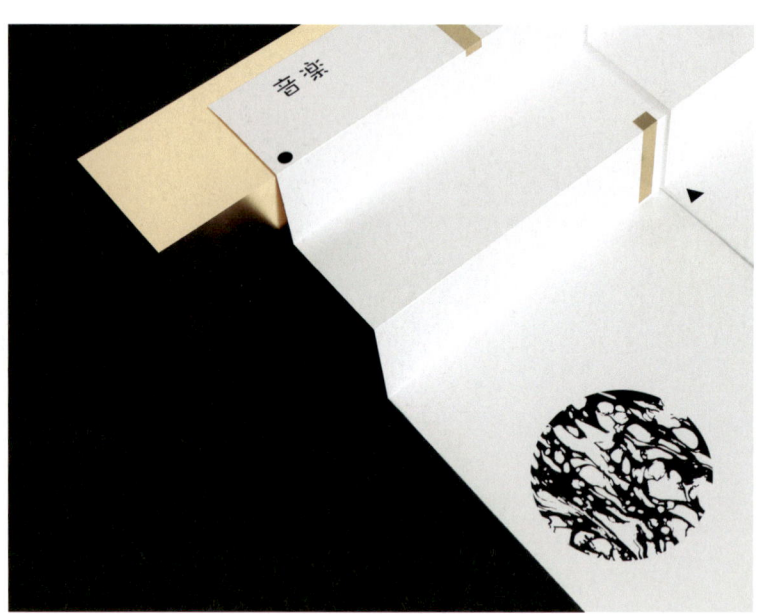

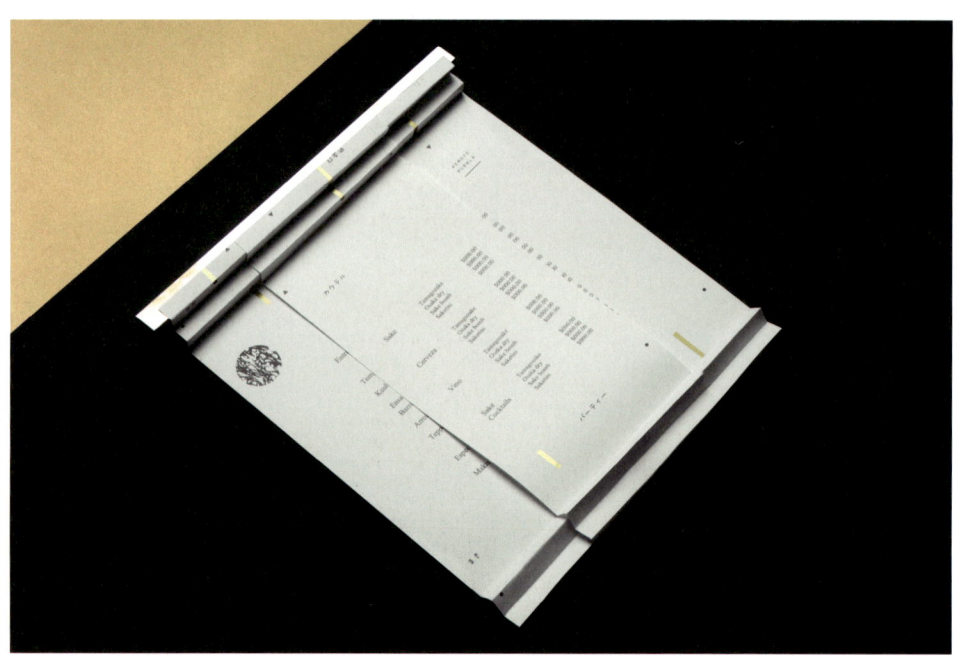

Remoto House

References to minimal art and modern Japanese architecture permeate _FUTURA_'s branding for this upscale restaurant.

Remoto House is an exclusive Japanese restaurant located in Puebla, Mexico. When developing the establishment's identity, Futura referenced the minimalist forms found in Tadao Ando's architectural work and Walter de Maria's art installations. The result is a dark, hard-edged identity system layered with an organically inspired icon. Gold foil stands out against the monochromatic color palette, and highlights text and visual details across all collateral, including wine labels, business cards, and chopsticks. It also references the orchestration of light in Ando's building structures.

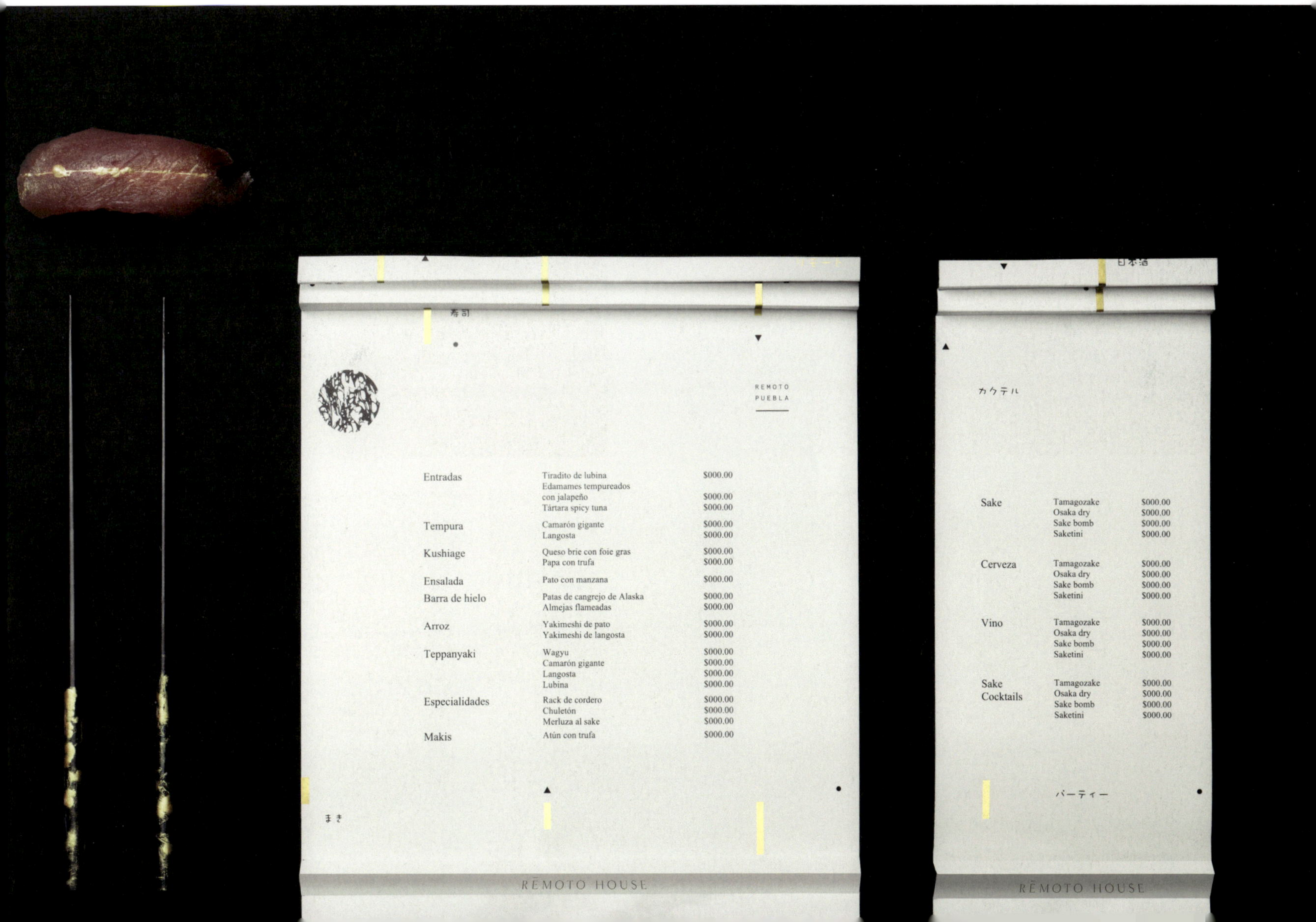

Gowanus Inn & Yard

<u>SAVVY STUDIO</u>'s branding for the neighborhood hotel marries classic Americana style with a contemporary sensibility.

Set in the heart of Brooklyn's revitalized Gowanus neighborhood, the Gowanus Inn & Yard is designed for both travelers and residents, with cozy yet luxurious rooms, common areas, a bar, and a restaurant. Savvy Studios' brand concept is expressed through the industrial aesthetics of the building that houses dark wood interiors and custom-made furniture, all of which are complemented by the minimal design of everything from menus to stationery. Together, these diverse elements reflect the vibrant spirit and optimism of quintessential Americana, and balance the past with the present.

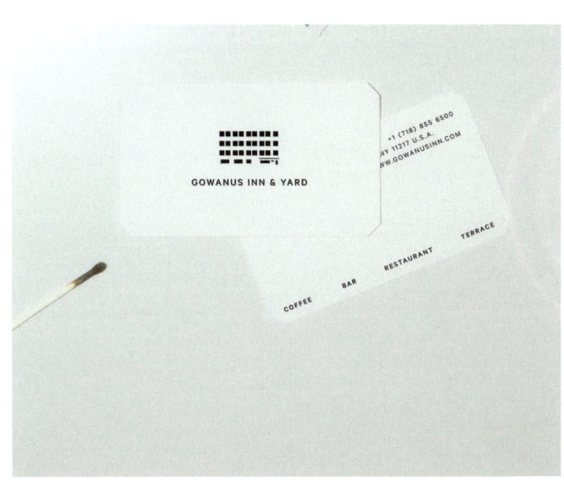
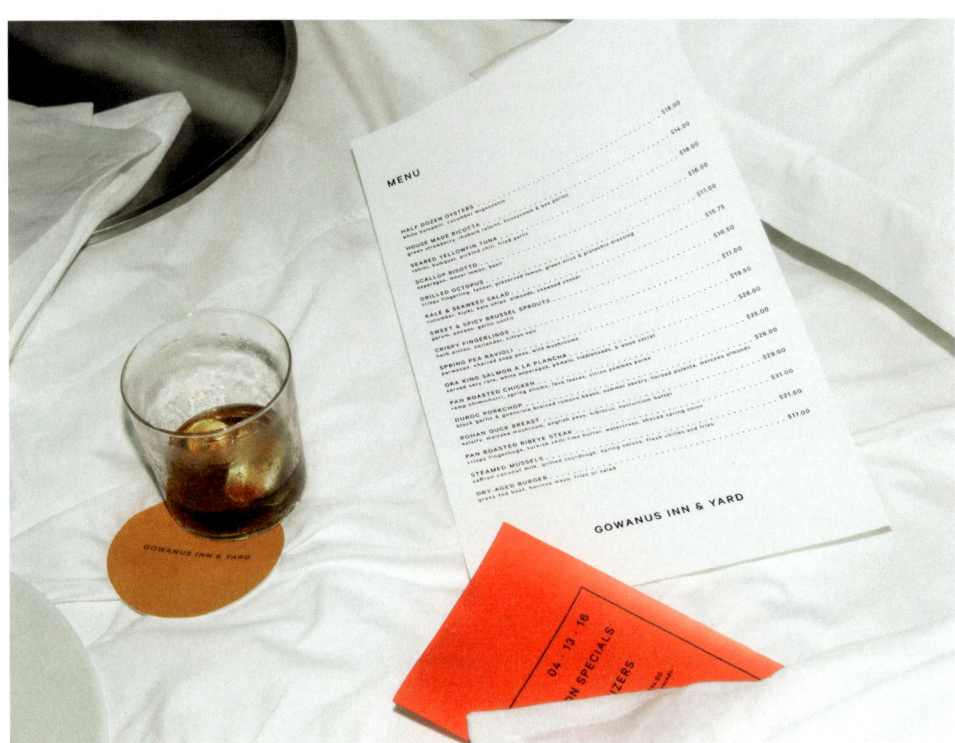

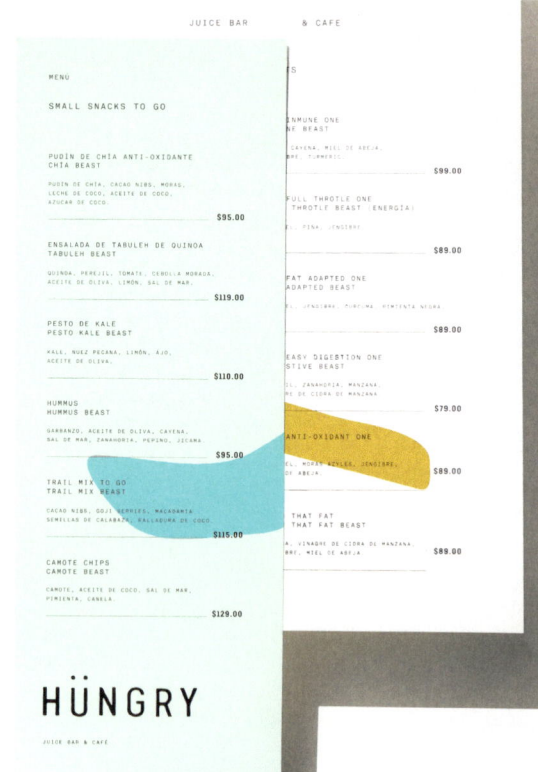

Hüngry Beast

SAVVY STUDIO's combination of crisp graphics and colorful brand photography promote the lighthearted spirit of the juice bar and health food cafe.

The menu at Hüngry Beast in Mexico City features dishes made with fresh ingredients, and prepared with creativity and joy, evoking a less serious attitude than many other health food cafes. Savvy Studio's identity system for the juice bar and cafe incorporates abstract shapes in the same colors as its food. This aesthetic is maintained across cups, boxes, napkins, and tote bags to add a pop of color while allowing the name to stand out. Bright and colorful photographs of the cafe's ingredients further emphasize Hüngry Beast's commitment to whole foods and to the health and happiness that eating well can bring.

Dig Inn

A restaurant chain focusing on community building gets a clever rebrand by *HIGH TIDE*.

The team behind New York's Dig Inn believes in the power of the communal table to bring people and ideas together over good food. Despite its commitment to serving fast and casual meals, the restaurant's food is grown locally and prepared lovingly. This successful combination eventually led to several new locations and the need to rebrand. High Tide redesigned the restaurant's collateral, including menus, signage, and packaging, inspired by the Dig Inn's minimal but cozy Scandinavian-style interior. The identity aligns with their mission as they continue to expand; and the idea of community and coming together is reinforced in many packaging choices, for example, the matchboxes, which need a pair to complete the full brand name.

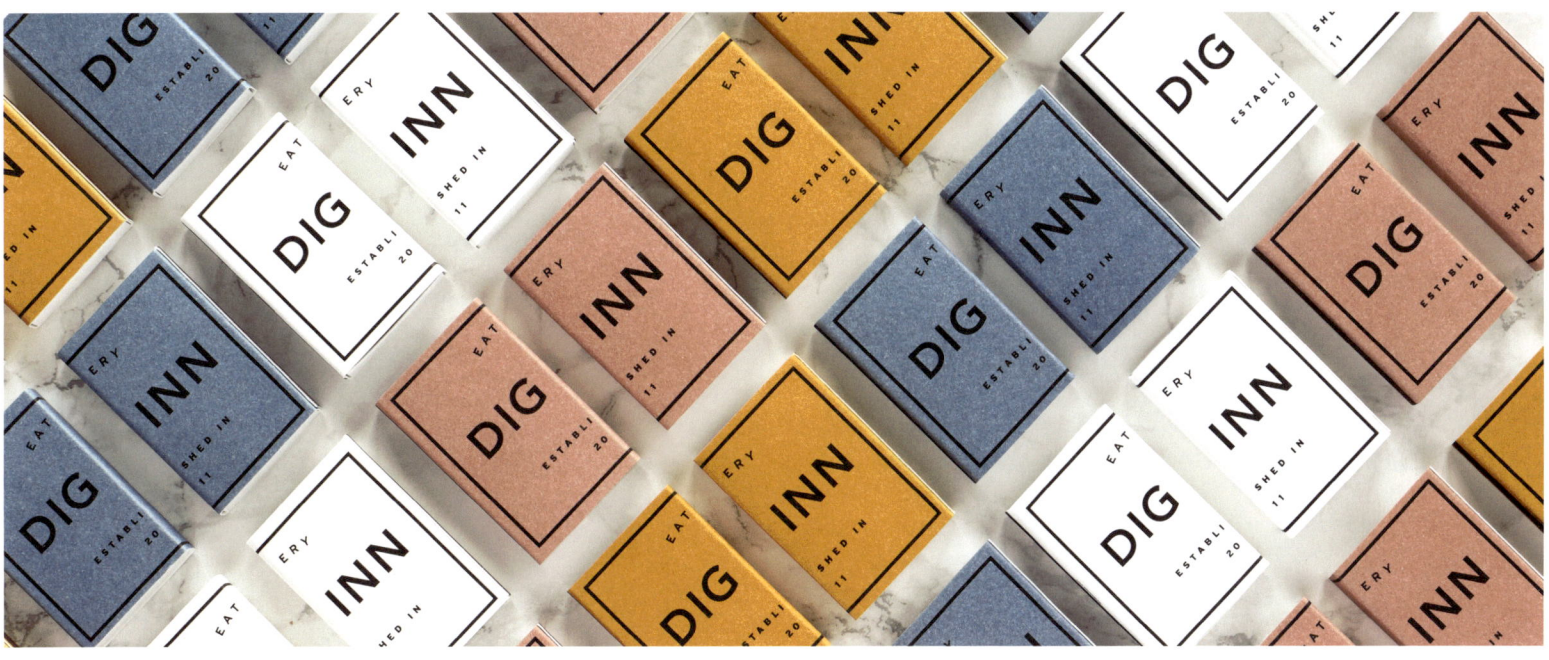

And The Friet

ANJE JAGER's illustrations celebrate the art of making french fries the Japanese way.

And The Friet specializes in European-style french fries. After many years of success as a food truck in Tokyo, the business expanded into brick-and-mortar restaurants in Japan and Korea. Anje Jager's pen and ink line drawings for the packaging and collateral depict a series of portraits of a family, with both the front and back views of each person's head. The distinctive illustrations help unify the brand's food trucks and international restaurant locations. When the company created its dried friet snack, Jager expanded the family with five more children's portraits to represent each new flavor. In addition to the packaging, Jager's drawings are on the oil and mayonnaise packets, snacks, tote bags, and signage.

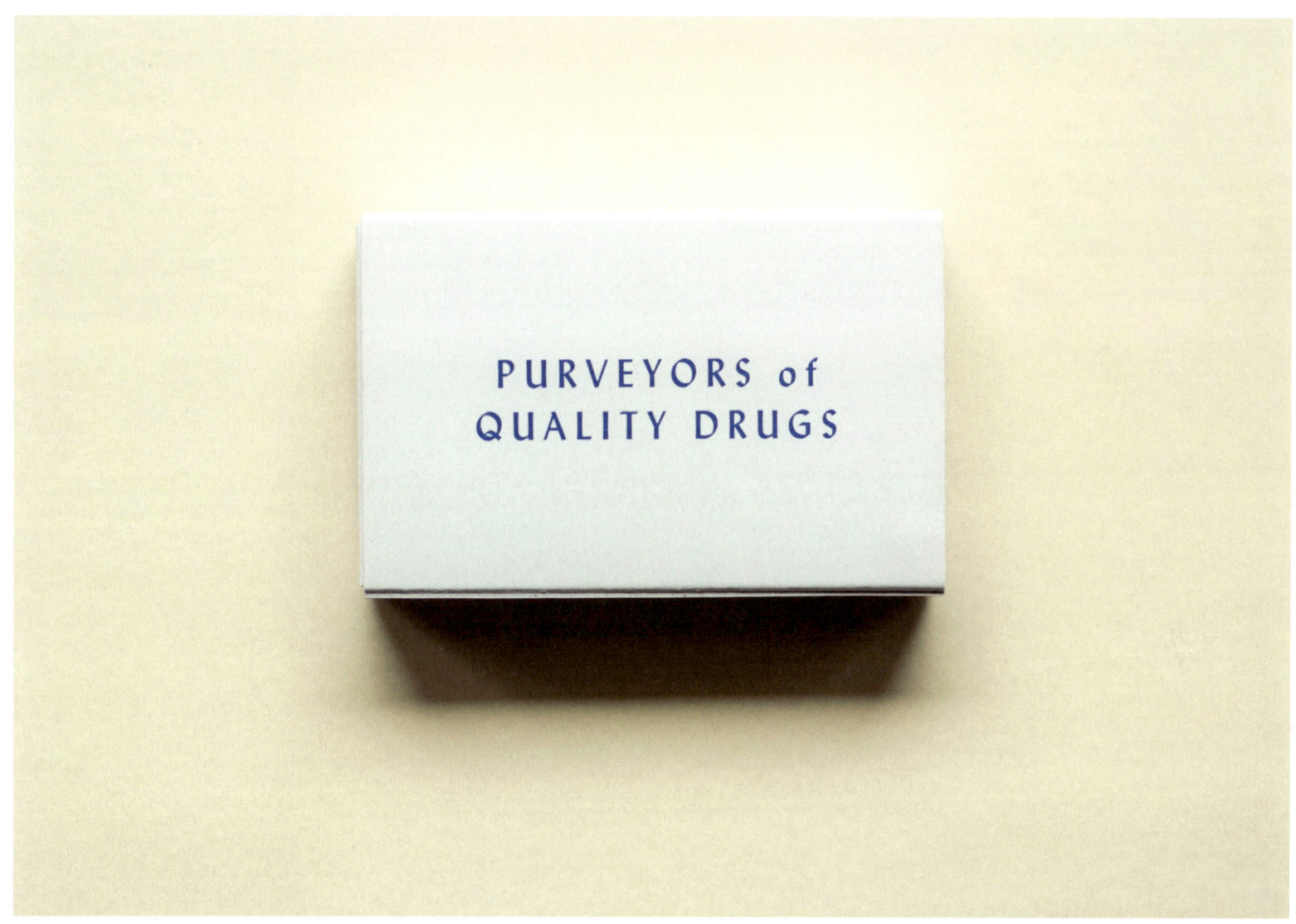

CASE STUDY: Serra

Portland-based cannabis dispensary Serra has a mission to "set the bar for progressive pot culture." Designed by *OFFICIAL MFG. CO.* and brimming with both art and agricultural references, the brand reaches out to those who, along with a good high, appreciate design that exceeds the industry standard.

In Italian, serra means greenhouse, but the stores of the same name present themselves in a bold blue inspired by minimal artist Yves Klein. In the art world, Serra is the surname of Richard, another minimal artist and contemporary of Klein. Entering a Serra boutique, one finds display cases and cabinets similar to those installed in museums and art galleries. Presented within are one-off artisanal objects produced by local creatives. Taking a decidedly artistic approach, the sophisticated pot boutique steers clear of the shady stoner image that many of its competitors cannot get out of their system.

"We wanted Serra to be artful, from the name, to the design, to the products on our shelves," says Cambria Benson Noecker, brand director at Groundworks Industries, Serra's parent company. She developed the strategy and positioning in close collaboration with Portland-based design firm Official Mfg. Co. (OMFGCO), whose Co-founder and Creative Director Jeremy Pelley adds: "The most important thing when developing a brand is to figure out why it exists in the first place. Everything else falls out of that."

According to Benson Noecker, Serra's raison d'être was to fill a yawning gap in the market. "I had gotten into the cannabis industry through another channel and the more time I spent in that realm, the clearer it became that

32

> "We wanted to create a beautiful experience that allowed our customers to be put at ease and enable them to explore cannabis."

there wasn't a brand or retail experience that resonated with me," she recalls. The experience she envisioned would not only break the stoner stereotype and be more attractive to a discerning clientele, but make the culture around cannabis more socially acceptable. "We wanted to create a beautiful experience that allowed our customers to be put at ease and enable them to explore cannabis," Pelley adds. "In a way, Serra was conceived as a gateway store for those that were curious, but didn't want to go to a weed shop." With all aspects of the design, the brand's makers wanted to push the limits of what pot culture can be.

According to Benson Noecker, all projects helmed by Groundworks Industries aim to "push limits through leading." The vertically aligned company integrates cannabis production (through its own grow brand Pruf Cultivar), processing (through extraction and a workshop that creates its edibles), retail (through Serra and its sister brand Electric Lettuce), and distribution. The company also takes responsibility for all respective accounting, compliance, and human resource services and marketing measures.

With Serra, Groundworks Industries caters to a growing crowd of conscientious consumers. "Our customers want to know what farming method is used when they buy their produce," Benson Noecker says. "They are savvy consumers who appreciate good design and quality in all other areas. If they want to know what ingredients are in their skincare, why not in their cannabis?"

Serra opened three stores in 2016: the first one in Eugene, Oregon, an approximate two-hour ride away from Portland; the second in the city's retail and residential district Belmont; and the most recent addition, the flagship in downtown Portland. By the end of the year, the progressive pot boutique had already been applauded on the pages of many of the world's leading design magazines. "The most sophisticated cannabis dispensary in the city, if not the country," *Wallpaper** wrote. The architectural and interior design platform *Dezeen* focused on the impressive space, mentioning the

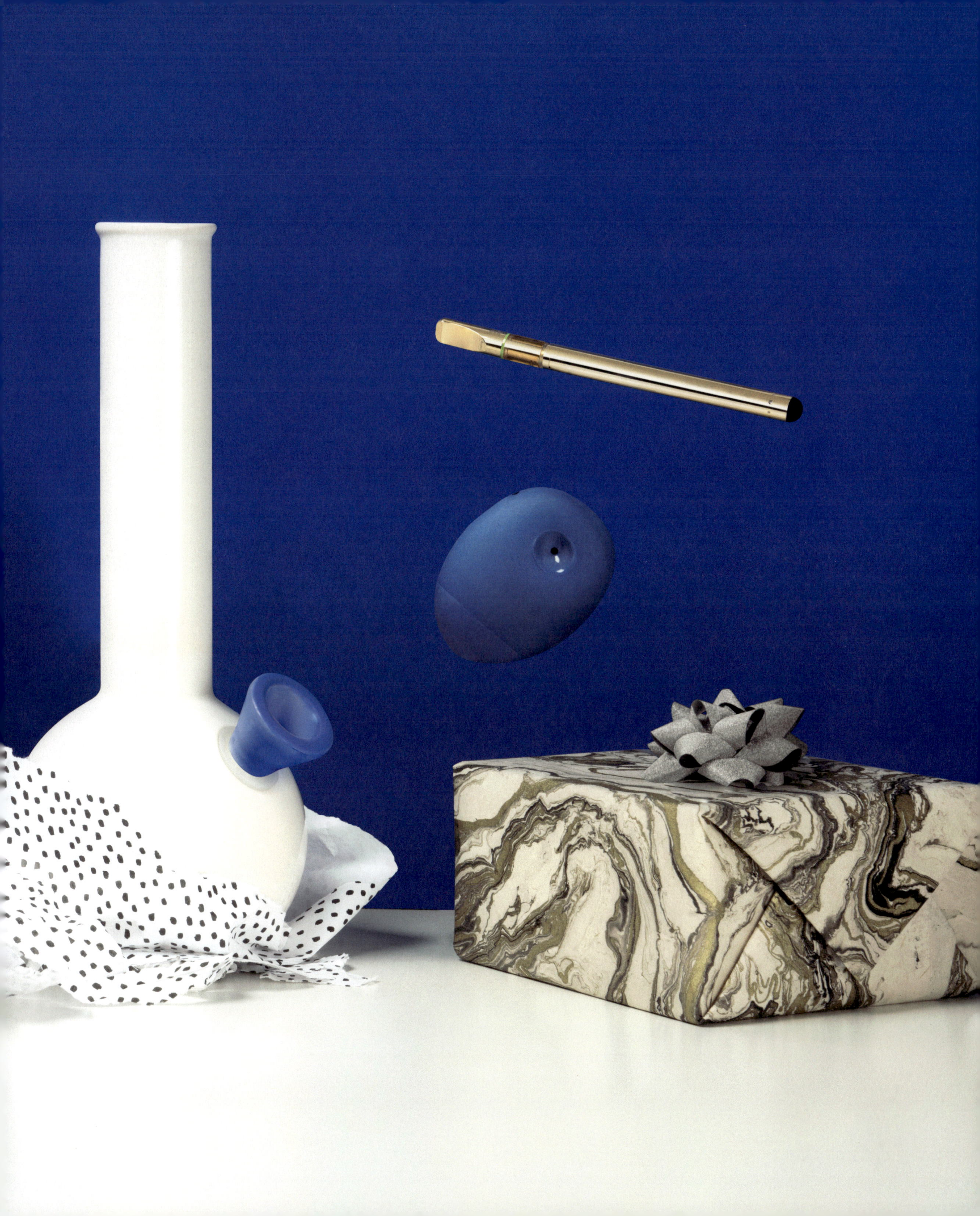

"Variations of Serra's signature blue crop up everywhere, from the packaging and signage all the way to the store's fine selection of non-pot products."

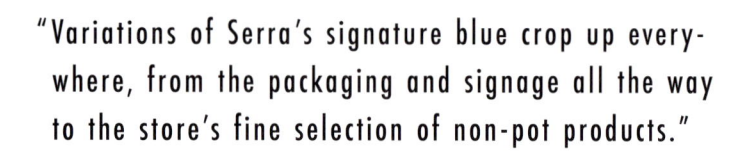

large-scale lighting fixtures by local designer Matthew McCormick, as well as OMFGCO's mesmerizing floor tiles, whose pattern is also taken up, for example, in the graphics of the packaging.

"Working with both print and interiors is our favorite thing to do—it makes it possible to let the brand speak in so many different ways," Pelley comments. With support from multidisciplinary design firm JHL Studio in the execution, OMFGCO was responsible for the overall concept of Serra's retail spaces, which tie in with the Italian meaning of the brand's name. "We worked with traditional and humble materials of a greenhouse, and used them in elegant ways," Pelley explains. "For the custom shelving and display cases we chose wrought iron, wood, glass, and brass. We also tried to weave in the natural greenery of live plants into the store experience itself."

The 'elevated greenhouse' concept has been central to the entire visual identity exploration, say the designers. To elevate the experience, they looked into the art and lifestyle world for inspiration. "For the Serra logo, we created a custom sans serif typeface that would also live comfortably among today's fashion set," Pelley explains. "We also began writing lines to help the logo lock-up feel anchored and balanced, and added a little voice with tongue-in-cheek lines from the past, such as 'Purveyors of Quality Drugs.'"

OMFGCO had some drug experience before branding Serra. In fact, it had just completed the identity for a sleek and stylish vaporizer pen called Quill, which was also designed to speak to a sophisticated pot audience too. Serra, however, was the studio's first foray into the cannabis retail space. To facilitate the shopping experience and help newcomers navigate through the product range, the designers came up with a visual system centered around feelings. "Most cannabis shops simply lead with the technical information, which can be quite overwhelming even for the experienced smoker," Pelley argues. "Everyone knows how they want to feel though, so we figured it would be best to come up with feeling categories and create a series of graphic symbols for them. Once you know how you want to feel, these icons help guide the way to a consistent experience."

Asked about other specific challenges of designing in the cannabis industry, OMFGCO's co-founder and creative director points to the administrative chaos it involves. "It is just the wild west right now, when it comes to the laws, rules, and regulations—things are changing constantly, and you have to fend for yourself. We had lots of awkward design constraints on everything from the package design for the Serra/Woodblock chocolate bar to the space design and layout, like the required signage that we have to create for legal reasons. That sort of stuff is notoriously a wart on what is otherwise a nicely designed space. You just do your best to make something amazing, regardless of all the red tape."

OMFGCO was nifty enough to turn the red into blue; into that strong blue very close to Yves Klein's, which, according to Pelley, "proved to be beautiful, but a real pain in the production phase, as it was very difficult to make consistent across different mediums." It may not be one uniform shade, but variations of Serra's signature blue crop up everywhere, from the packaging and signage, all the way to the store's fine selection of non-pot products.

Many of these items are custom-made exclusives, produced in limited editions. Benson Noecker is always keen to collaborate with local artists and designers on wearables, houseware, and smoke accessories. The results include a series of bubble bongs by glass designer Gary Bodker, the Summerland x Serra Chongo, and an artisan clay pinch pot by Haley Ann Robinson. "I'm constantly exploring new artists through social media," Benson Noecker says. "The goal is to find or partner on pieces I would have on my shelf at home and that you shouldn't be able to tell if it's art or a pipe."

She shares that there are fresh product ideas in the pipeline already, as well as plans to open more Serra stores in the near future. With a new flagship Los Angeles dispensary, the brand is now beginning to expand beyond the Oregon region. "Is blue the new green?" one might ask, looking at Serra's success. "Do we perceive reality, or do we perceive our perception of reality?" Pelley asks back, assuming the voice of a very sophisticated pothead.

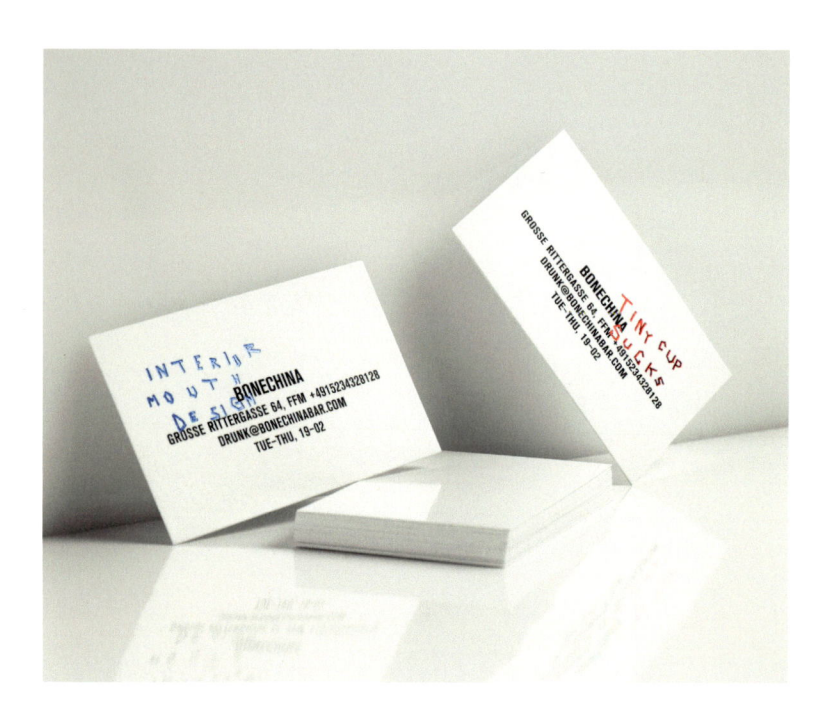

Bonechina

A bar with no bartender gets an unconventional identity system by design studio _DEUTSCHE & JAPANER_.

The experimental Bonechina bar in Frankfurt's Sachsenhausen neighborhood has neither a bar counter nor a bartender. Instead, customers blend their own drinks using premixed concoctions and an assortment of prepared garnishes. The tiny space seats just 12 guests and features custom-made tile walls and an elephant fountain spouting tonic water in the center. Deutsche & Japaner's branding highlights the bar's unconventional vibe. It communicates standard information, such as address and menu items, in a black sans serif font, with cryptic messages referring to the quirks of the bar in a colorful, hand-lettered script stamped on top.

39

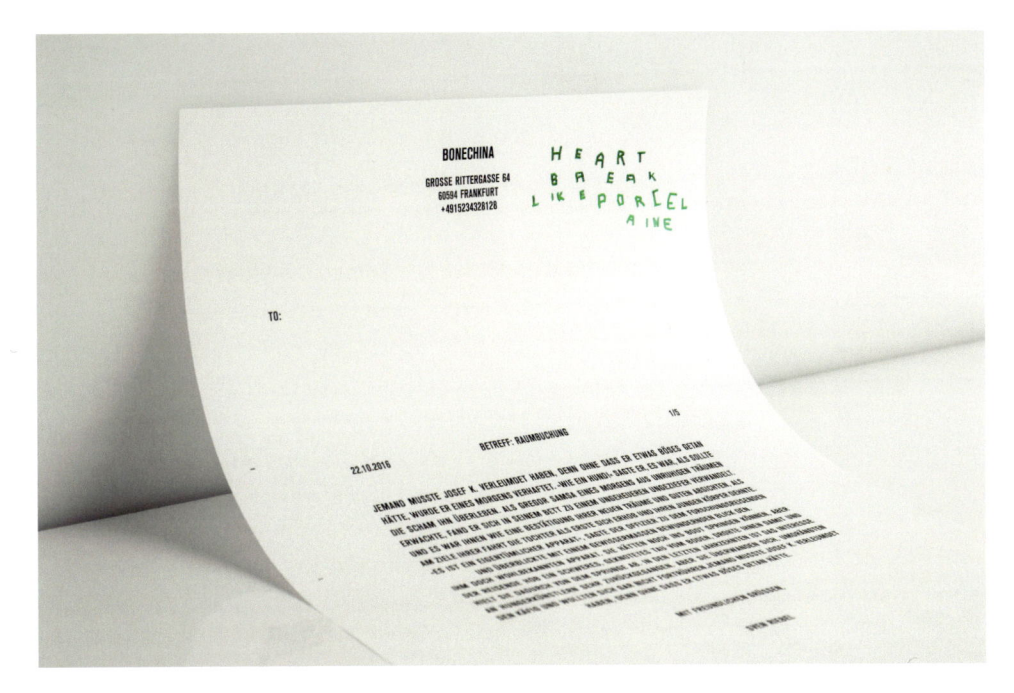

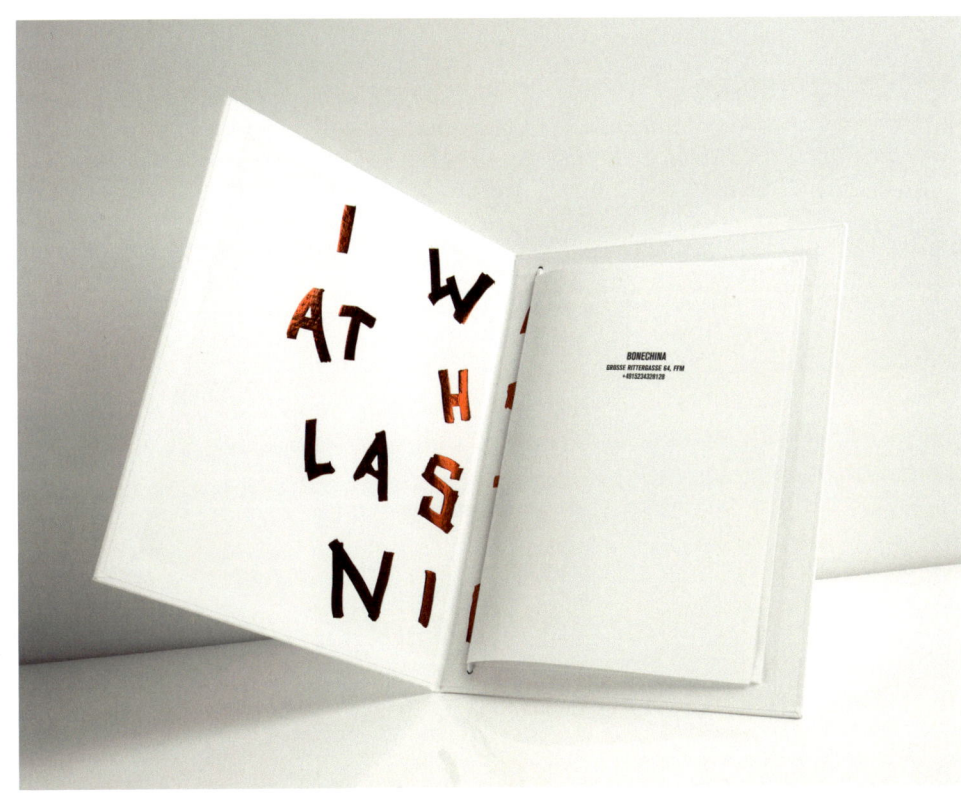

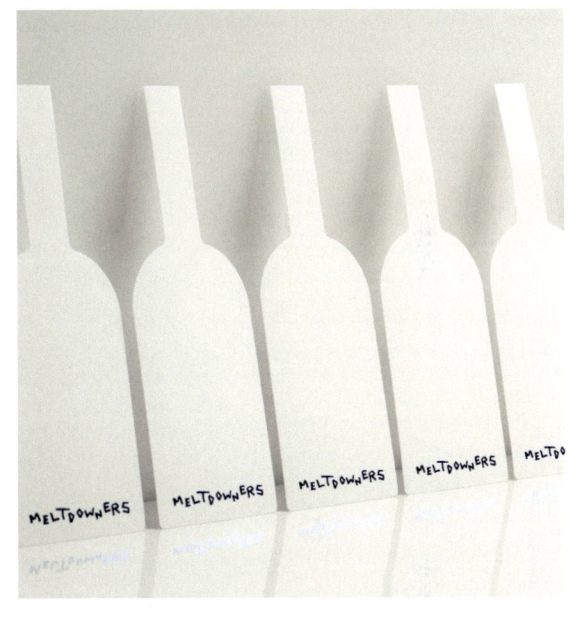

40

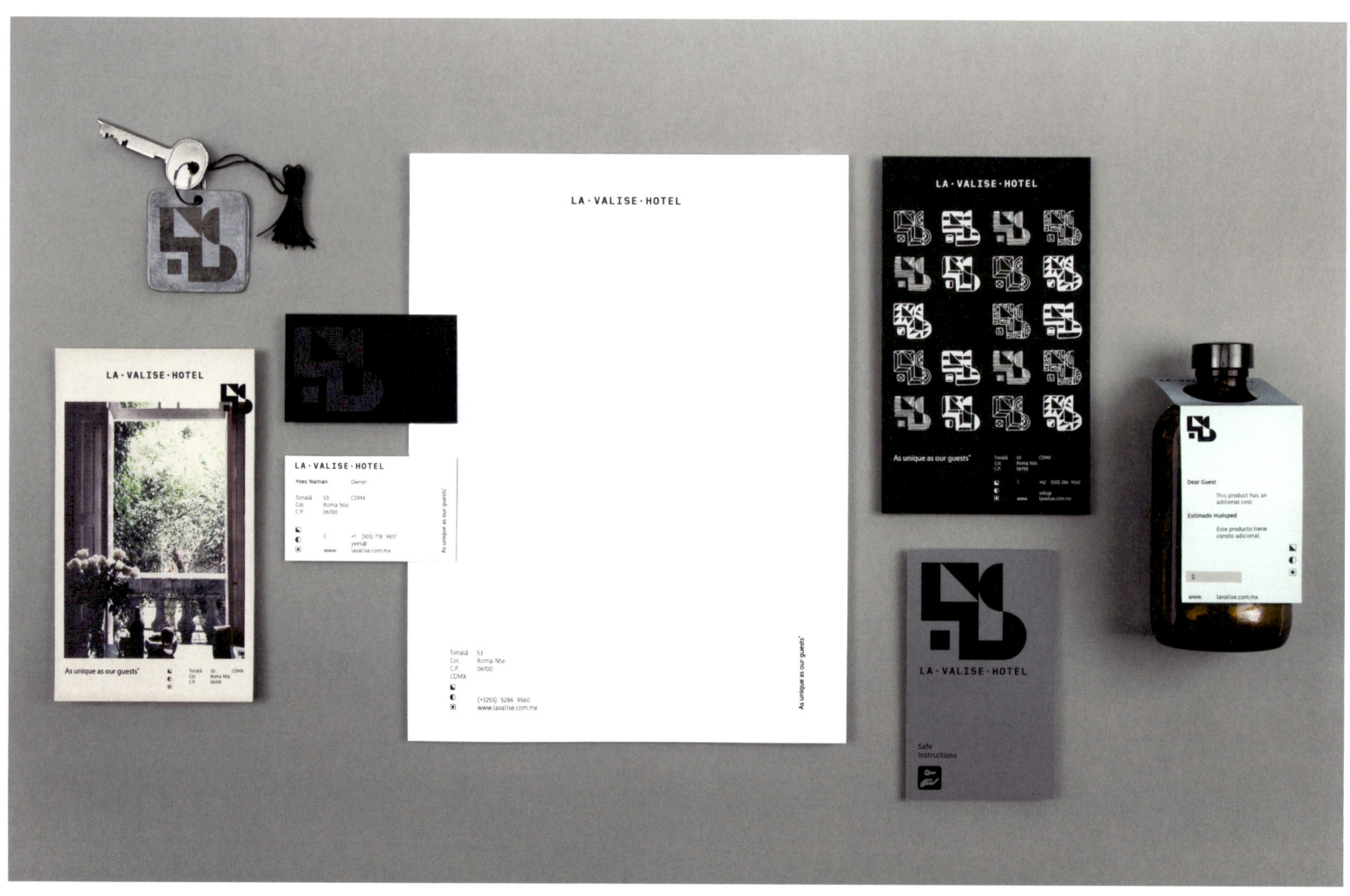

La Valise

An abstract logomark designed by _BIENAL_ incorporates geometric shapes that reference the hotel's three guest rooms.

With a worldwide reputation of being a small hotel with a unique personality, Mexico City's La Valise provides guests with a beautiful and peaceful retreat in the middle of the city. Inspired by the travels of owner Yves Naman, the hotel has only three luxurious rooms, in which every detail has been thought of. Bienal designed a logomark that contains the La Valise initials, as well as geometric shapes that represent its three rooms: Patio (square), Terraza (triangle), and Luna (circle). Using pre-Hispanic and abstract patterns, the outline of the logomark can be filled in to create different effects; and the designers developed the versions into a pattern for use on printed collateral.

42

Summerhill Market

BLOK DESIGN's rebrand for the boutique grocery store marries the market's proud heritage with its progressive spirit.

Since 1954, Toronto's Summerhill Market has led the way in the boutique grocery store model. The family-owned business, which houses a florist, a deli, a butcher shop, and a bakery, also produces its own line of high-quality goods. When the time came to develop a new identity that would give the store a fresh voice, while maintaining its warmth, Blok Design started with its logo and packaging system. The designers developed a monogram that gives a nod to the store's rich heritage, opting for a modern san serif type, chosing an inviting pastel color palette, and creating the new tagline, "Your Other Kitchen". Combined with clean graphics and minimal illustrations, the market's new look and feel is simple and approachable.

43

FULL
OF 福
LUCK
乐
CLUB
FULL OF LUCK CLUB
DIM SUM 点心
Steamed Shrimp Dumplings
(4 pcs)
Steamed Chicken Siew Mai Dumplings with Fish Roe
(3 pcs)

福乐
FULL OF LUCK CLUB
CANTO KITCHEN & BAO BAR
BRENDEN NG
ASSISTANT RESTAURANT MANAGER
243 HOLLAND AVE
SINGAPORE 278977
TEL: 6208 6845
BRENDEN@FULLOFLUCK.CLUB
INTERNET:
WWW.FULLOFLUCK.CLUB
YOUR LUCKY NUMBER
9781

FULL
OF 福
LUCK
乐
CLUB

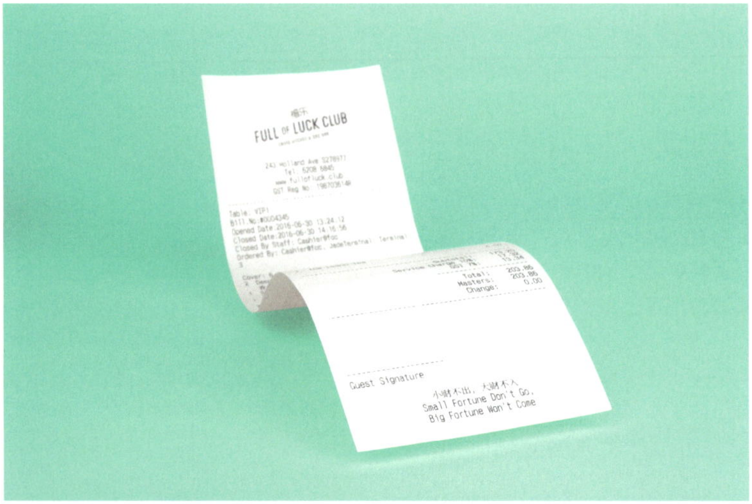
FULL OF LUCK CLUB
Guest Signature
Small Fortune Don't Go,
Big Fortune Won't Come

FULL OF LUCK CLU
DIM SUM 点心
Steamed Shrimp Dumplings with Bamboo Shoot
Steamed Chicken Siew Mai Dumplings with Fish Roe
Deep-fried Crispy Prawn Rolls with Mango
Steamed BBQ Pork Buns 叉烧包 (3 pcs)
Baked BBQ Pork Puff 脆皮叉烧酥 (3 pcs)
Crispy Beancurd Skin Rolls with Shrimps and Chives
Steamed Scallop and Vegetable Dumplings
Stir-fried Radish Cake with X.O. Sauce
Steamed Rice Rolls with Shrimp/Char Siew
$7.20
$6.20
$6.00
$5.40
$5.40
$6.00
$6.00
$6.80
$6.80
LIGHT BITES 小食
Golden Sand Corn with Salted Egg Yolk
$4.80
SHARING PLATES
BAO 包
Kung Pao Fried Chicken 宫保鸡
Classic taste of spicy chicken, lettuce, dried chilli and crushed peanu
Salted Egg Yolk Prawn 金沙虾
Braised Pork Belly
Portuguese Pork Chop
Juicy crispy pork chop in spicy sweet curry sauce, lettuce, fried shallots
& coriander
Panko-crusted Portobello
Golden fried whole Portobello mushroom in teri
cabbage slaw & grilled pineapples
Hokey-Pokey Ice Cream
in a fried bao

Full of Luck Club

Designed by BRAVO, a playful mix of colorful graphics expresses the restaurant's traditional-meets-contemporary feel.

Full of Luck Club is a modern Cantonese kitchen that serves authentic Chinese comfort food. Opened by the same team behind the upscale Li Bai Cantonese Restaurant in the city's Sheraton Towers, the Full of Luck Club is a more playful, casual eatery that serves classic dishes, such as roasted meats, fresh noodles, and dim sum, alongside contemporary options, including salads, specialty baos, and craft beers. Echoing this spirit of old meets new, the designers at Bravo combined a modern pastel color palette, bold lettering, and an abstract looping pattern with traditional touches of deep red and gold foil.

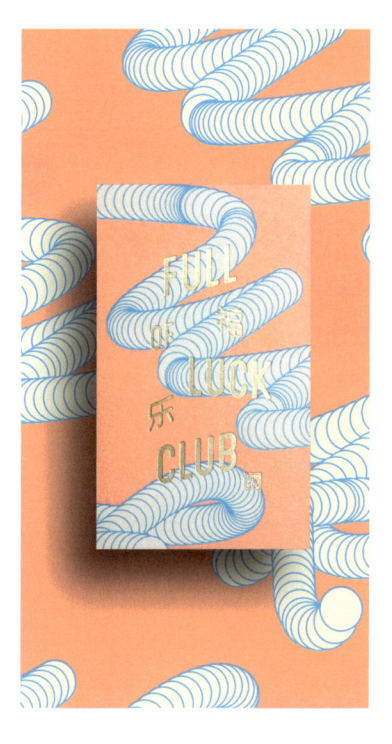

45

LE TURTLE
BOTTLES
BUBBLES
CREMANT D' ALSACE BRUT NATURE ROSE, DIRLER-CADE, 2012, ALSACE 64
WHITE
CHARDONNAY, MONTBARNIER, JOUVEAUX, 2013, BURGUNDY 73
SANCERRE, LES QUARTERONS, RIFFAULT, 2012, LOIRE VALLEY 70
CHARDONNAY, LES BOUTONNIERS, LES DOLOMIES, 2013, JURA 65
JACQUERE, LA PETITE ROBE, PERON, 2013, SAVOIE 65
GRENACHE BLANC/CARIGNAN BLANC, BLANC FRISANT, 2013, LANGUEDOC-ROUSSILLON 53
RED
CABERNET FRANC, HERLUBERLU, SEBASTIE
DAVID, 2013, LOIRE VALLEY 49
PINEAU D'AUNIS, BRENDAN TRACEY, 2014, LOIRE VALLEY 54
VOLNAY, DOMAINE DE CHASSORNEY, 2012, BURGUNDY 145
GAMAY, ROUE LIBRE, LE GRAIN DE SEN
2013, BEAUJOLAIS 47
TROUSSEAU/PINOT NOIR/POULSARD, DD ROU
TISSOT, 2013, JURA 63
PINOT NOIR, ULM, L'OCTAVIN, 2011, JURA 76
MONDEUSE, CHAMP LEVAT, PERON, 2013, SAVOIE 62
FER SERVADOU, LA COQUILLE, DOMAINE ROLS, 2014, AVEYRON 51
GRENACHE/CARIGNAN, MANO A MANO, MATIN CALME, 2012, LANGUEDOC-ROUSSILLON 45
GRENACHE/CARIGNAN, FRIDA, LES FOULARDS ROUGES, 2013, LANGUEDOC-ROUSSILLON 66
BANDOL, CHATEAU STE ANNE, 2011, PROVENCE 68
LE TURTLE
CHEESE ST. STEPHEN, TOMME DE CHEVRE AYDIUS, EWE'S BLUE
ENDS MEAT SAUCISSON SEC, FINOCCHIONA, CACCIATORINI, LONZINO
LA QUERCIA ROSSA PROSCIUTTO BROADBENT COUNTRY HAM
LE TURTLE CHICKEN LIVER MOUSSE
SINGLE SELECTION 7 SELECTION OF THREE 18
BREAD 6 LE TURTLE BUTTERS
CRUDITÉ 14 RADISH, TURNIP, CARROT & PICKLED ROMANESCO WITH LOBSTER BUTTER
ROMAINE 14 GARLIC CONFIT EMULSION, ANCHOVY BREADCRUMBS WITH FIORE SARDO
KABOCHA & FRESH CHEESE 12 CIPOLLINI ONIONS WITH RYE
MAINE LOBSTER 29 PICKLED AJI DULCE & ASIAN PEAR WITH ALMOND CURD
KOHLRABI BISQUE 15 LAMB BELLY & SMOKED CABBAGE WITH PICKLED MUSTARD SEEDS
PICKLED CAULIFLOWER & BROCCOLI RABE 16 WATERCRESS WITH FENNEL LABNE
COCKLES & PARSLEY ROOT 16 GRILLED LEMON & PARSLEY EMULSION
OXTAIL 35 CELERY BREADCRUMBS & FRESH HORSERADISH
LAMB 28 DELICATA SQUASH & ROASTED CARROT WITH PUFFED AMARANTH
GRILLED WAGYU 32 JAPANESE SWEET POTATO & PERSILLADE WITH NASTURTIUM SOUBISE
WHOLE SASSO CHICKEN FOR TWO 49 BITTER GREENS & SORREL WITH PUMPKIN VINAIGRETTE
MUSHROOMS 29 PERIGORD TRUFFLE & SALSIFY WITH OYSTER-BRIE EMULSION
LE TURTLE
LE TURTLE
LE TURTLE
LE TURTLE
LETURTLE.FR

Le Turtle

<u>LETA SOBIERAJSKI</u> combines bright colors with raw materials and a dash of club culture to create unforgettable brand identity for the modern French restaurant.

Founded by a team of food and wine professionals, Le Turtle is a new-wave French restaurant in New York with only 18 tables. Its vibrant interior features neon lights, pink velvet, Horween leather, and French hip-hop on the sound system. The staff are also part of the experience, wearing baggy, steel-gray prison jumpsuits for their uniforms. Leta Sobierajski's branding takes inspiration from psychedelic symbology and visual occult, using references to painting and architecture. It combines angular patterns, bright-pink backgrounds, and raw materials to create an unmistakable visual language. The project also has a bespoke typeface across its print and digital collateral.

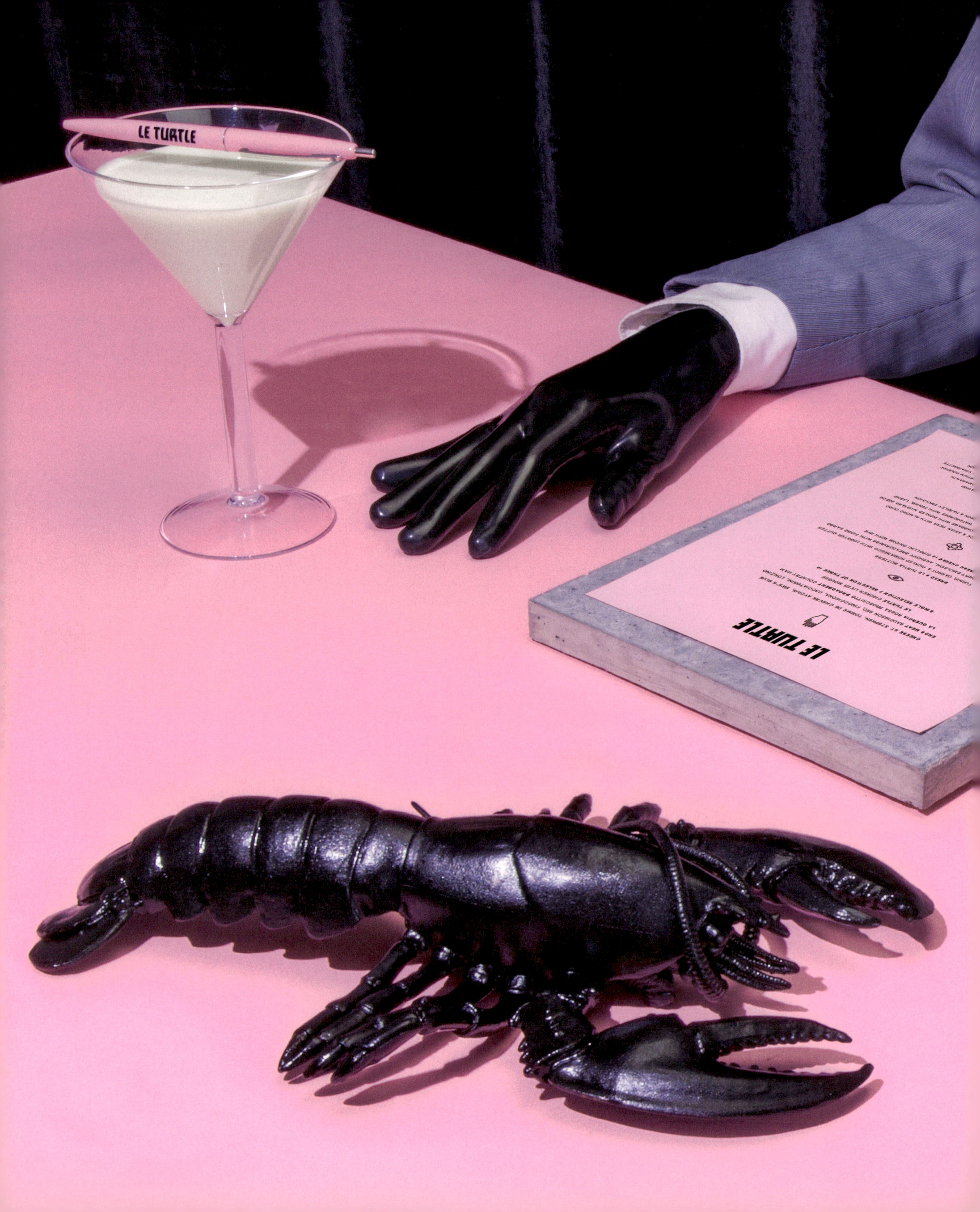
LE TURTLE
LE TURTLE

LE TURTLE

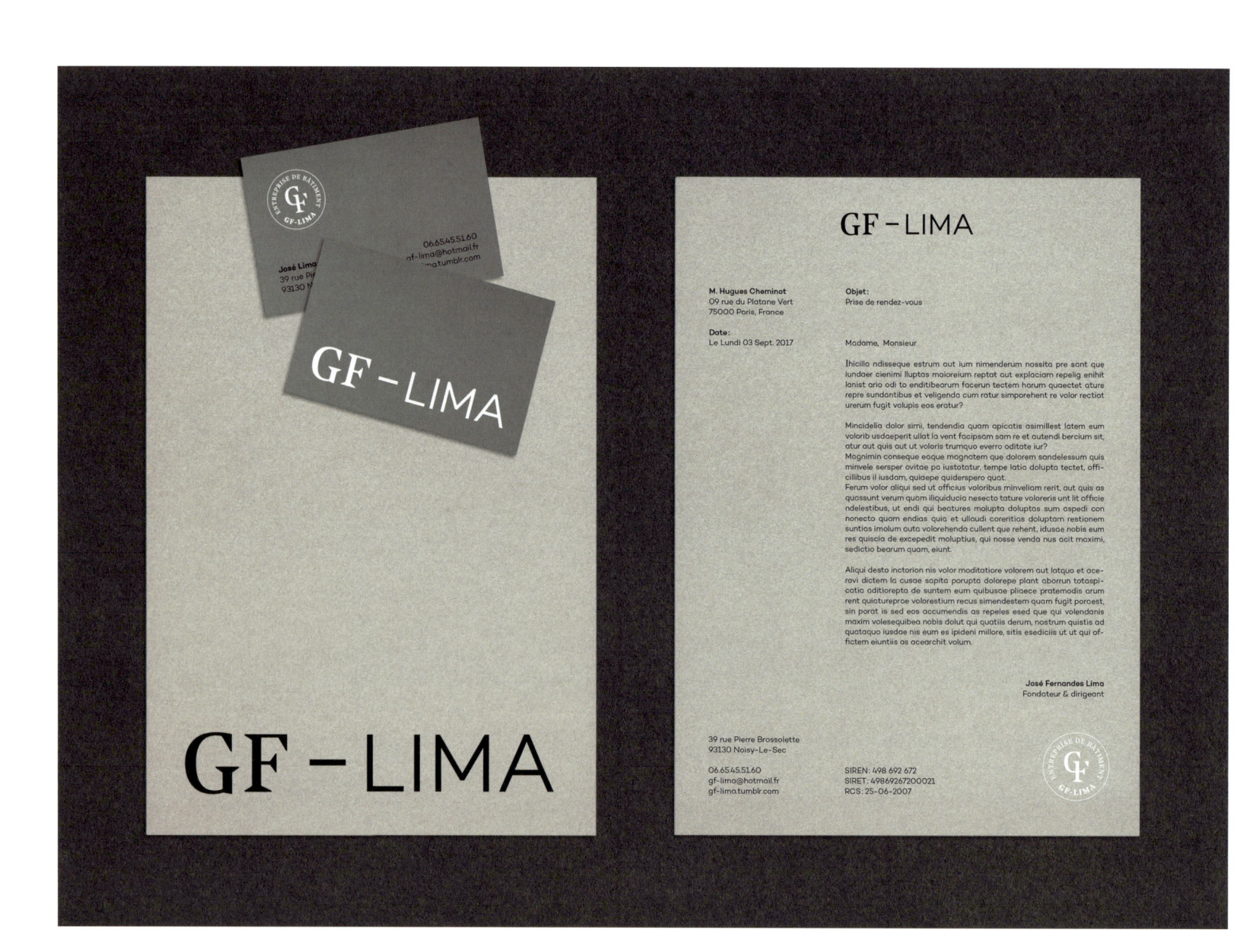

50

GF—LIMA

STUDIO IMPULSO lets contrasting typefaces communicate the construction company's core values.

The construction company GF—LIMA brings more than 10 years of experience to its projects. The logo design by Studio Impulso uses two different typefaces to communicate the brand's character: a strong serif font emphasizes the company's trustworthiness, while a more delicate sans serif font highlights its attention to detail. The designers used a matte gray paper, reminiscent of concrete, for the stationery and business cards, reinforcing the nature of the GF—LIMA's business. Artful black and white photography further demonstrates the construction company's high aesthetic standard.

52

Kolme Perunaa

Designed by **KUUDES**, this playful graphic system illustrates the art production firm's unconventional name.

The Helsinki-based visual arts production platform Kolme Perunaa (three potatoes) realizes art projects all over the world, including exhibitions, films, and books. Developed by local design firm Kuudes, the production company's visual identity is a simple interpretation of its unusual name. The humorous design features yellow potato shapes that are used in a trio for the logomark, and en masse for a larger pattern. The result is a bold and playful graphic system that can be applied to a wide range of brand elements, including stationery, business cards, tote bags, and shipping containers.

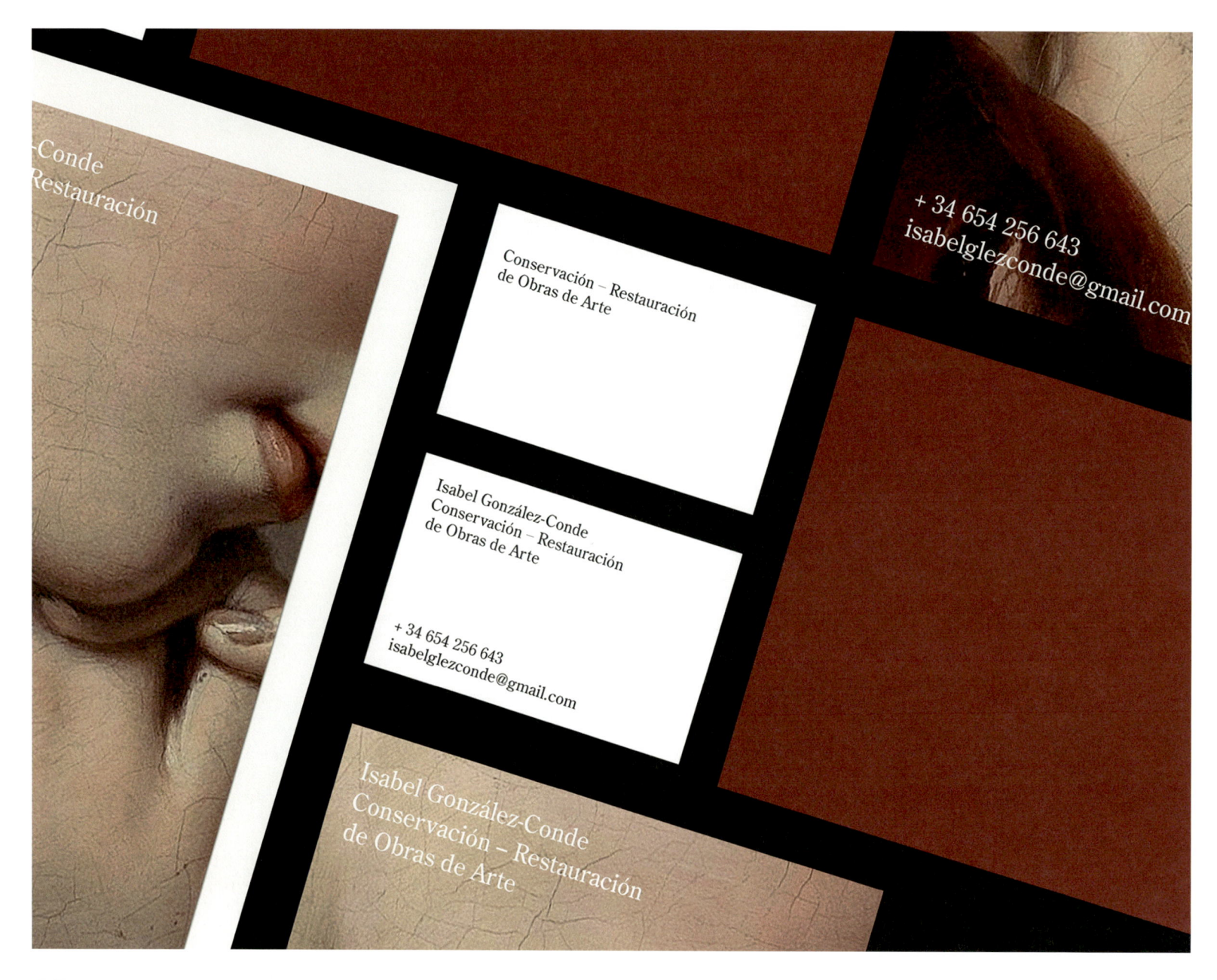

IGC Art Conservation & Restoration

Inspired by the old masters, <u>SONIA CASTILLO STUDIO</u> highlights the art conservator and restorer's attention to detail and her commitment to tradition.

From her workshop in Madrid, art conservator and restorer Isabel González-Conde has collaborated with institutions throughout Spain, including Museo Nacional del Prado and Museo Reina Sofia. Sonia Castillo's visual identity and stationery for IGC Art Conservation & Restoration reflects the patience, dedication, and delicate touch required for the profession. A deep-red and earthy color palette echoes the characteristics of the pigments used by the old masters and complements an up-close image representing IGC's work. An elegant serif font finishes the identity by reinforcing the restorer's commitment to tradition and allowing the image to take center stage.

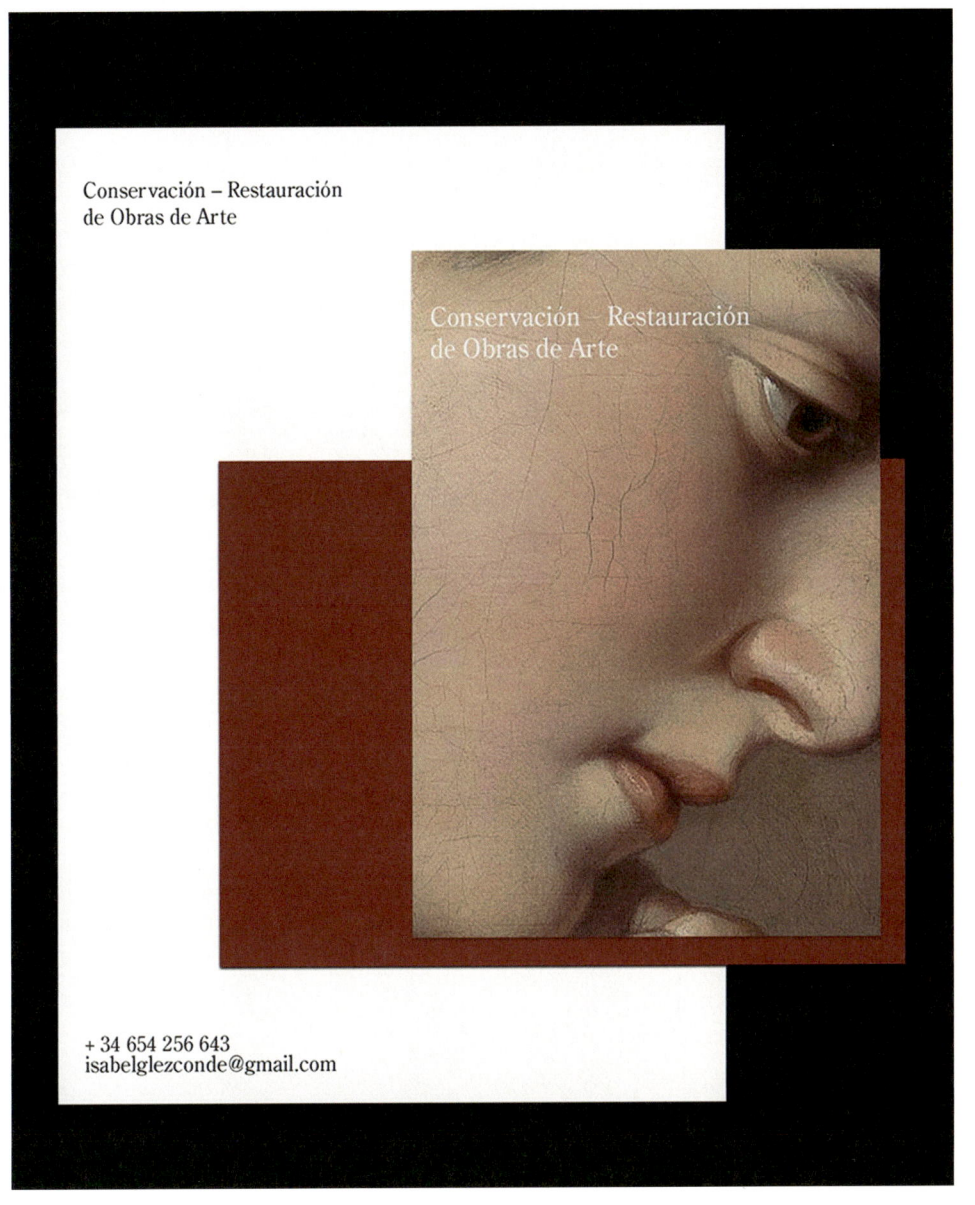

55

56

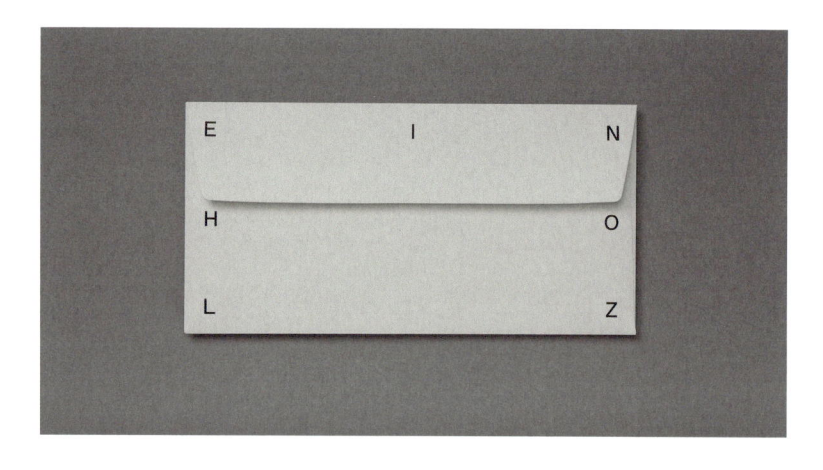

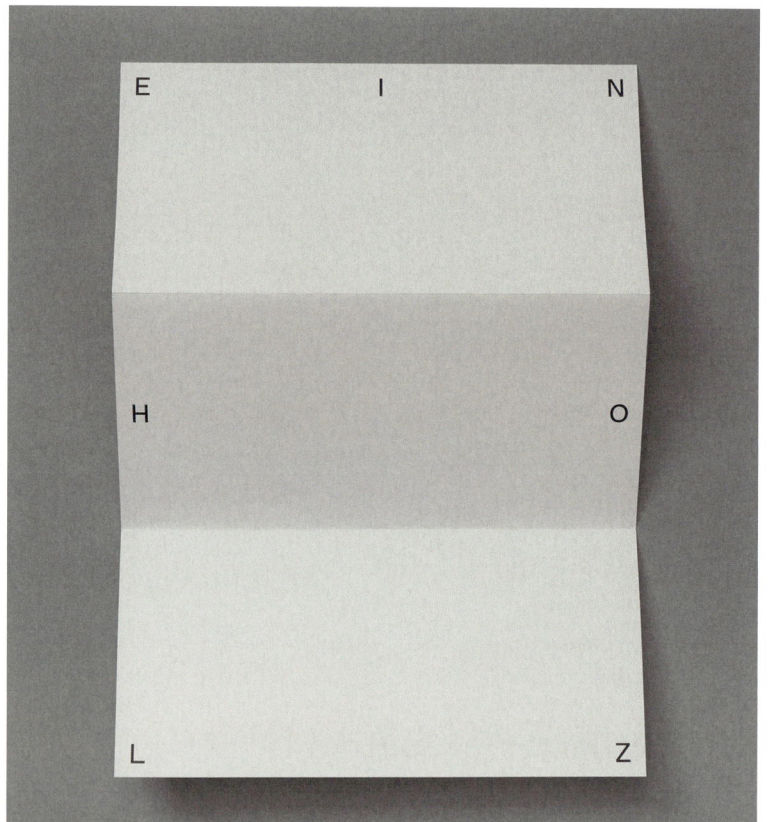

Einholz

BUREAU COLLECTIVE uses real wood varieties to underscore the unique properties inherent in the woodworker's projects.

Woodworker Ueli Reusser founded his carpentry shop One Man Show in 2014. Working with Bureau Collective to rebrand the business, they changed the name to Einholz (Monowood) because of its close phonetic relationship to the German word Einhorn (unicorn), a creature embodying the very notion of uniqueness. The wordplay reflects the rare mix of special skills needed by self-employed carpenters to create quality work. By setting each letter of the name on a grid, the designers call attention to the skill set Reusser brings to each project. The business cards are printed on real wood varieties, which highlights the unique properties of the materials Reusser uses in his work.

Kafi Franz

BUREAU COLLECTIVE's brand identity for the Swiss restaurant and café features an adaptable menu with a fun flourish.

Two friends founded the Kafi Franz restaurant and cafe in St. Gallen, Switzerland. It has an inviting, easy going atmosphere and serves food prepared with fresh, local, seasonal, and organic ingredients. Because the restaurant changes its dinner menu on a monthly basis, Bureau Collective created a template that the owners can easily modify. In addition to new dishes, the owners can include vintage black-and-white photos or paintings of a man who will represent that month's Franz. It is a humorous touch to an otherwise simple identity, using an understated selection of off-white, gray, and kraft papers for stationery, packaging, and menus.

Das St.Galler
Stadtkafi
mit offenem
Garten

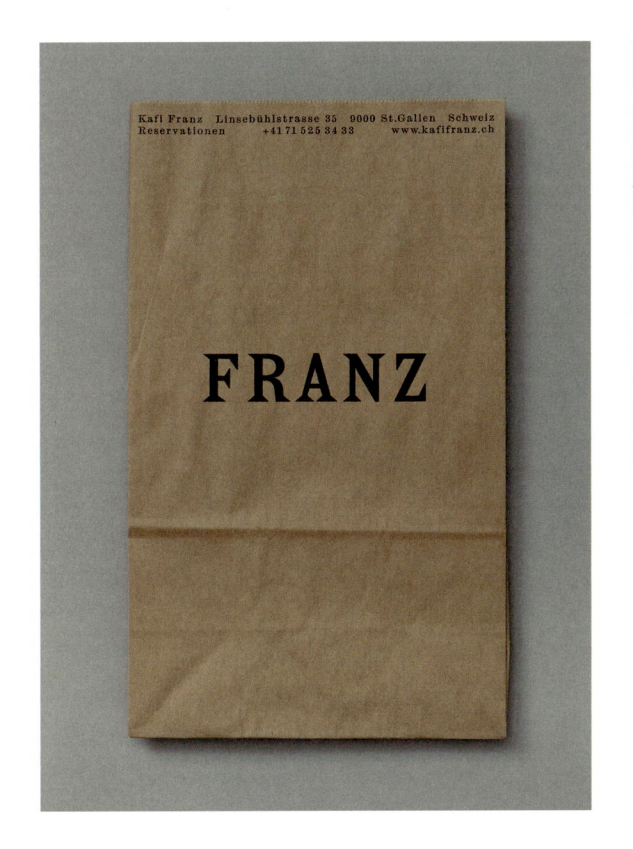

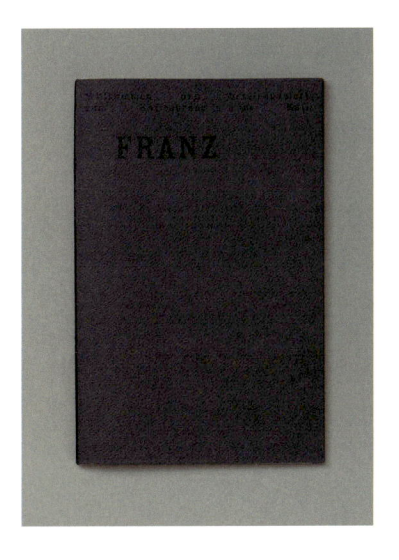

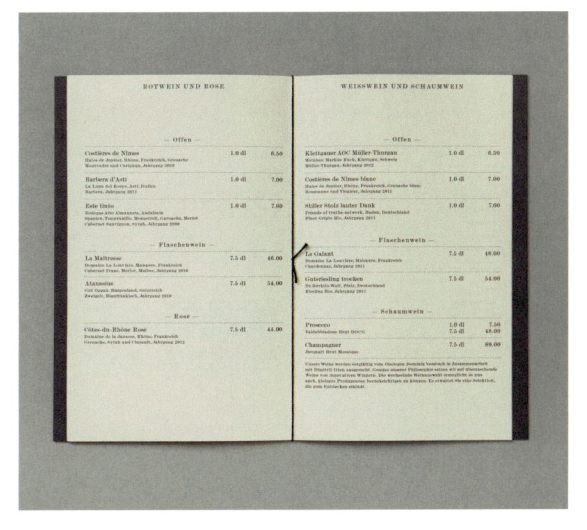

60

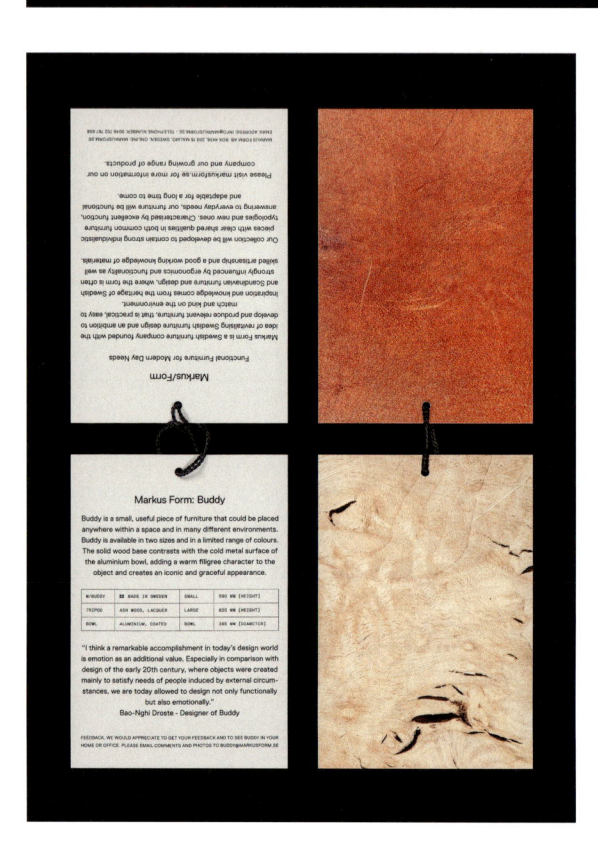

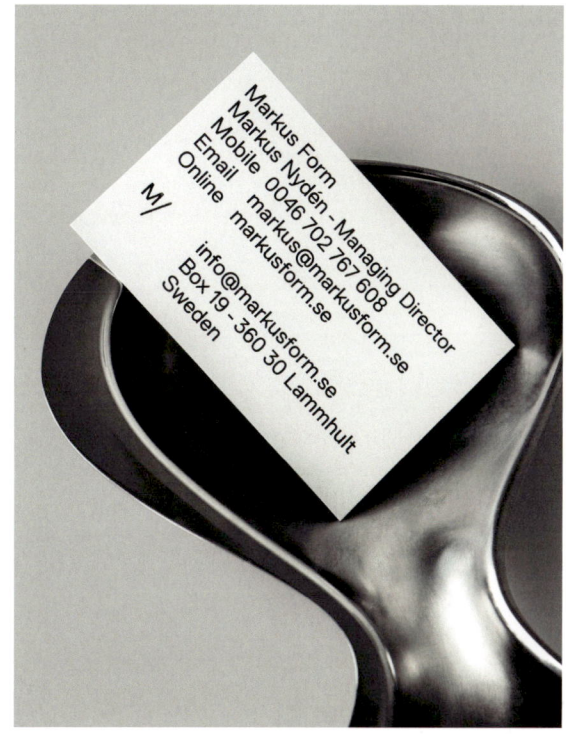

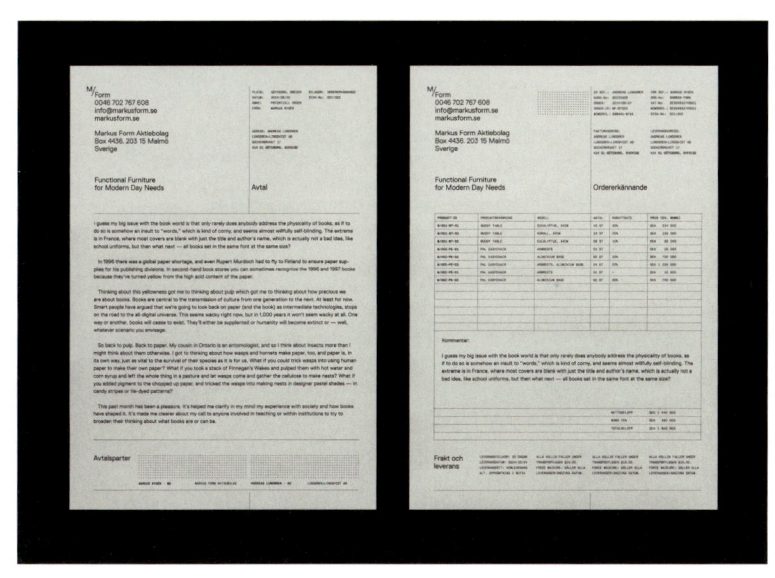

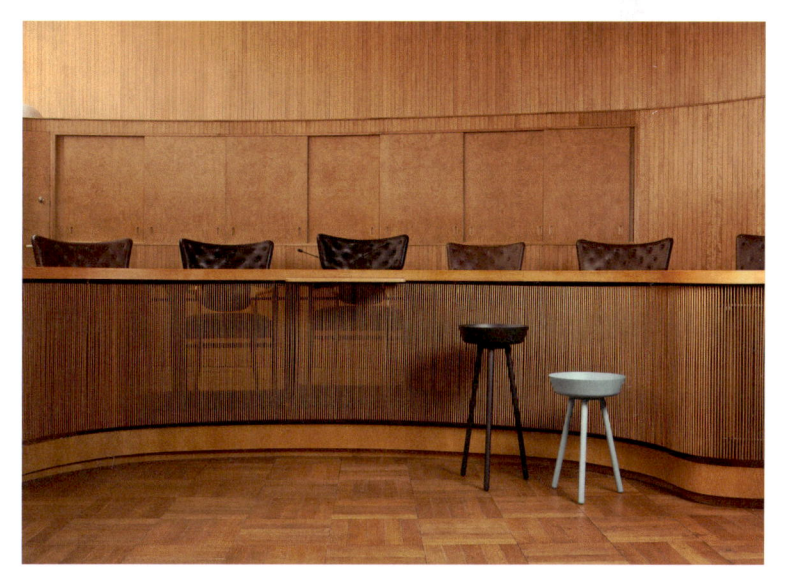

Markus Form

__LUNDGREN+LINDQVIST__'s identity for the Swedish furniture company includes a series of photographic essays.

The founding mission of Markus Form is to revitalize the Swedish furniture industry by producing products that are practical, attractive, and environmentally friendly. Lundgren+Lindqvist developed its identity, from its name to its printed collateral and website. The designers also produced a series of photographic essays showcasing the furniture in more than 20 locations to illustrate the versatility and durability of each product. All stationery and printed collateral has subtle high-end finishes, such as foil blocking and varnishes on Fedrigoni paper stock.

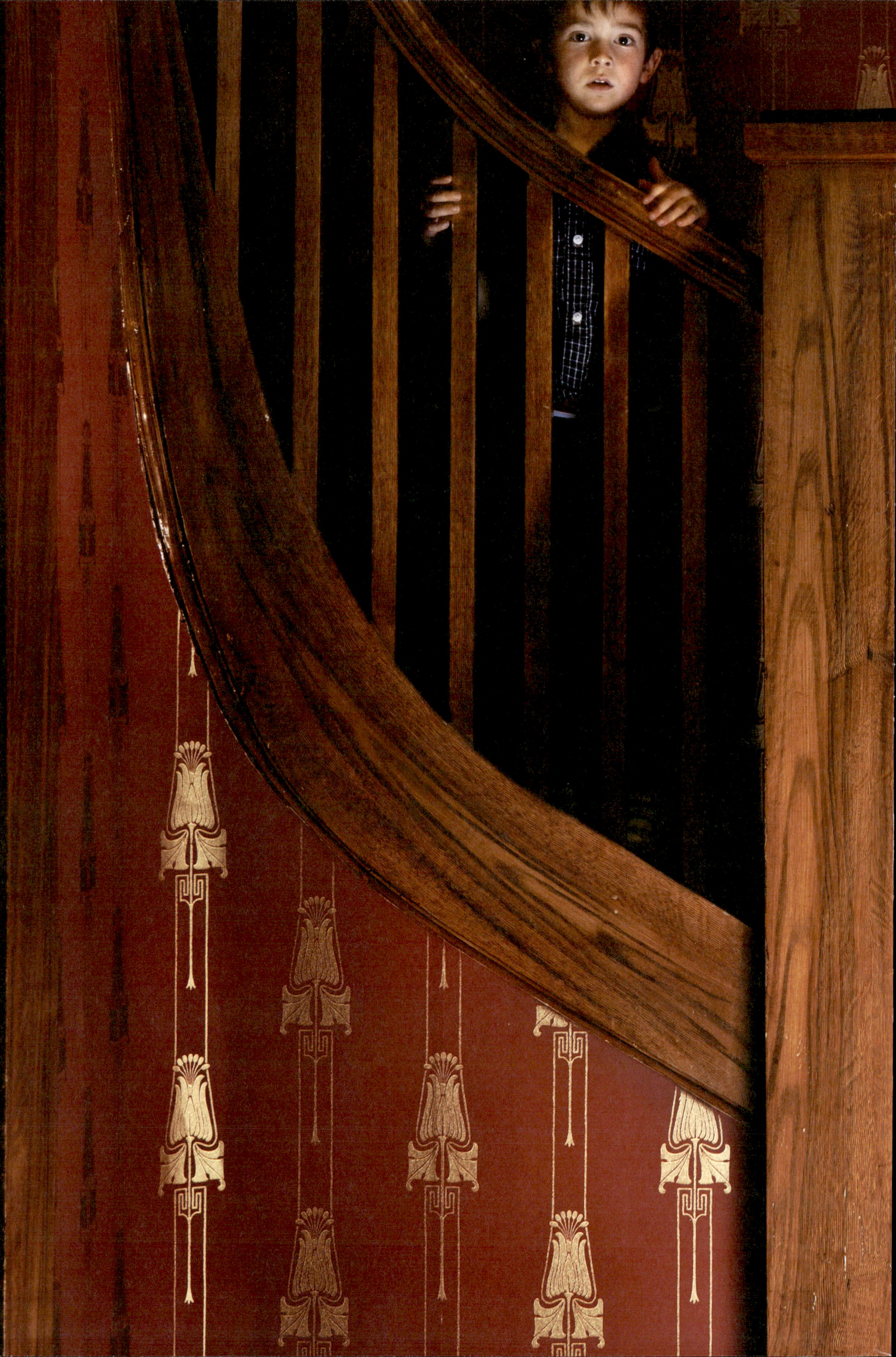

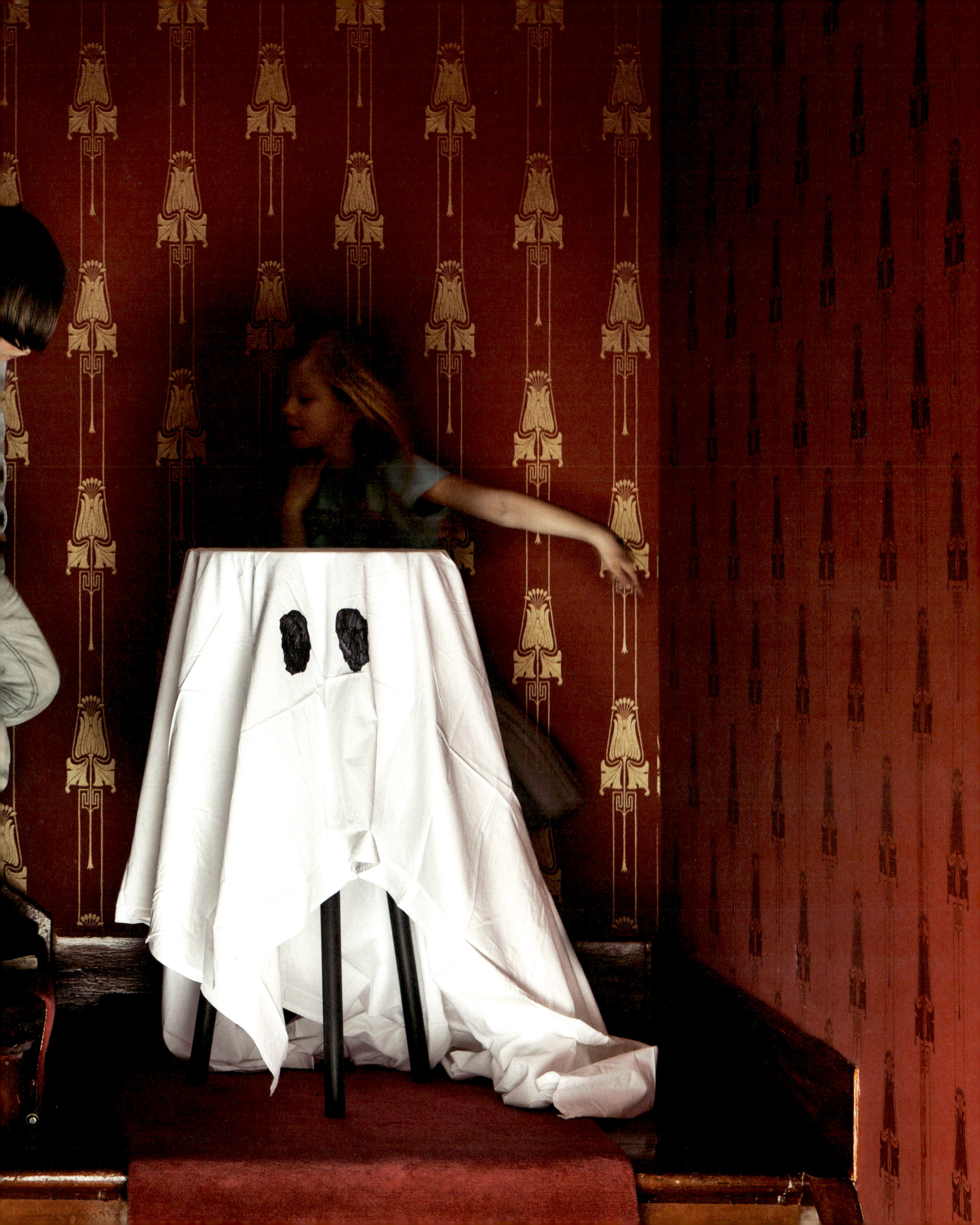

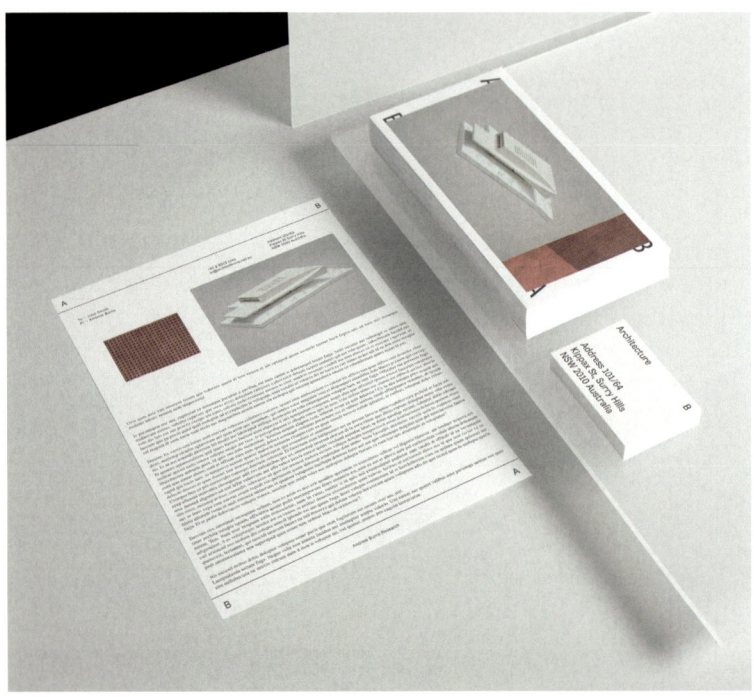

Andrew Burns Architecture

A flexible brand identity system by *SP-GD* helps define the two sides of the Australian architecture firm's practice: research and realization.

Andrew Burns Architecture specializes in heavily researched projects for private and commercial clients. It asked SP-GD to create a graphic language that sends a subtle and research-oriented message to potential clients. SP-GD's solution divides the company's work into two main areas: research and realized projects. After defining the studio as a parallel practice, the designers projected this theme in the identity system. It uses the initials AB and its reflection BA, as well as two typefaces, serif and sans serif, to indicate the two sides of the company and how each supports the other.

65

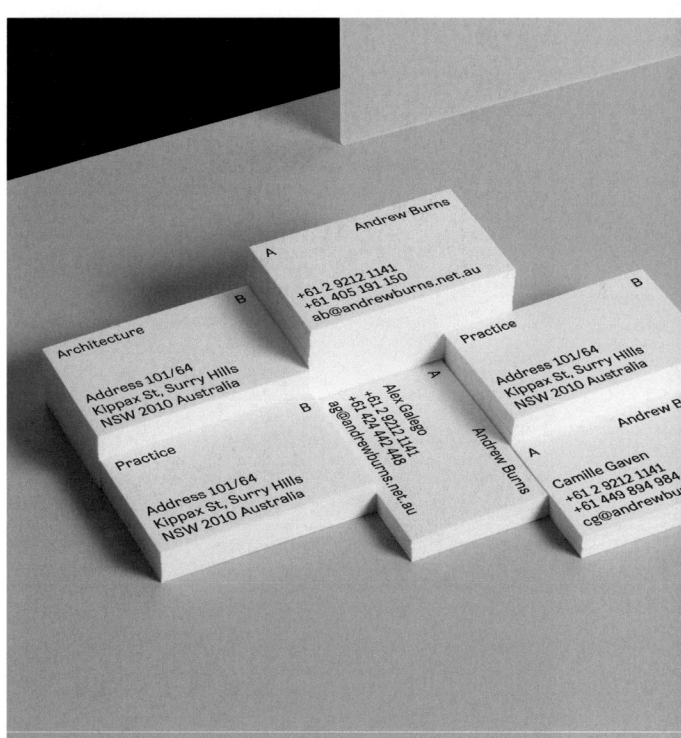

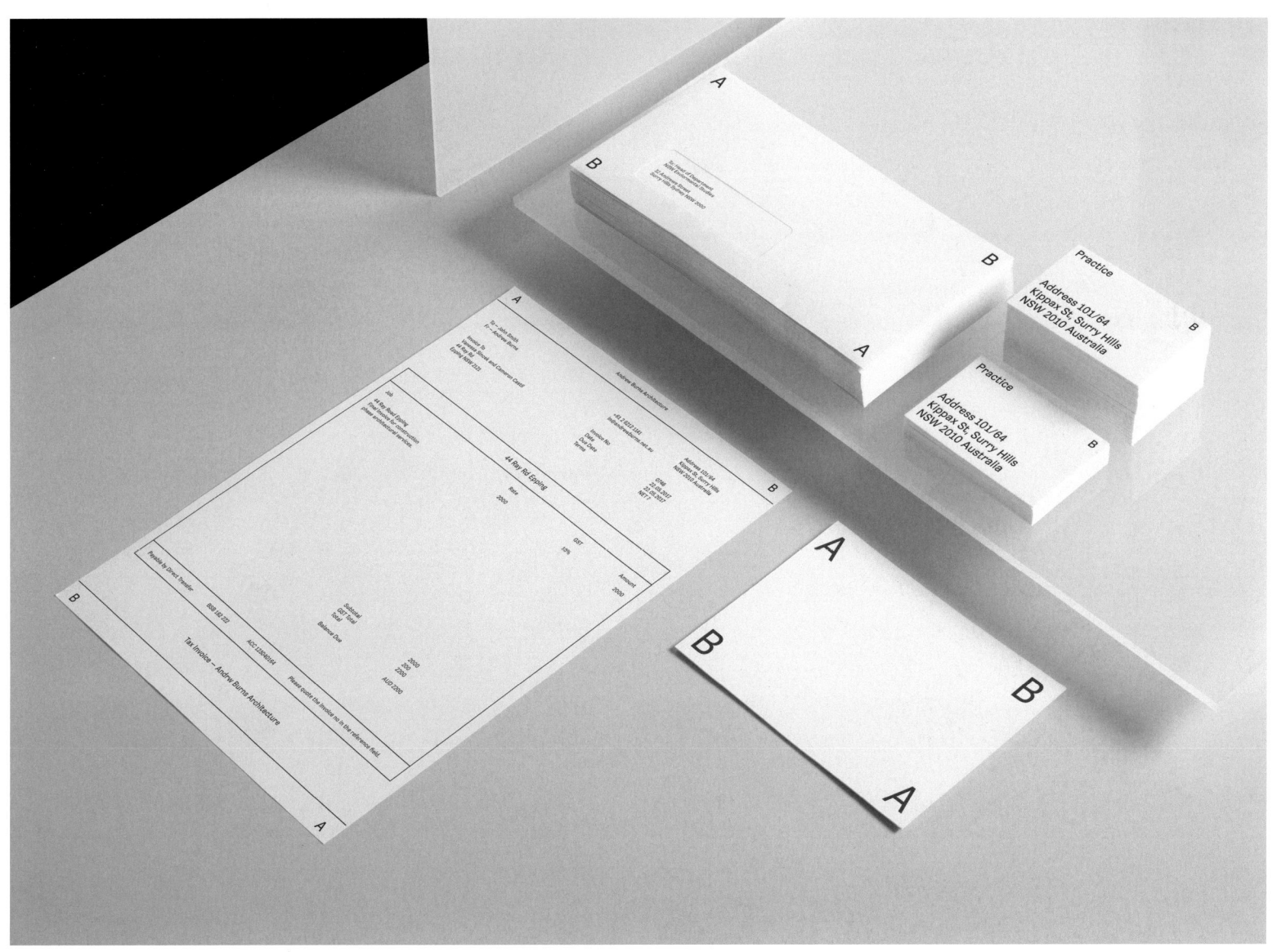

hello@formbar.no
+47 992 35 131

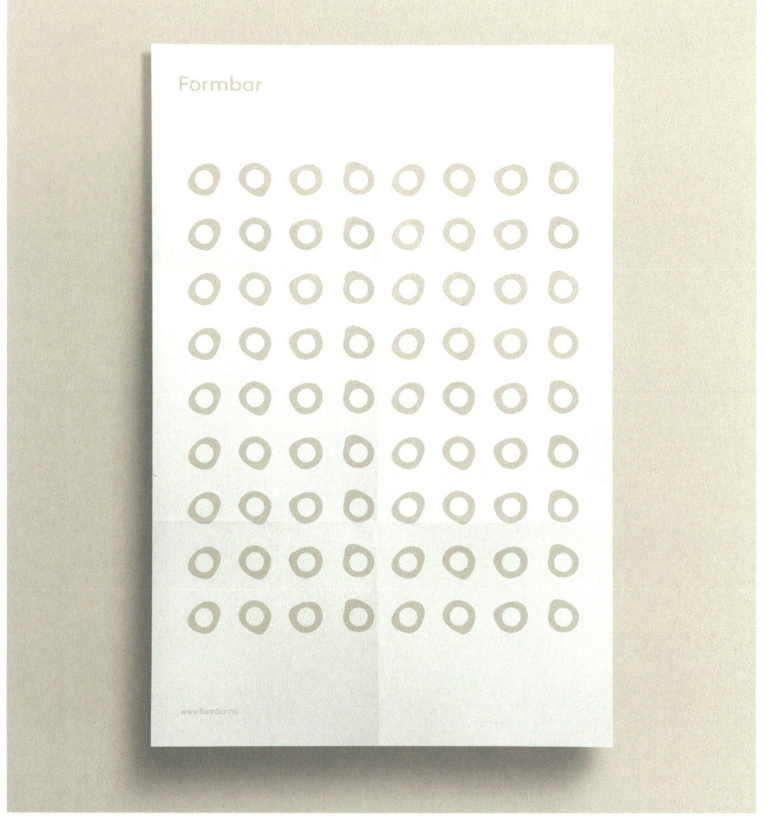

Formbar Glassverksted
www.formbar.no

Formbar
Glassverksted

Org. Nr. 917 765 049
www.formbar.no

Formbar

Formbar

A simple yet expressive logo system by **LARSSEN & AMARAL** echoes the unique properties that define the Norwegian glass studio's artisanal products.

The Norwegian glass studio Formbar creates high-end handblown tableware and glass art. Because of the nature of glass blowing, each object is slightly different. Larssen & Amaral therefore decided to develop a logomark that is organic in form and allows for infinite variation and applied it to the stationery, packaging, signage, and catalog. The designers also used printing techniques, such as embossing, to stamp Formbar's name into the business cards, creating an effect that echoes the transparency of glass.

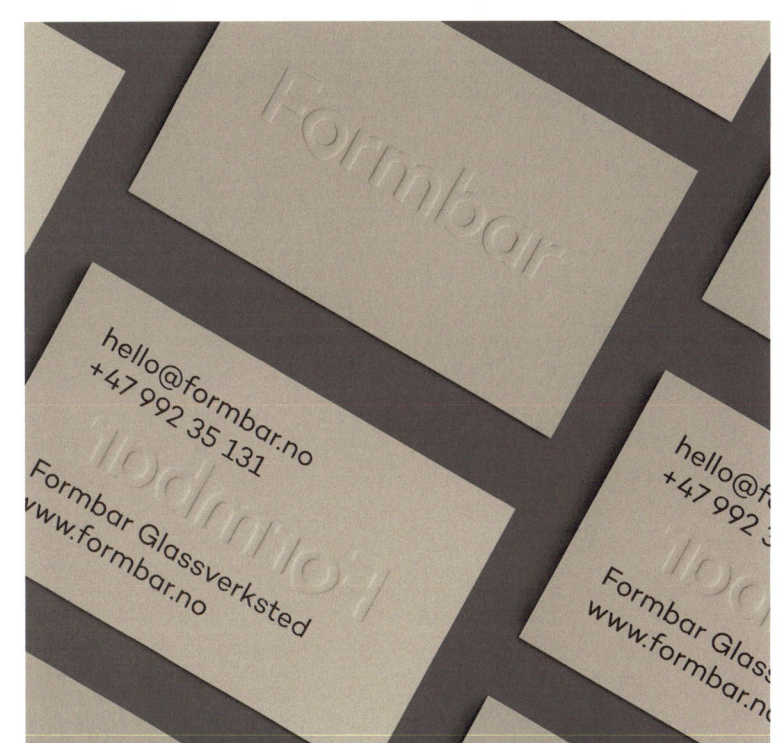

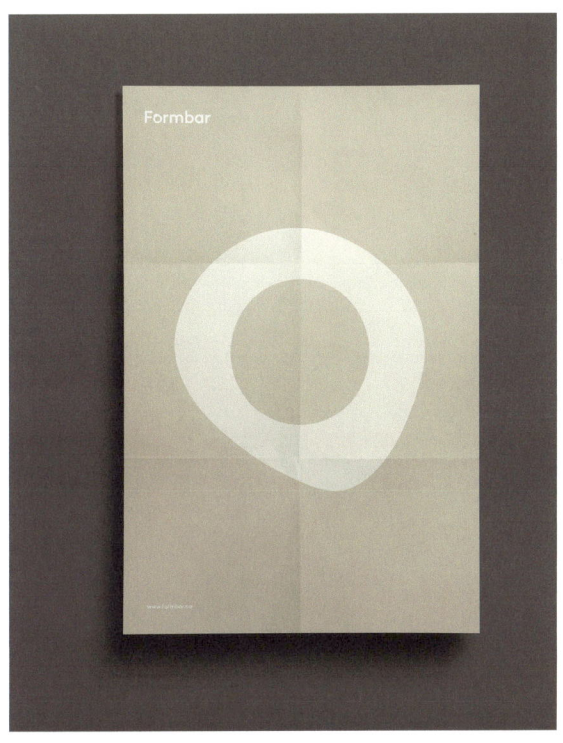

67

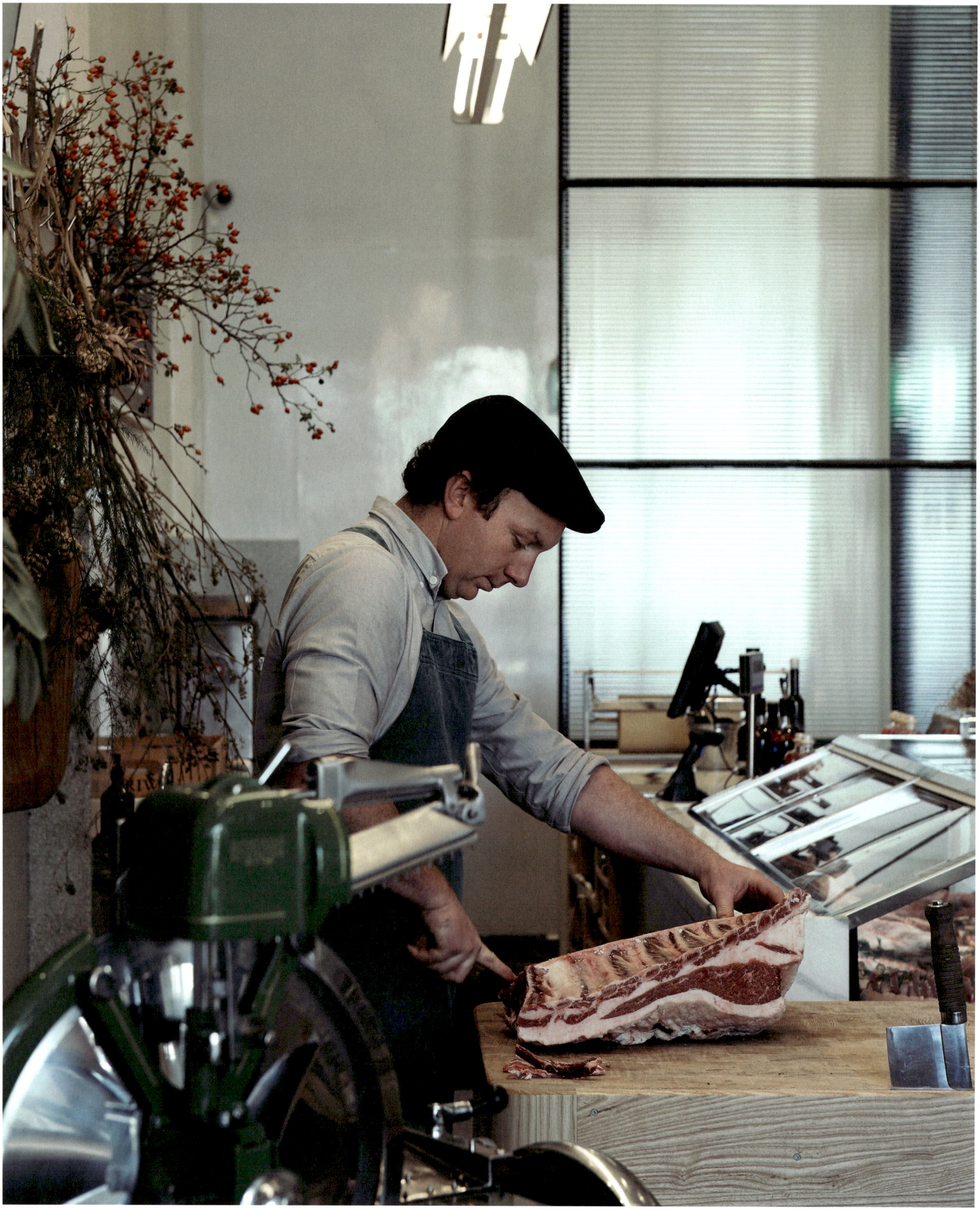

CASE STUDY: **Meatsmith**

Meatsmith caters to responsible consumers and restaurateurs, offering a selection of ethically reared meats from regional farmers. Whereas big butchery chains court customers with innocent illustrations of fictional farms, the Melbourne-based meat specialist gives them a birds-eye view over the homelands of roaming livestock. Crafted by local design studio ROUND, the Meatsmith brand is built around a series of aerial photographs by Tom Blachford, which bring consumers closer to the source of the butcher's produce by offering picturesque and almost abstract views of the rolling landscape.

When celebrated chef and gastronomer Andrew McConnell teamed up with artisan butcher Troy Wheeler to move into the meat business, the duo's venture was destined to make Australia's culinary critics applaud. A Melbourne-based food journalist and blogger titled Meatsmith "the carnivore's delight," not long after its first store opened in the Fitzroy neighborhood. "The Gucci or Prada of butchers," she wrote. Enraptured by the butcher's "bright, marble-countered space, with its high ceilings," *Broadsheet Melbourne* was quick to announce the rise of a veritable "meat emporium." "Brace yourself for a sausage party, Melbourne," advised the gourmand's go-to website *Good Food*.

With a rich, almost decorative display of cold meats, the butcher shop is a meat-lover's land of plenty—a land of milk and salami, if you will. But this isn't your folksy sausage party; nor is the atmosphere haughty and aloof, like that of a luxury fashion retailer. Rather than positioning Meatsmith as a high-end meat boutique for well-heeled hipsters, the founders see their

"Meatsmith's range features housemade sauces, stocks, and pickles that come neatly packaged in glasses with classy white type."

brand as a contemporary incarnation of the old-school local butcher shop. While distinguishing themselves with ethically sourced quality foods, they emphasize that their business is, above all, based on human relationships.

To develop a deeper understanding of where the meat comes from, McConnell and Wheeler maintain close liaison with the farmers they work with. They also look back on their own longstanding business relationship. Wheeler, who previously managed Peter Bouchier, one of Melbourne's finest butchers, first met McConnell during the renovation of Builders Arms Hotel in Fitzroy, one of the restaurateur's many hospitality projects. McConnell was on the lookout for someone to help him develop a high-end meat aging room and, having found the ideal candidate in Wheeler, the two men have worked together since. For many of McConnell's restaurants, the seasoned meat specialist came on board as a buyer, consultant, and instructor conducting butchery demonstrations for employees. With Meatsmith, the pair have extended their fruitful collaboration, to the benefit of Melbourne's thriving culinary scene. Besides meat-loving locals and McConnell's own diners, their joint butchery also supplies other select gastronomy businesses with high-quality meaty ingredients.

As a matter of both principle and practicality, Meatsmith offers regional deliveries only, but connoisseurs from around the world can at least salivate over the range of products online. There are rare beef varieties from old-school British breeds and the Japanese Wagyu; and a large selection of produce comes from O'Connor, Australia's top supplier for grass fed beef. Meatsmith also retails fresh gourmet sausages, rare breed pork belly, pastrami, and ham. There is a housemade mortadella, a selection of poultry products, and native Australian meats such as kangaroo and emu. "It is all limited runs, so one might only see particular produce every few weeks, or once every season," Wheeler explains. Besides seasonal meat, Meatsmith's range features freshly prepared dishes for customers to pick up or to eat in store, terrines and pâtés prepared by McConnell's team in the Builders Arms kitchen, as well as housemade sauces, stocks, and pickles that come neatly packaged in glasses with classy white type.

McConnell's impeccable taste is not restricted to food; the seasoned chef is a long-term client of Melbourne design firm Round. For more than a decade,

"We've intentionally avoided the stereotypes of butcher branding such as heavy typography, cute cows, and knives."

McConnell has commissioned the studio to develop visual identities for his manifold restaurant and hospitality ventures, along with editorial designs for his cookbooks. "It is always inspiring to see how passionate Andrew and his team are about their profession. They work extremely hard behind the scenes to put delicious food on our table," says Michaela Webb, Round's creative director. Together with her team, Webb has been responsible for the design of McConnell's all-day diner Cumulus Inc. and its sister-bar Cumulus Up.; the fine-dining venue Cutler & Co. and its adjoining wine bar Marion; and Ricky & Pinky, the gilt-lined Chinese restaurant that represents the most recent gastronomy addition

71

"Round's design is beautifully minimal and really leaves the landscapes to do the talking."

to the Builders Arms Hotel, amongst many others. For Meatsmith, Round's designers "intentionally avoided the stereotypes of butcher branding such as heavy typography, cute cows, and knives." Instead they worked with a combination of classic and contemporary typography and a simple black-and-white color palette, which brings the butcher's products to the fore. Most distinctively, they centered the brand around a series of birds-eye view photographs to reflect the business

"We needed to rise high above the ground to share the perspective of the wide, open fields—the free-range pastures that provide a natural food source for the livestock to graze."

founders' respect for the farmers, their land, and their livestock—the true pivots of anything Meatsmith.

To portray the provenance of the produce, Round collaborated with Melbourne-based photographer Tom Blachford who specializes in aerial shots. Together, they went on a helicopter flight over the farmland. "We needed to rise high above the ground to share the perspective of the wide, open fields—the free-range pastures that provide a natural food source for the livestock to graze—which seemed like a great idea until we absolutely froze in that open air helicopter on a winter's day," Webb describes. "For a brief like this, a real helicopter is crucial as the ground you can cover is infinitely greater than that of a drone, for example," Blachford explains. "While drones are legally only supposed to be visible by the naked eye, which gives you perhaps 500 meters at the most, during this flight we probably covered an area of 50 square kilometers in an hour. It also allowed me to use much longer and heavier lenses."

Blachford's fascination with aerial photography stems from his interest in discovering unexpected details. "Being high up in the air offers perspectives that we never really get to see, particularly when shooting with a superzoom lens that allows you to focus in on tiny scenes and see beyond the limits of your own senses. The process is very visceral and primarily based purely on instinct, as everything moves incredibly quickly. I'm trying to capture these fleeting moments of natural composition, texture, and shadow before they disappear in the blink of an eye," the photographer says. "This was an incredibly memorable flight. At one point we found a huge mob of kangaroos and followed them across the landscape for probably 10 minutes. It was mesmerizing seeing them move together and looking so powerful. It's something I'll never forget."

There are more reasons why Blachford speaks of the Meatsmith project as a special experience. Although he frequently shoots from the air for commercial clients, the photographer rarely finds his images front and center of a brand, or comparably well-integrated in its different applications. "Round's design is beautifully minimal and really leaves the landscapes

MEATSMITH

OPEN DAILY

MONDAY TO SATURDAY
9.00AM — 7.00PM

SUNDAY
10.00AM — 5.00PM

"We wanted to bring back a sense of tradition, service, and overall ambience of a local butcher."

to do the talking. It all ties in perfectly; and I always get a thrill seeing people walk down the street with the bags or coolers that carry my pictures."

Since Meatsmith outgrew its first store in Fitzroy only two years after its opening, the butcher's photo-printed bags are now seen more often in Melbourne's south as well—particularly around the St Kilda neighborhood, where Meatsmith opened a second location in mid 2017. Local interior design practice Herbert & Mason designed both retail spaces, working very closely with Round. "We shared our creative concepts in the same sessions, which resulted in a shared understanding of the brand, and allowed the interior and graphic approaches to naturally complement each other," Webb says. "It also enabled very active conversations about a shared vision for what the retail experience could be." Matthew Herbert and Lucinda Mason describe the common objective as bringing back "a sense of tradition, service, and overall ambience of a local butcher." Based on an open format, their bright design focuses on the interaction between butcher and customer. "A standard solution would have conflicted with the brand's sense of tradition, formality, and ambience, so we reinterpreted the space, and added an atypical product display, as well as custom furniture crafted in our own Herbert Mason Workshop (HMW)," the interior designers explain.

While the Fitzroy butchery is housed in a former cafe, the St. Kilda store resides in what was the home of longstanding Gruner's Butcher & Deli, a Melbourne food icon. Notwithstanding the different settings, the second store still carries the DNA of the first through its materiality and signature elements, such as the custom-made marble counter. "The main difference was scale, so the design had to be edited to fit the new space, and a warmer palette assisted with its approachability," Herbert elaborates. To add personality and a hinge of nostalgia, both Meatsmith stores are adorned with select vintage items, such as an antique meat slicer, which the designers and their client sourced from "from small pockets around the world." For the bespoke signage boards that express quotes and the daily specials, Round commissioned their former employee Ryan Ward, "a very talented maker" whose company United Measures focuses on fine-art frame fabrication.

"There was a number of parties involved in the project, including Troy Wheeler's wife Brittney, who managed production of all collateral," Webb says. Asked about the specific challenges they faced in regards to the design and its implementation, she mentions intermittent difficulties in combining their approach with service and environmental needs, such as providing environmentally friendly packaging that can hold bloody meat products, while remaining easy for service staff to use. "However, we eventually learned that it is possible to make meat look fresh and delicious in a vacuum packed bag," Round's creative director adds, stressing that, all in all, they look back on the process as a very rewarding experience. "The project taught us to always wear thermals in helicopters. And it confirmed our conviction that it's great to buy less meat, and therefore choose high-quality produce," she says. As a direct translation of the less-but-better approach, Round's branding solution for Meatsmith gives fresh flavor to an old design dictum.

HANNES
REEH
WEIN AUS ANDAU

Nicht jede
Traube
hat das Glück,
eine
sonnenverwöhnte
Andauer Traube
zu sein.
HANNES REEH

HANNES REEH
HANNES REEH
HANNES REEH

HANNES REEH
UNPLUGGED X
CUVÉE ROT
HANNES
REEH
ZUSAMMENKOMMEN
HANNES REEH
UNPLUGGED X
CUVÉE ROT
HANNES REEH
UNPLUGGED X
CUVÉE ROT
HANNES
REEH

Hannes Reeh

Rebranding by _MOODLEY BRAND IDENTITY_ for the established Austrian winery builds on the company's history while expanding on its philosophy.

The enjoyment of the product is at the core of Hannes Reeh's production philosophy. Moodley Brand Identity expressed the winemaker's passionate spirit by placing it at the root of his new visual identity. In order to preserve existing recognition of the brand, the designers retained the basic look of the wine labels and focused on enriching the brand story with two additional labels, as well as new images, illustrations, and text. They also created a range of marketing materials and products, including a 16-page newspaper, branded folders, pencils, notebooks, wooden product boxes, and stamps that complement and integrate with the existing look of the award-winning vineyard.

77

HANNES REEH
HANNES REEH
WEIN AUS ANDAU
HANNES REEH
WEIN AUS ANDAU
hannesreeh.at
HANNES REEH
HANNES REEH
HANNES REEH

Augasse 11, 7163 Andau
+43 2176 27011 wein@hannesreeh.at
Burgenland, Austria
hannesreeh.at
HANNES REEH
HANNES REEH
HANNES REEH
HANNES REEH

Kitz

Welcome to the woods: <u>HOCHBURG</u>'s brand identity for this Swabian hotel with an extensive cocktail and gin bar features a series of forest-inspired illustrations.

Located in southwest Germany, Kitz is a luxurious boutique hotel offering its guests cosmopolitan amenities in the city center of Metzingen. Its lush-green and timeless aesthetic is carried though from the facade to all graphic applications, such as custom-made wallpapers, menues, and stationery, which are adorned with woodland scenes of plants and animals. As part of the project, Hochburg also designed a booklet that showcases the bar's renowned gin selection in detail. Featuring one gin brand per spread, it introduces each with an illustration of the bottle and the main botanical used in the distillery process, as well as a description of its main characteristics.

longdrink

Sei dein eigener Mixologe.
Jeder Mensch hat seinen eigenen Charakter.
Genauso facettenreich ist das aromatische
Empfinden. Werde deshalb zu deinem eigenen
Mixologen und kreiere deinen individuellen
Genussmoment – für Kehle und Seele.

Spirit 4cl + Soda Water
Spirit 4cl + Coca Cola, Sprite, Säfte
Spirit 4cl + 1724 Tonic Water
Spirit 4cl + Fentimans (Tonic, Indian Tonic)
Spirit 4cl + Fever Tree (Indian Tonic, Mediterranean To
Spirit 4cl + Schweppes (Dry Tonic, Indian, Tonic)
Spirit 4cl + Schweppes Pink Pepper Tonic
Spirit 4cl + Thomas Henry Tonic
Spirit 4cl + Qyuzu Tonic

50+ gin
du in u
botani

81

MALDINI
MALDINI
MALDINI
MALDINI
MALDINI
MALDINI

MALDINI
RASMUS MOBERG · 076-1680060
RASMUS@MALDINISTUDIOS.SE · MALDINISTUDIOS.SE
MALDINI
MALDINI

Maldini Studios

JENS NILSSON developed a tactile identity system for the carpentry and interior design studio.

Interior designer Elina Johansson and carpenters Rasmus Moberg and Theo Klyvare are partners at the Maldini Studios, a Stockholm-based interior design and carpentry firm. When developing the studio's identity, designer Jens Nilsson used texture to visually link the materials the team uses in its work. He also created Donadoni, a custom typeface that combines hand-drawn and geometric qualities which also underscore the mix of elements at use in their work. Each piece of the branding is letterpress printed on textured papers purchased from quality producers G.F. Smith and Arjowiggins.

84

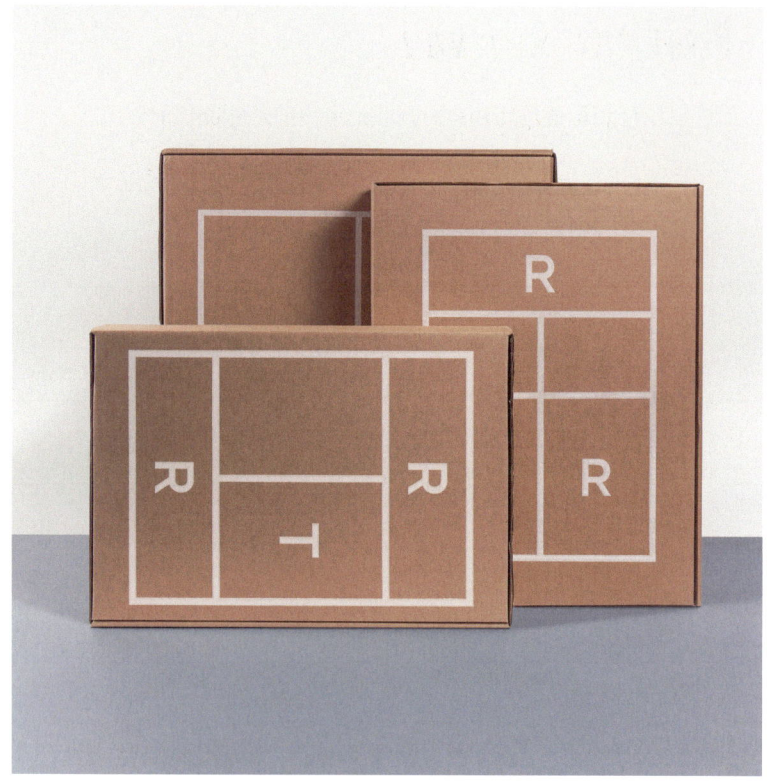

Rent the Runway

LOTTA NIEMINEN STUDIO's versatile visual identity system encapsulates the company's essence into modular shapes.

Rent the Runway loans designer dresses and accessories to its clientele so that they don't have to pay full price. Under this subscription model, clients receive four designer pieces per month, which they can wear and return before receiving the next set. This steady rotation has become the key component of Lotta Nieminen's work on the rebrand. The company's logo represents the ever-changing closet that the brand offers with its flexible grid structure that allows for multiple variations. A muted color palette maintains the brand's signature high-end feel and contrasts its otherwise playful aesthetic. Overall, it is a highly versatile system that can be applied to all digital and printed elements by the in-house design team.

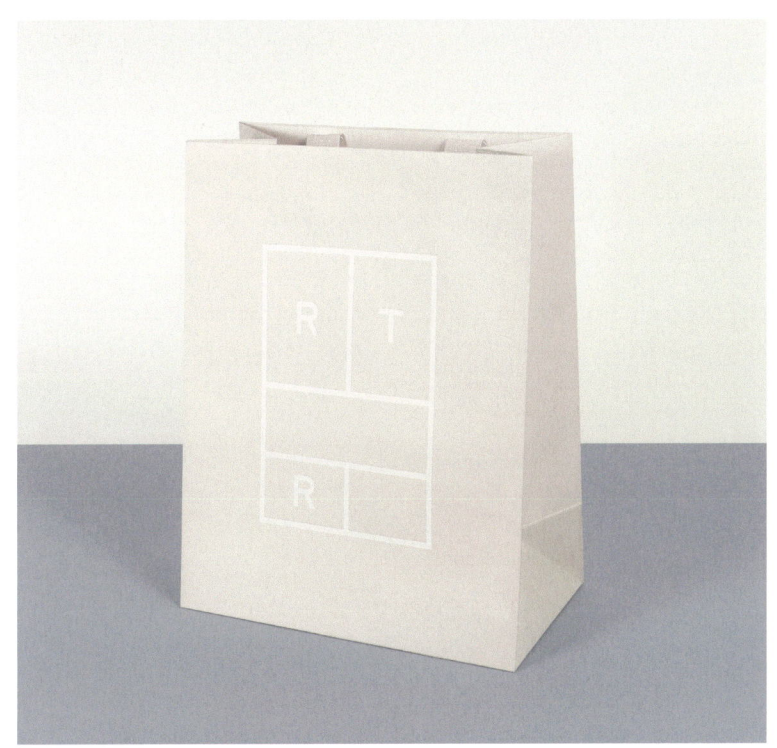

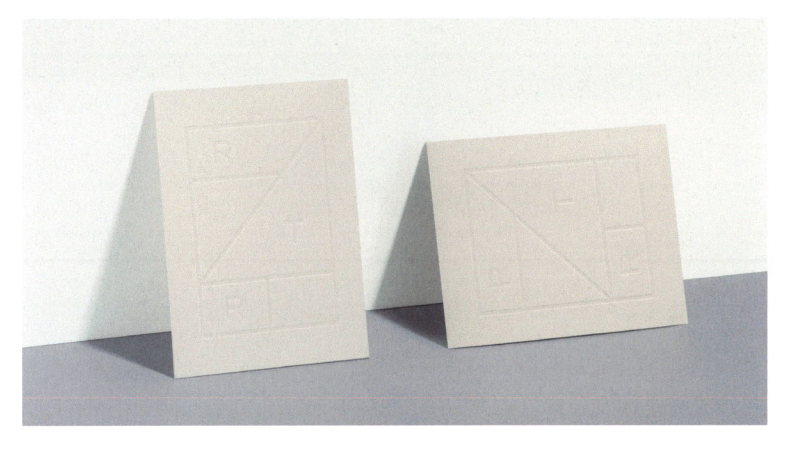

85

THE BIG GROUP
A CREATIVE HOSPITALITY AGENCY

OLIVIA BARRY
HUMAN RESOURCES MANAGER

THE BIG GROUP
A CREATIVE HOSPITALITY AGENCY

38–40 Cubitt Street
Richmond Vic. 3121 Australia

jill.ireton@thebiggroup.com.au
thebiggroup.com.au

PO Box 2031
Richmond South Vic. 3121

M. +61 (0) 447 121 387
T. +61 (03) 9429 0910

THE BIG GROUP
A CREATIVE HOSPITALITY AGENCY

"CREATIVITY IS PIERCING THE MUNDANE TO FIND THE MARVELOUS."
— BM

THE BIG GROUP
A CREATIVE HOSPITALITY AGENCY

RECEPTION FIRST FLOOR
(PRESS BUZZER AND SAY HELLO)

KITCHEN DELIVERIES*

*FITZGIBBON ST LOADING BAY
(VIA SIDE ENTRANCE)

The Big Group

Bold type and quote-driven signage by ROUND reposition the established catering company as a creative hospitality firm.

For the past 25 years, catering and event company The Big Group has organized events ranging from corporate Christmas lunches to weddings and bar mitzvahs. Its founders Bruce and Chyka Keebaugh engaged Round to help move the business in a new direction by repositioning it as a creative hospitality agency. Round's branding strategy repositioned The Big Group as a "creative hospitality agency" with an identity system to reflect that spirit. The logomark is simple but powerful and uses a sans serif font in black and white. Quotes about creativity are used throughout the signage to further underscore the company's new life as an agency for creative hospitality.

Institute

Key card inspired branding by <u>COMMISSION</u> for a low-profile creative agency that works with high-profile clients.

Led by creative director Nathaniel Brown, Institute works with some of the world's most elite brands and creatives. It operates with discretion when working for the high-profile client base, which allows the work of Institute's clients to come to the fore. Commission designed a new brand identity that reflects the agency's under-the-radar working philosophy. The solution is inspired by the magnetic strip on the back of a key card, as a symbol of a modern-day artifact that can open doors. Institute's wordmark is embedded in the graphic strip and camouflaged with a security pattern using the micro-foiling printing technique. The logo form is a long strip that can be used across the company letterhead, envelopes, and business cards.

89

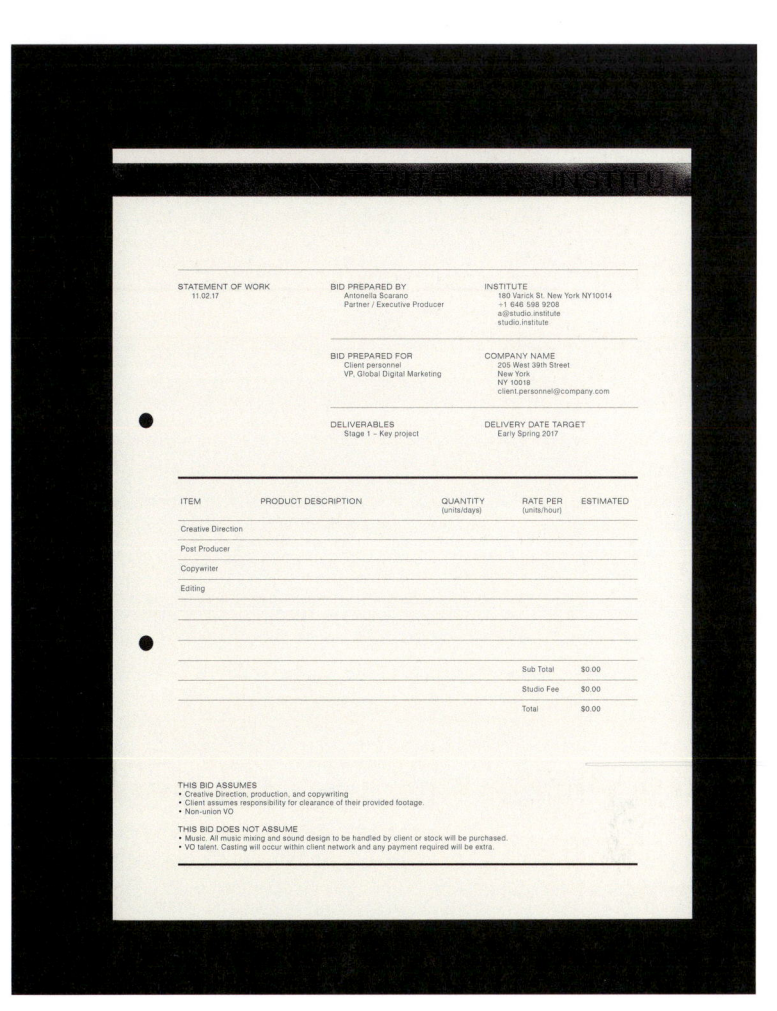

© William Kentridge, 2015

du mercredi au dimanche
12h – 20h

le mardi sur rendez-vous
01 48 04 70 52

Librairie Marian Goodman

Portraying birds in flight in the branding for a modern Parisian bookstore, *A PRACTICE FOR EVERYDAY LIFE* reminds us that reading lends wings to the senses.

Librairie Marian Goodman is located on Rue du Temple in Paris, a few doors from the larger Marian Goodman Gallery. A Practice for Everyday Life provided art direction for the exterior façade and interior renovation with a concept that exploits the dimensions of the space. The flexible display system can be reconfigured to accommodate a wide range of objects; and its open shelving units were designed to feature a variety of formats. The tables in the center of the space have two metal surfaces for displaying books on top and extra copies below. Working closely with architects OMMX to realize the design concept, A Practice for Everyday Life developed the signage, labeling, and packaging, which includes wrapping paper, stickers, and tote bags.

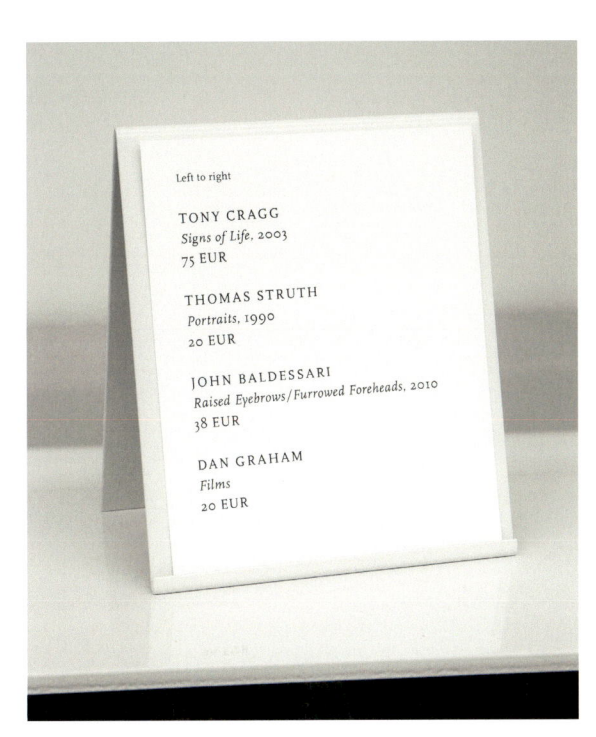

Left to right

TONY CRAGG
Signs of Life, 2003
75 EUR

THOMAS STRUTH
Portraits, 1990
20 EUR

JOHN BALDESSARI
Raised Eyebrows/Furrowed Foreheads, 2010
38 EUR

DAN GRAHAM
Films
20 EUR

92

44 Build & Tradesmith

<u>TRACTORBEAM</u> put their stamp on this Dallas-based custom fabrication workshop and retail space.

Located in the Deep Ellum neighborhood of Dallas, 44 Build is a custom fabrication workshop with a retail storefront, Tradesmith. The workshop specializes in using reclaimed and locally sourced materials for its authentic handmade pieces. Next door, Tradesmith sells the handmade furniture, clothes, and goods. Tractorbeam's brand identity highlights 44 Build's affinity for craft and authenticity; and like their products, it is flexible enough to work with a wide variety of materials. At the heart of the system is a set of 44 stamps developed for use on collateral and hang tags. They have an old-school look and analog function to communicate information in a visually pleasing way that aligns with the company's values.

The Informal Anymade Cafe

Black-and-white illustrations by ODDDS set the tone for this cafe and coffee brand whose house roasts provide fuel for creative insomniacs.

Oddds's branding for The Informal Anymade Cafe in Singapore is inspired by black coffee. A meditation on the hot drink's darkness, the visual identity uses a black and white palette along with moody product photography. Illustrations of hands appear across the design, symbolizing the brand's target market: creatives who work late into the night, fueled by caffeine. The illustrations are used individually on packaging, coasters, and other collateral, and are also arranged into a pattern with the logomark—the 'in' of informal has a line through it—and the names of its three house roasts: Cigarette Dust, Walking Hours, and Chanterelle Toss.

95

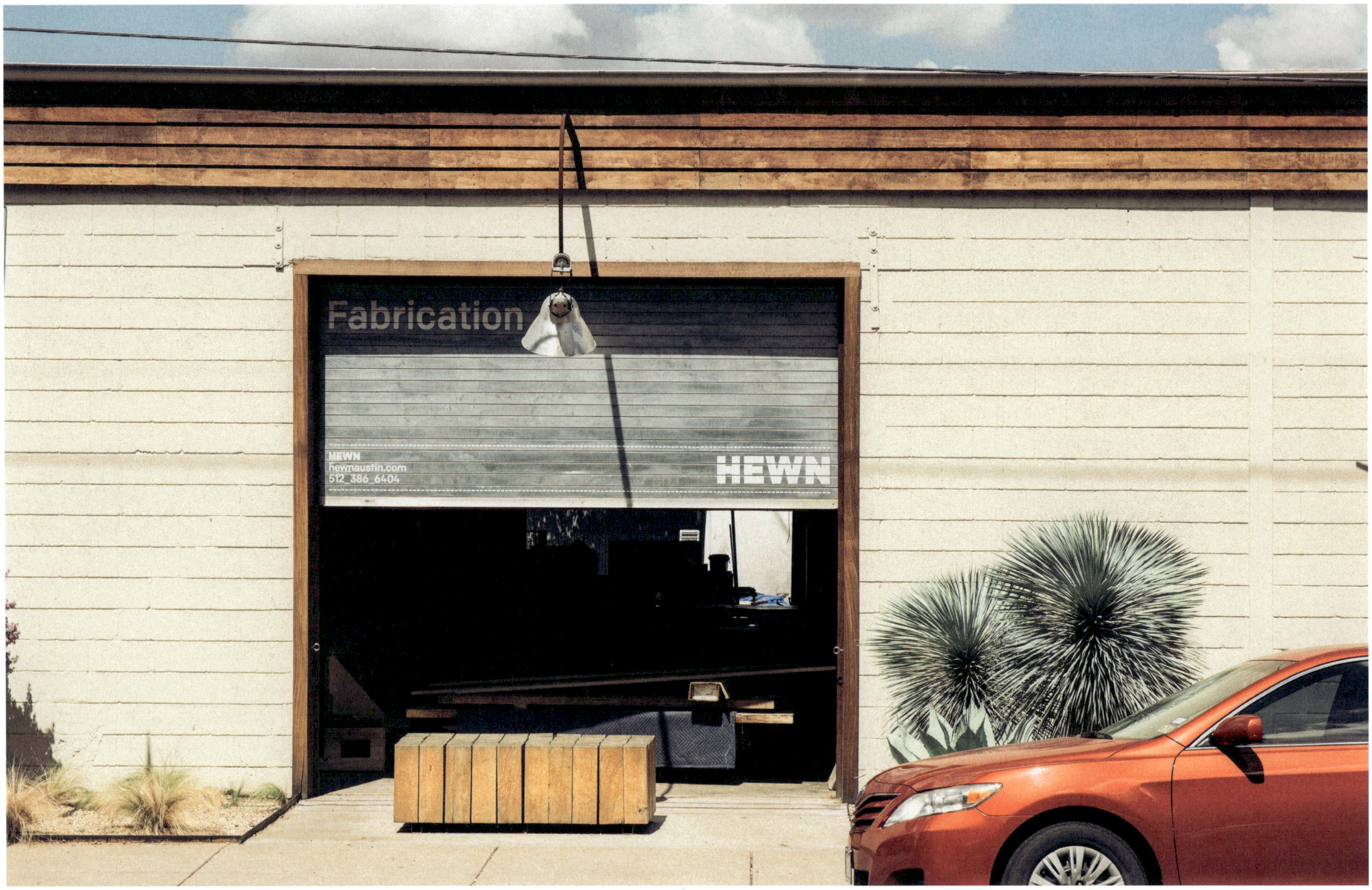
Fabrication
HEWN
hewnaustin.com
512_386_6404
HEWN

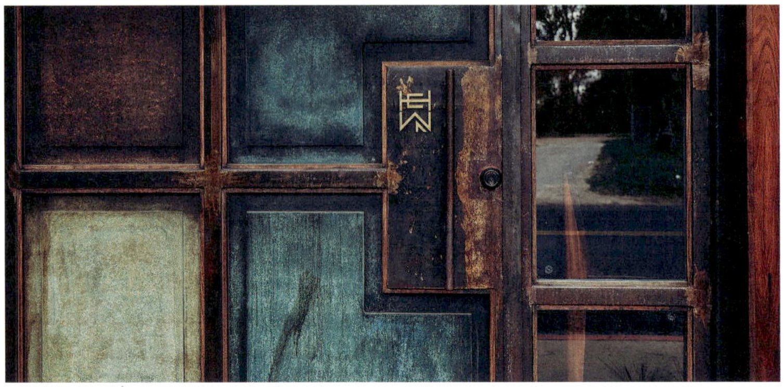

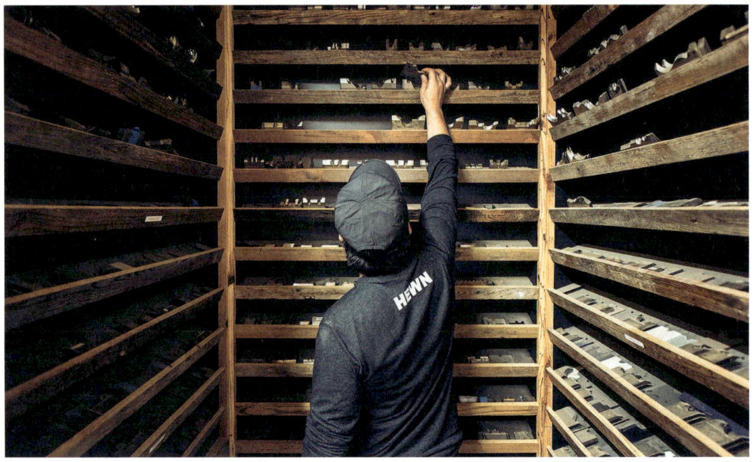
HEWN

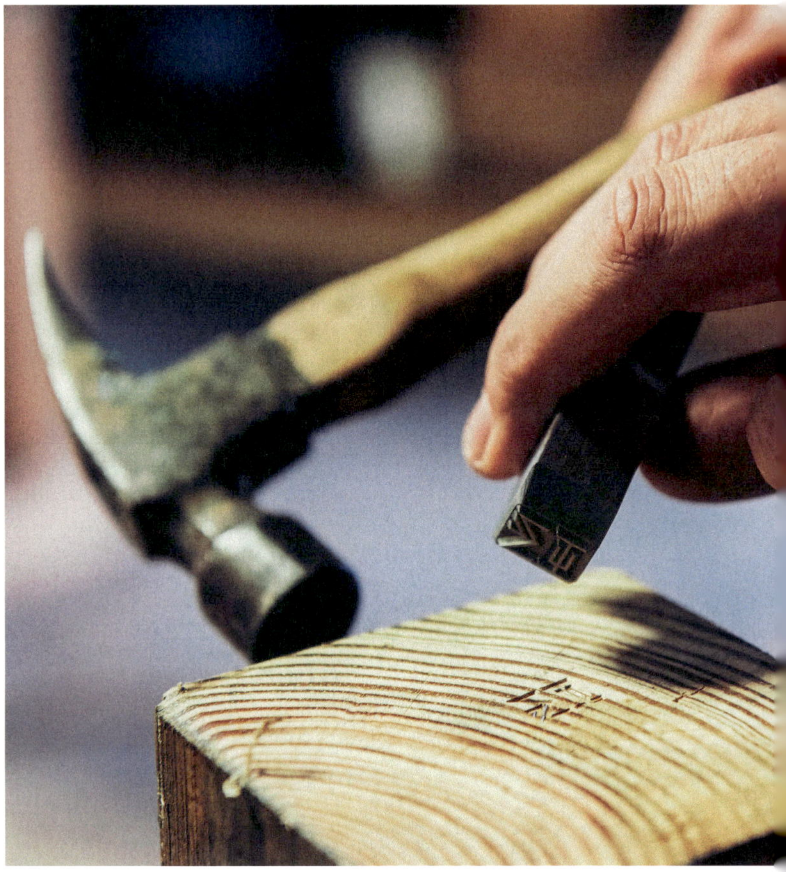

Hewn

FÖDA's rebranding communicates the Texan woodworking collective's dedication to quality building.

The master craftspeople at Hewn specialize in custom woodwork, high-end residential and commercial millwork, metal fabrication, and custom furniture, as well interior and exterior detailing using reclaimed and rare wood. Hewn engaged Föda to develop a new brand identity that would help it secure market share, ensure longevity, and lay the groundwork for future leadership transitions. Focusing on Hewn's reputation as a company with a local legacy and national presence, Föda created a new name, brand, identity system, environmental graphics, and operational kit. The Hewn logo is the focal point of the project, and its four letters are artfully rearranged to connect, overlap, and intertwine, just as the components of its building projects do.

Belmont Hotel

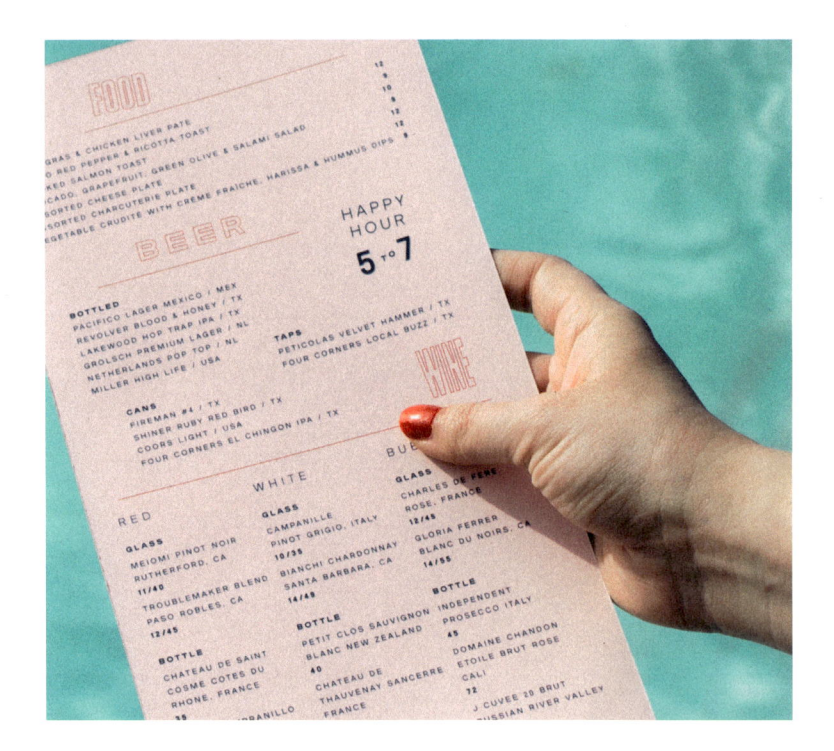

<u>TRACTORBEAM</u> combines mid-century ephemera and vintage photographs with contemporary graphics to give this former motor lodge a new lease of life.

Belmont Hotel is one of Dallas's most well-known properties. Opened in 1947 as a motor lodge, it has become beloved over the years for transporting its guests to a place unlike any other in the city. Tractorbeam's refreshed the branding by bringing the mid-century history of the Dallas icon to the forefront in order to speak to a new generation of guests. Digging through archives and old publications, Tractorbeam collected ephemera and photos from the hotel's past and used these to create a richly layered brand story. The photos and films they discovered also became a library of images to use across the hotel's website and social media accounts. The rebrand is authentically timeless like the property itself.

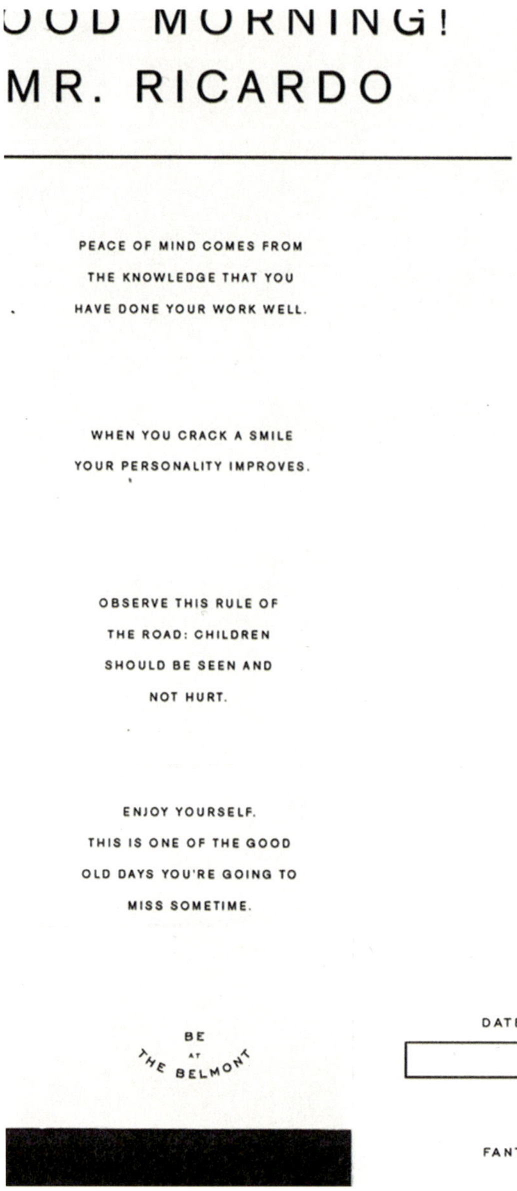

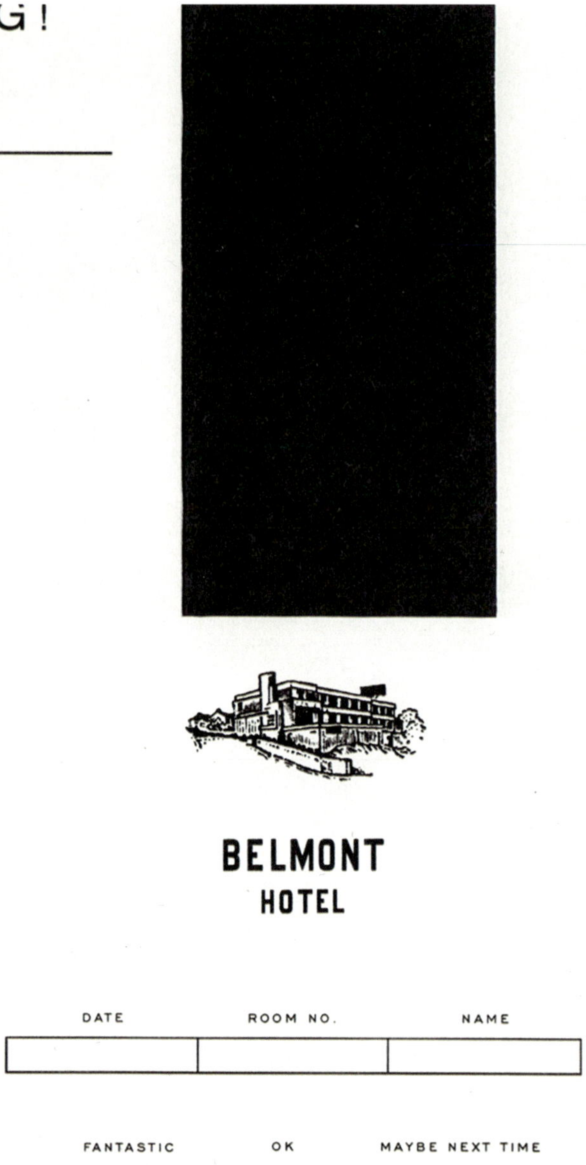

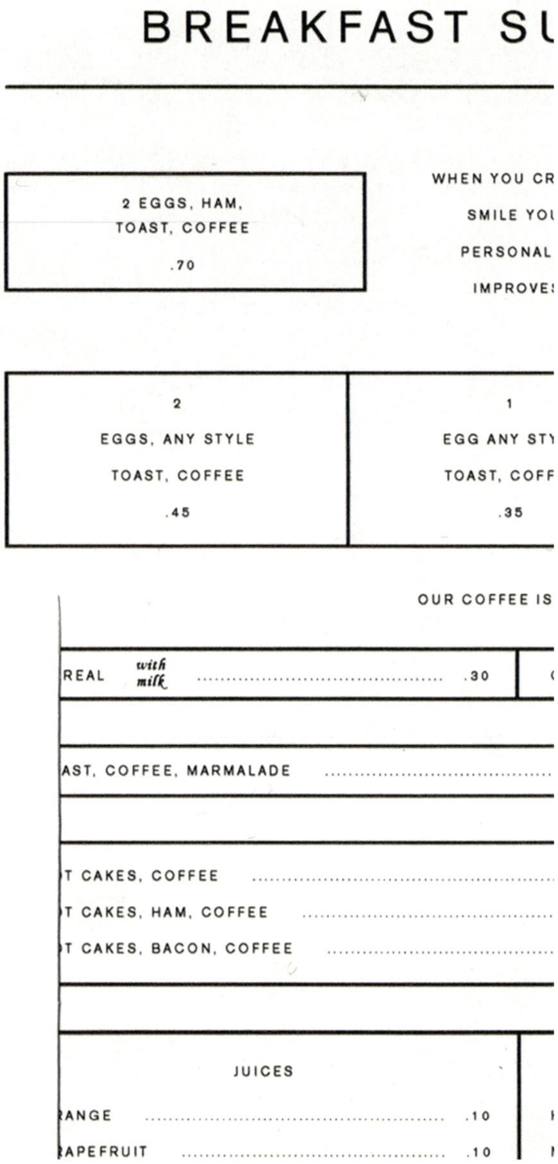

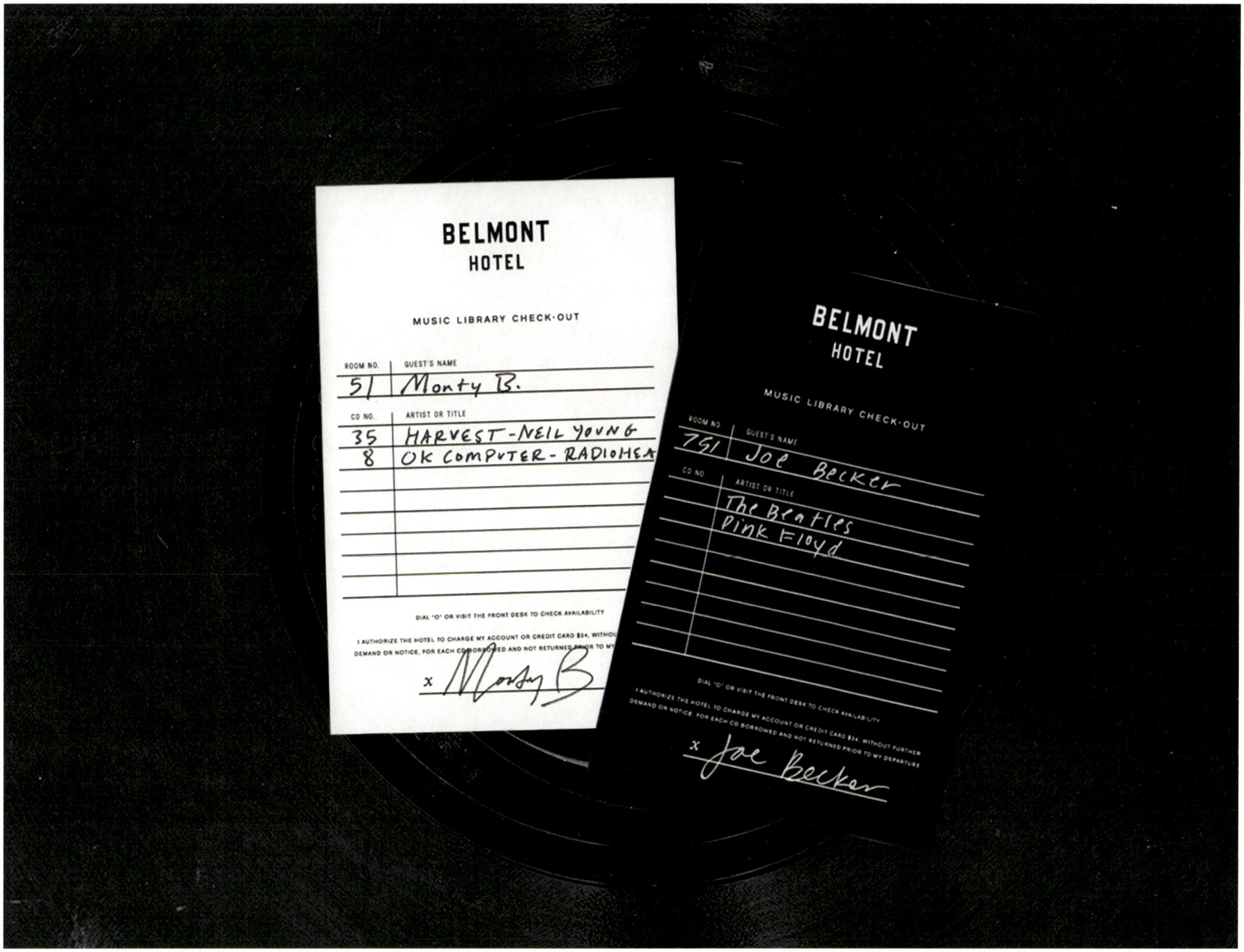
BELMONT
HOTEL
MUSIC LIBRARY CHECK-OUT
ROOM NO.
GUEST'S NAME
51
Monty B.
CD NO.
ARTIST OR TITLE
35
HARVEST - NEIL YOUNG
8
OK COMPUTER - RADIOHEA
DIAL "O" OR VISIT THE FRONT DESK TO CHECK AVAILABILITY
x Monty B
BELMONT
HOTEL
MUSIC LIBRARY CHECK-OUT
ROOM NO.
GUEST'S NAME
751
Joe Becker
CD NO.
ARTIST OR TITLE
The Beatles
Pink Floyd
DIAL "O" OR VISIT THE FRONT DESK TO CHECK AVAILABILITY
I AUTHORIZE THE HOTEL TO CHARGE MY ACCOUNT OR CREDIT CARD $24, WITHOUT FURTHER DEMAND OR NOTICE, FOR EACH CD BORROWED AND NOT RETURNED PRIOR TO MY DEPARTURE
x Joe Becker

BELMONT
HOTEL

Formal Opening
BELMONT Motor HOTEL
The Hotel with the Sky View!
Below, interiors at distinctive Belmont! Rooms with singing colors ... suites with unusual appointments ... each accommodation styled for convenience and comfort. Eye-catching color schemes emphasize the rare atmosphere created by resort-type architecture. Specially-built furnishings accent the note of refreshing hospitality which characterizes Belmont —the "Hotel With the Sky-View."
Today
Starting at 5 P.M.
Dallas reaches a new high in hospitality! You are invited to the spectacular event which launches "The Hotel With the Sky View" ... magnificent, unique Belmont Motor Hotel, Fort Worth Avenue. Only by SEEING will you believe such BEAUTY.
This afternoon at five, continuing until ten tonight, music will be provided by two orchestras— Ted Pasino's Serenaders, familiar to KRLD audiences, and the Dude Ranch Buckaroos from WFAA.
Sky-stabbing searchlights will guide your path this evening—to the brilliant setting for a 7:30 parade of Fall Forecast Fashions. Lovely models will show styles from Nardis, Donovan, Brogan-Jennings, Stockton, Marcy Lee, L & L, and Felix Chapeaux. Ken Lowell of the "Early Birds" will share M.C. honors at the public address microphone with Miss Lillian Caldwell, Fashion Commentator.
You'll have opportunity to see the handsome hotel with remarkable appointments— single and double rooms, cottages and suites. Explore the colorful rooms, year-round air-conditioned, gorgeously furnished. Meet Chef Damommio and have an early dinner in his air-cooled restaurant, then you'll be present for the open-air Fashion Parade. Meet Mr. and Mrs. J. B. Malone and Mr. Walter R. Smith, managing owners, who are today receiving congratulations for building in Dallas the beautiful Hotel with the Sky-View, Belmont Motor Hotel.
On the Spot Broadcast
WFAA 570, 3:00 to 3:30 P. M.
FEATURING "THE BUCKAROOS"
CONTRIBUTING TO THE LUXURY AND BEAUTY OF MAGNIFICENT BELMONT HOTEL
THESE DALLAS - FT. WORTH FIRMS EMPLOYED THEIR PROFESSIONAL ARTS AND SKILLS
CHARLES S. DILBECK, Architect • BURFORD CONSTRUCTION COMPANY
HARRIS-BEEMAN CO., Fort Worth • D. G. STRATHDEE, Ceramic Tile, Fort Worth
WM. F. KAUN & SON, Plumbing and Heating-Kohler Fixtures • HIDELL HARDWARE CO.
JESS CAMPBELL INSURANCE CO., Wichita Falls, Geo. Cooper, Dallas Representative
W. H. TRICE & SON, Floor Coverings, Dallas-Houston • THE SMILEY ELECTRONIC CO., Radios
Electrical Installations by SOUTHWEST ELECTRIC • PAINT CONTRACTING CO. of Texas
MISTER BUSTER STUDIO FURNITURE CO. • CUSTOM-BILT FURNITURE STUDIO
GARDNER HOTEL SUPPLY CO., Restaurant Supplies • J. F. ZIMMERMAN & SONS, Neon Signs
Congratulations from friends in Henderson, Texas

101

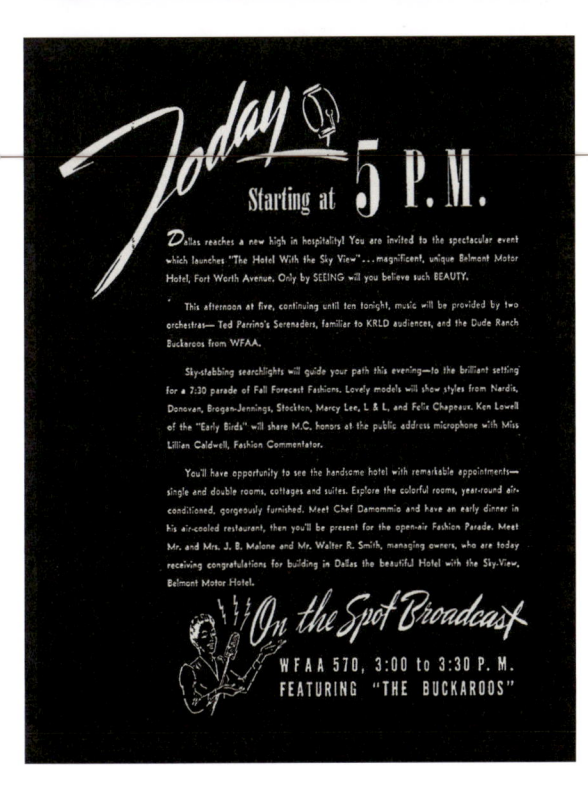

BELMONT
HOTEL

RE - LAX
YOU -
ARE -
HERE —
INTERNET ACCESS
COFFEE
ROOM SERVICE
LAUNDRY AND
DRY CLEANING SERVICE
END
EVERY SHEEP NEEDS A SHEPARD
DOODLE PAD
MIND
YOUR
SELF
TODAY / /
HIGHLIGHT OF THE DAY:
I'M THANKFUL FOR:
WHAT DID YOU LEARN TODAY?
I HOPE THAT:
USE
YOUR
TIME
WISELY

103

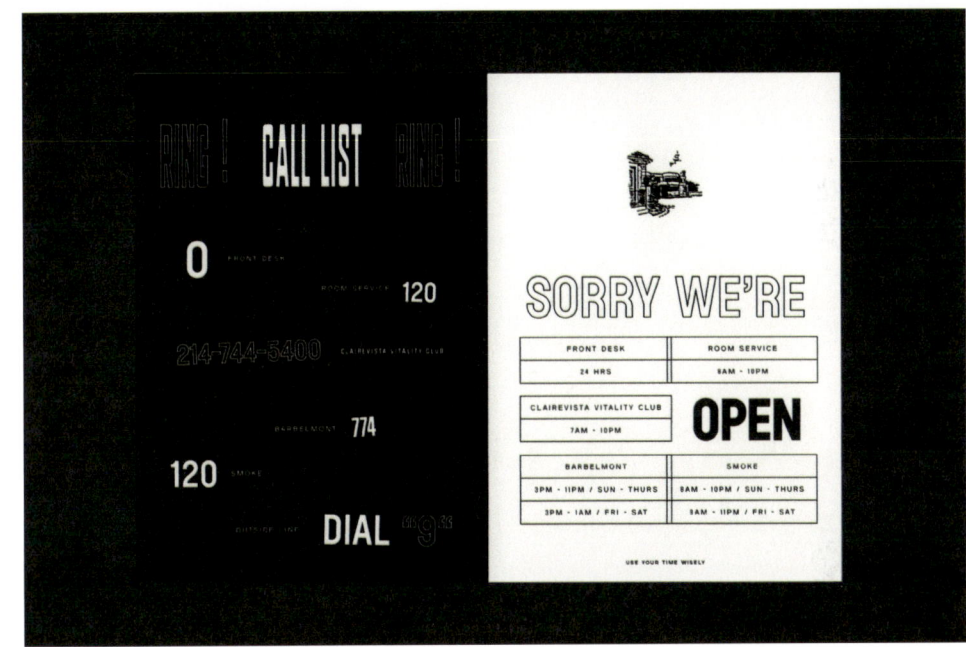

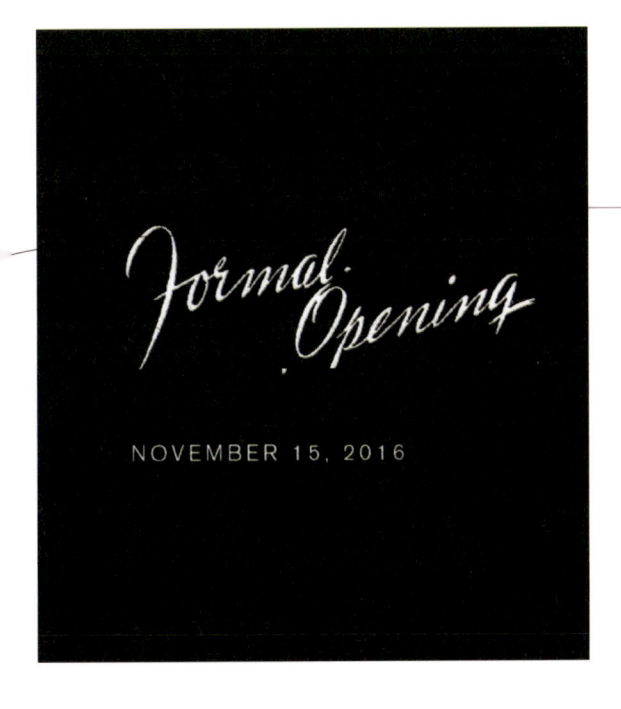

Velvet Coat

KIKU OBATA & COMPANY uses a subtle blend of typefaces and font sizes to create a visual identity with edge for this fashion retailer from Iowa.

Velvet Coat retails clothes and accessories by established and emerging designers. With a focus on casual luxury items that can be worn every day, its two inviting retail locations in Iowa also accommodate regular cultural events. Kiku Obata developed Velvet Coat's visual identity using characters from three different typefaces, as well as InDesign GREP styles, which gives a subtle edge to the traditional look. The collateral uses letterpress printing on affordable materials to align with the fashion retailer's commitment to providing luxury goods that are accessible and wearable.

Black Friday Sale

360 Sweater
Bella Dahl
Chinti & Parker
Citizens of Humanity
Ecru
Frame
Lilla P
Margaret O'Leary
Rag & Bone
Raquel Allegra
Trina Turk
Velvet
Vince
…

Fall Collections
40–50% off

Fri, Sat, Sun
November 25–27

Velvet Coat

Image © Loeffler Randall

Opaak

Sensual and sleek, <u>DEUTSCHE & JAPANER</u>'s brand identity for the Cologne-based bodywear company redefines the visual language of lingerie.

Opaak designs contemporary bodywear for women in search of something bold rather than frilly. The company's striking style combines technology with sensuality, a visual language that is reflected in its branding by Deutsche & Japaner. The studio's liberal use of black provides a dramatic backdrop for the company's minimal serif logo, as well as its packaging, where it allows the garments to take center stage. A gridded dot pattern echoes the mesh material often used in its products, while pops of red and blush underscore the brand's sensual nature. By juxtaposing strong typography with erotic product photography, the designers created a sexy yet assertive look that is meant to empower rather than to objectify women.

107

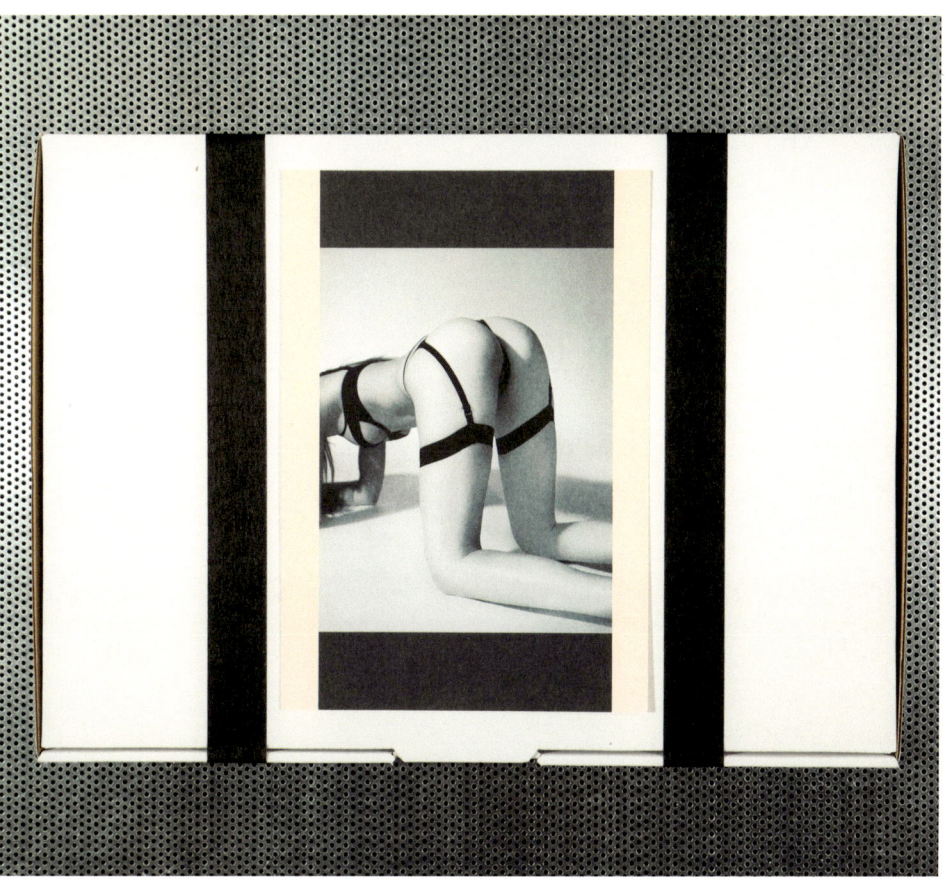

108

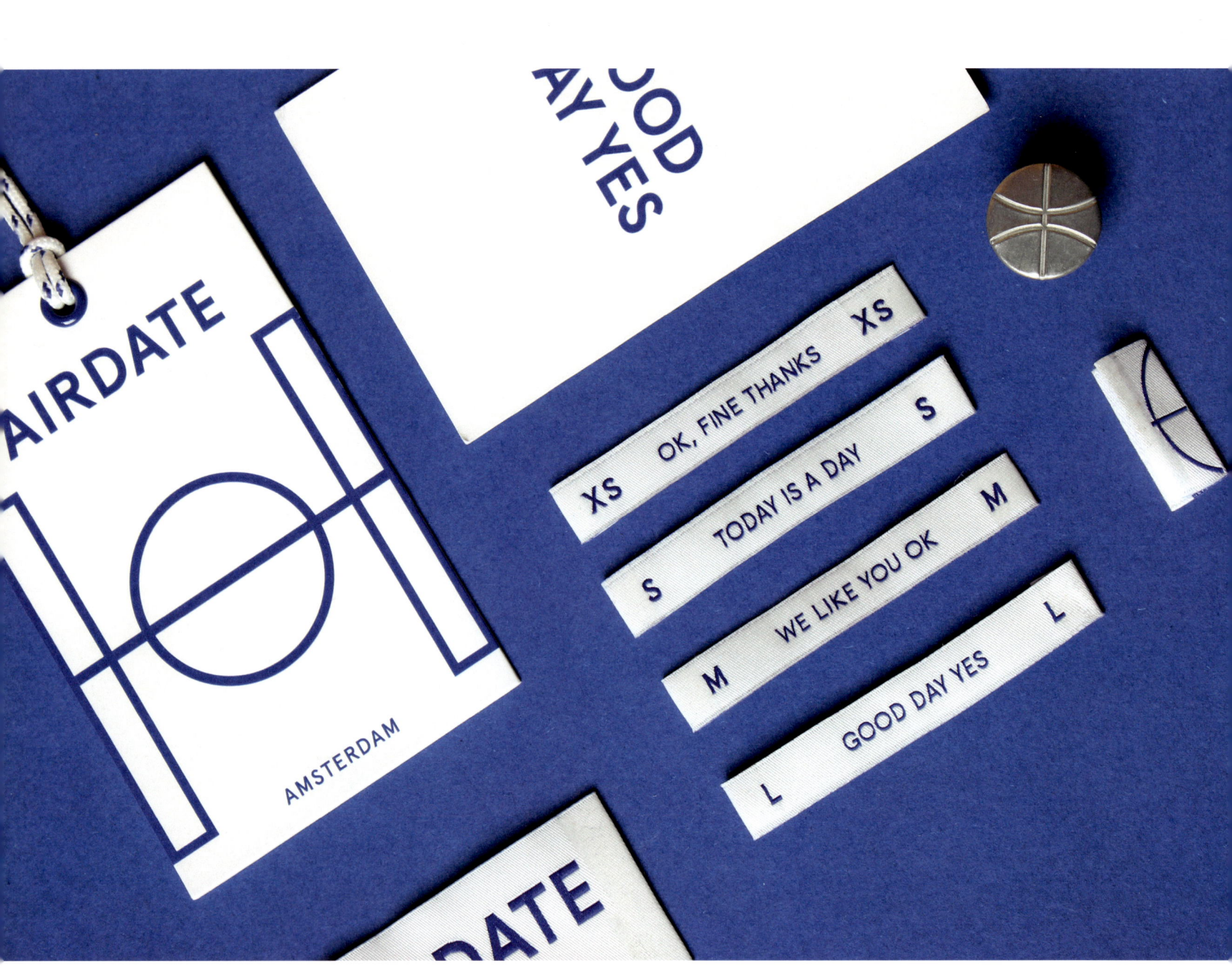

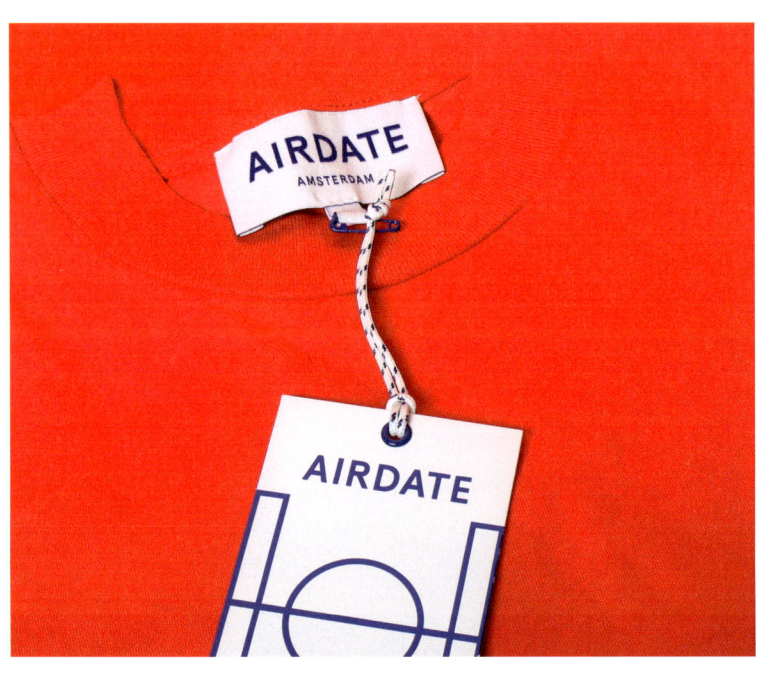

Airdate

MARTA VELUDO's sporty identity for the female fashion brand plays with graphic icons and fresh colors to reflect the label's nonchalant reputation.

When creative agency Men at Work started their own fashion label, they asked Marta Veludo to help develop and design the branding. The Amsterdam-based designer's solution is simple, casual, and extremely flexible and uses a variety of graphic icons that work across Airdate's collateral, including tags, tote bags, coffee cups, and its digital presence. The royal blue and white color palette emphasizes the geometric forms of the basketball-court icon. Unpretentious, cool, and pleasantly straightfoward, Veludo's visual language speaks to the relaxed and confident modern woman it is made for.

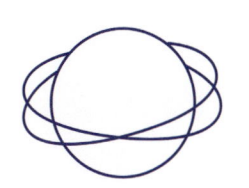

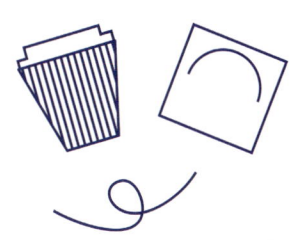

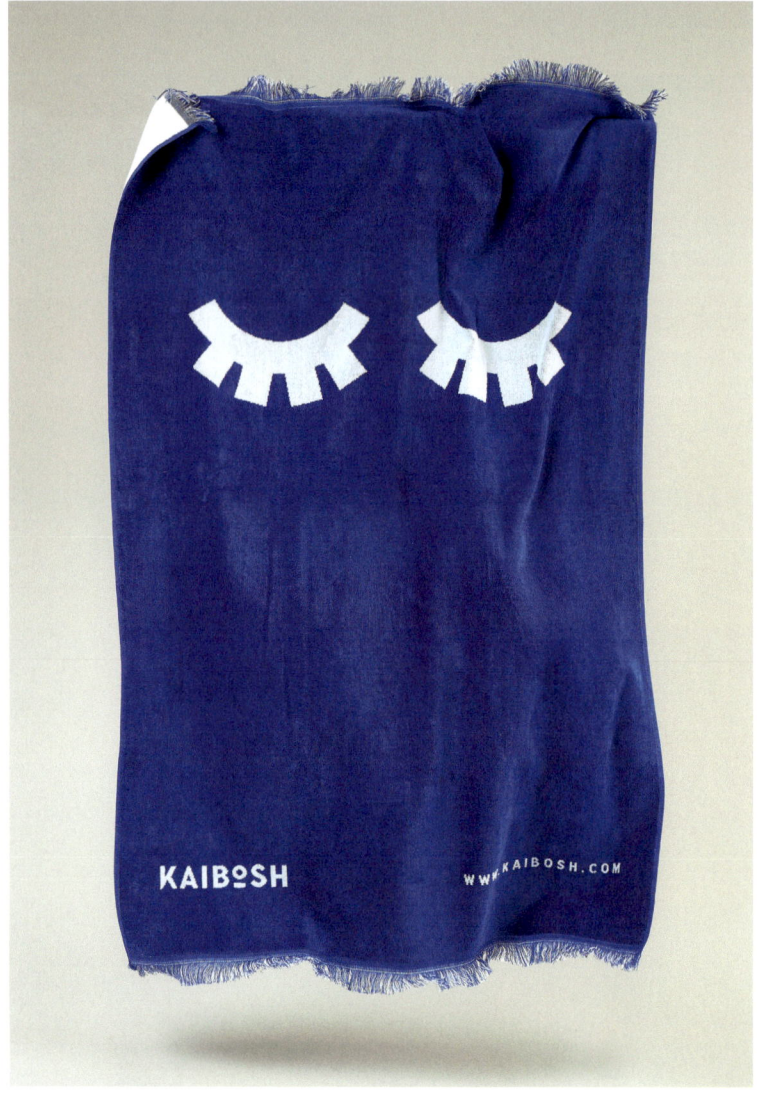

Kaibosh

SNASK takes a playful approach to let the eyewear brand's outgoing personality shine through.

The original identity of Norwegian eyewear brand Kaibosh was too minimal and subdued to accurately reflect its trendy and bold personality. Stockholm-based studio Snask created a more expressive look while retaining the original logotype. Snask's solution started with establishing the tone of voice, as the branding strategy relies heavily on creative copywriting and typography used across promotional materials and the interior of the store. The designers introduced a set of eyelashes, as a fun and distinctive graphic element that appears on signage and packaging. They also designed the brand's flagship store, including shelving, murals, and colors.

100% KAIBOSH DESIGN

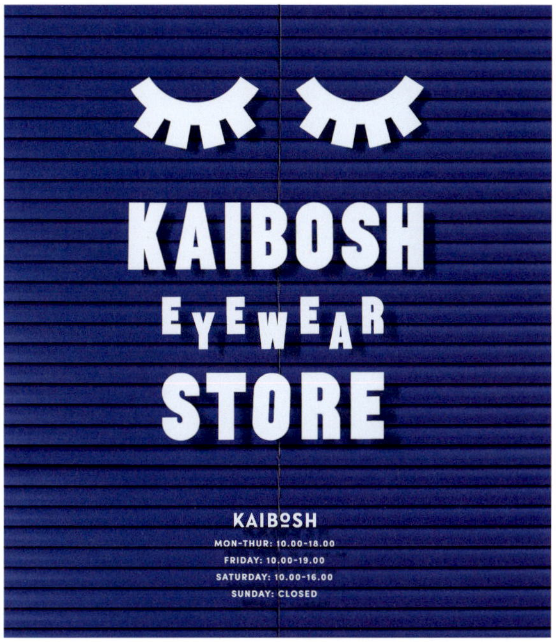
KAIBOSH
EYEWEAR
STORE
KAIBOSH
MON-THUR: 10.00-18.00
FRIDAY: 10.00-19.00
SATURDAY: 10.00-16.00
SUNDAY: CLOSED

OUTTA
(UNKNOWN)
BOOM BOOM
MISS JOPLIN · MISS JOPLIN ·

FEELING BLIND?
DON'T BE SAD.
WE DO EYE TESTS!

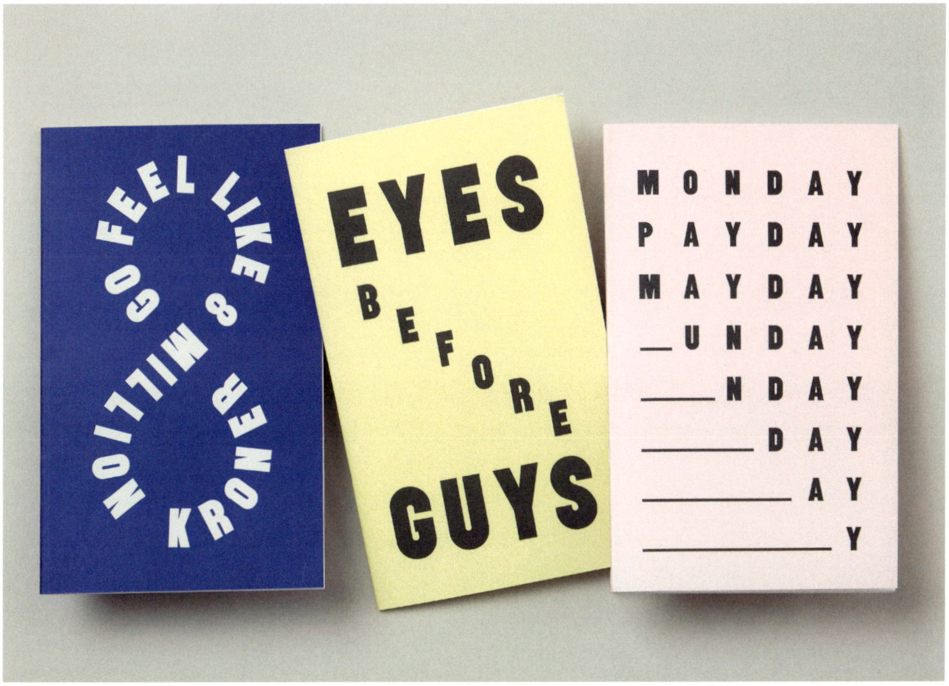
GO FEEL LIKE 8 MILLION KRONER
EYES BEFORE GUYS
MONDAY
PAYDAY
MAYDAY
_UNDAY
___NDAY
____DAY
_____AY
______Y

KAIBOSH
GO MAKE
CUSTOM
FEEL LI
MILL
KRON
KAIBOSH STAFF HAND BOOK -> VERS
WWW.KAIBOSH.COM
OUTTA
OUTTA
SIGHT
KAIBOSH
KAIBOSH SCANDINAVIAN EYEWEAR CONCEPT
WWW.KAIBOSH.COM · @KAIBOSH_CO

EYES BEFORE GUYS

IT'S A WRAP! A WRAP!

WiNE LIST
FOOD MENU
ViNKöKET
A MEAL WITHOUT WINE IS CALLED BREAKFAST
SPARKLING BY THE GLAS
WHITE BY THE GLAS
LE ROUGE WINES
REDS
SNACKS
SMÅRÄTTER
MELLANRÄTTER

SÉGURET
2011
Moulin à Vent
2015
REY MORO
2012
SIERRA DE GREDOS
FAUGÈRES
2012
DOMAINE LEON BARRAL

Vinköket

<u>LOBBY DESIGN</u>'s branding for the restaurant and wine bar in Stockholm underscores the establishment's appreciation of casual enjoyment and community.

In the basement of a historic building in Stockholm's old town resides a restaurant and wine bar with the intimate atmosphere of a private dinner party. Vinköket has a first-class menu, and yet its visual identity, cafted by Lobby Design, is decidedly unpretentious. Inspired by the noble drops served by the bar and restaurant, the designers created a wine-inspired color palette and combined it with materials found on a wine bottle, such as the cork and gold foil, which appear on menus and business cards. Pictures on the wall feature vintage black-and-white portraits with bright splashes of color like wine marks, adding a final touch of humor.

Graze

<u>**MADISON TIERNEY**</u>'s moody identity for the wine bar and delicatessen marries historicity with hipness.

Graze's interpretation of the classic Italian enoteca, which traditionally serves wine and small plates of food, is a wine bar and delicatessen designed to be a place for friends to meet. Madison Tierney conceived the identity system as an homage to pre-nineteenth-century Europe, opting for a dark color palette and imagery inspired by sixteenth- and seventeenth-century still-life paintings. Instead of highly stylized, flat-lay food photography and sans serif typefaces, the designers chose a font called Blackletter, a Gothic script that has a long history in European graphic treatments and further emphasizes the brand's relationship to Italian tradition.

117

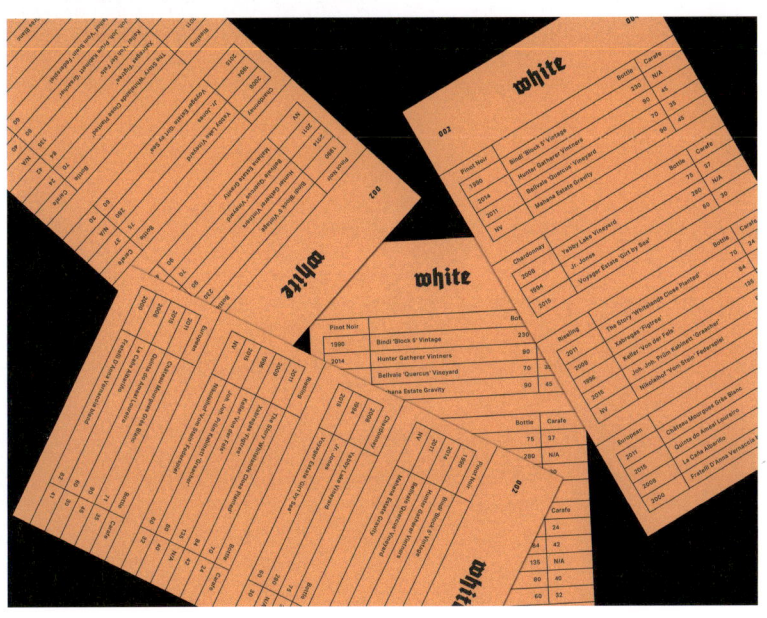

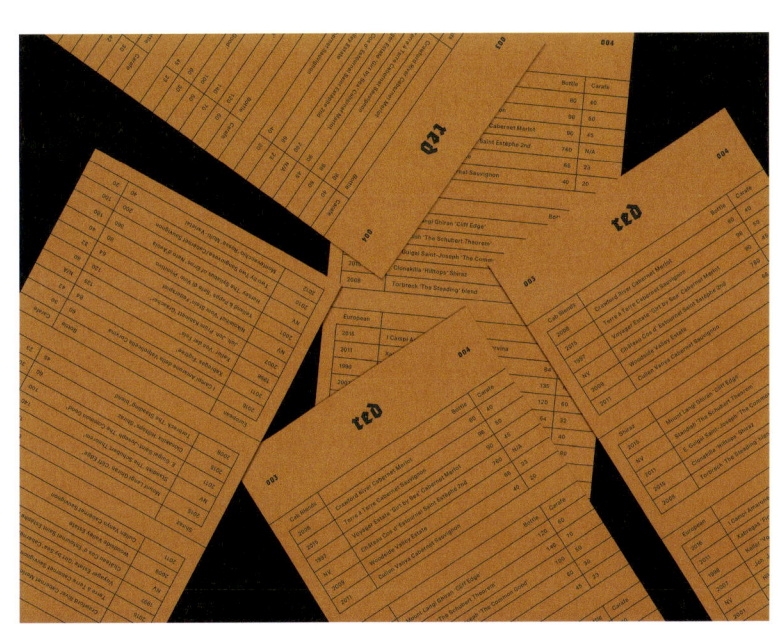

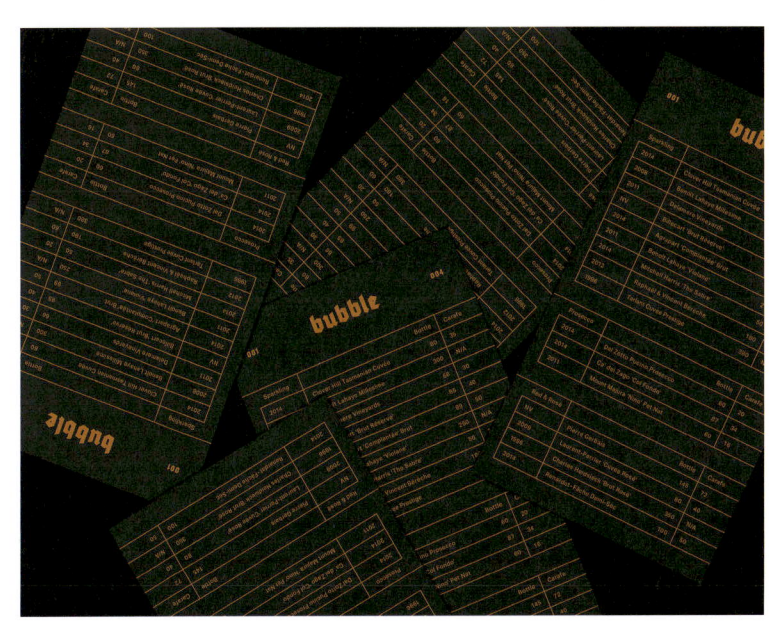

118

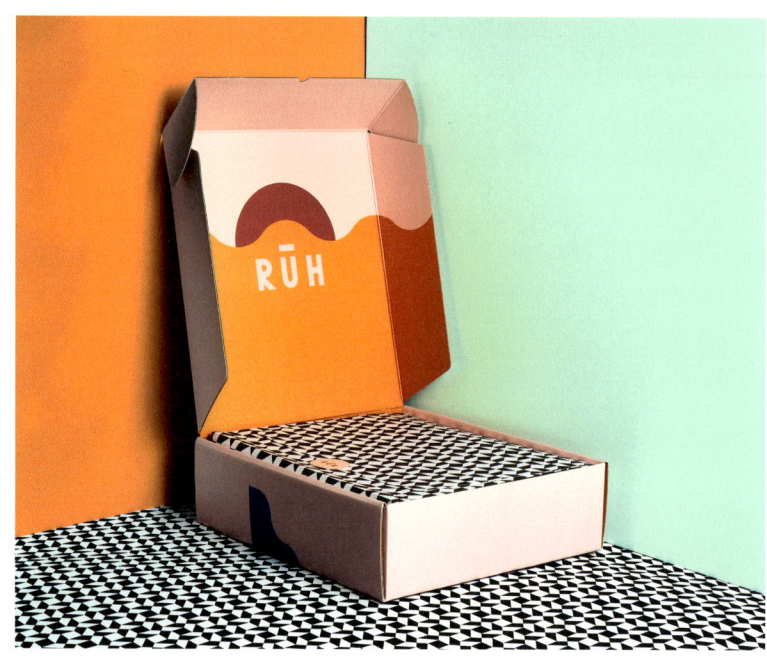

RŪH Collective

The modern spirit of the London-based fashion collective's Muslim clientele finds a voice in *LETA SOBIERAJSKI*'s boldly colored geometric design.

Founded by creatives from New York, London, and Istanbul, RŪH Collective is a London-based fashion brand for women who dress modestly but not quietly. The collective gives a retail platform to entrepreneurs who value respect and opportunity. Designer Leta Sobierajski's approach for RŪH's visual identity uses colorful geometric illustrations to convey the modern sensibilities of its fashion-forward clientele. The five colors in the palette are influenced by the five times a day that Muslims come to pray, while the geometric illustrations and patterns adhere to the same grid as the typographic identity. The final look is reminiscent of vintage block art and is finished with a touch of copper foil for a subtle shine.

Van Leeuwen

__PENTAGRAM's__ photogenic packaging for the ice cream maker encourages sharing on social media.

Brooklyn-based Van Leeuwen has been making ice cream with all natural ingredients since 2007. For its 10-year anniversary, the owners wanted to set the company apart in the now-crowded world of artisan ice cream. They worked closely with Natasha Jan from Pentagram to rebrand company by reducing the visual clutter on existing packaging and developing a color palette that reflects the purity of the ice cream ingredients. The move unifies Van Leeuwen's regular and vegan lines and helps customers easily differentiate flavors. The solution is easily adaptable for future product lines and so deliciously colorful that fans regularly share Van Leeuwen's products on Instagram, which has helped lead to a significant increase in sales.

CO-FOUNDER
PETE
VAN LEEUWEN
CO-FOUNDER
LAURA
O'NEILL
Van Leeuwen
CO-FOUNDER
BEN
VAN LEEUWEN

Van Leeuwen

Van Leeuwen
GIFT CARD
REDEEMABLE FOR GOODS AT
ANY VAN LEEUWEN STORE OR TRUCK
VANLEEUWENICECREAM
VLAIC
VANLEEUWENICECREAM.COM

HANDCRAFTED IN BROOKLYN SINCE 2008
ICE CREAM
&
VEGAN ICE CREAM
VAN LEEUWEN
56 DOBBIN ST
BROOKLYN
NY 11222
Van Leeuwen
@VLAIC
@VANLEEUWENICECREAM
EVENTS
EVENTS@VANLEEUWENICECREAM.COM
VANLEEUWENICECREAM.COM

122

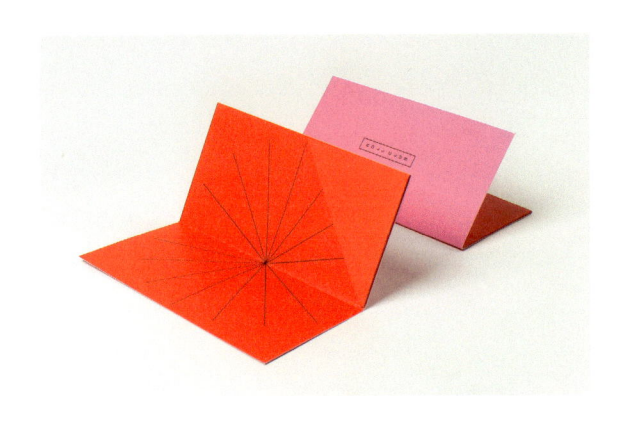

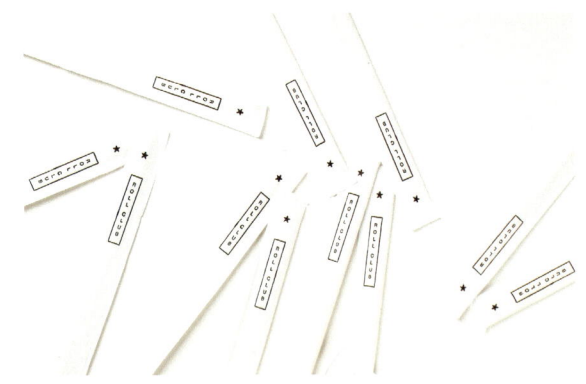

Roll Club

CANAPÉ translates the broad range of culinary options available from the restaurant and food delivery service into a tasty visual identity system.

Roll Club started as a food delivery service in the Ukrainian city Kharkiv before expanding into a restaurant in the city's center. Canapé developed a new identity system to bring both businesses together under one modern brand. The logomark and graphic patterns represent the different cuisines and countries on Roll Club's menu. The logo combines a tomato and fish to symbolize Western and Eastern cuisine, and the patterns include the stars and stripes for America and olives for Italy. The symbols and colorful palette are incorporated in the interior of the restaurant with design elements such as blue and pink floors, red stairs, and olive lamps.

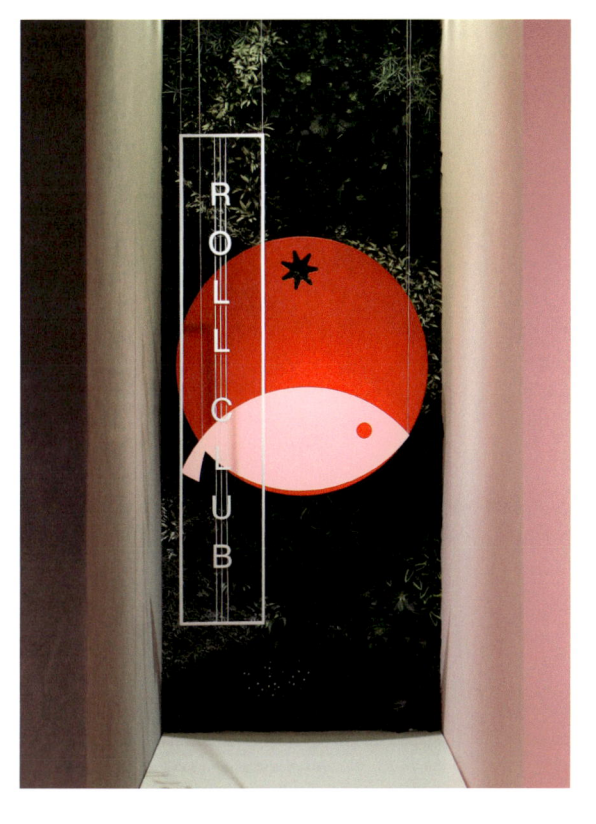

ROLL
CLUB

ОТКРЫТИЕ ПЕРВОГО
ФИРМЕННОГО РЕСТОРАНА
ROLL CLUB

РЫТИЕ
ЖДЕМ В ГОСТИ
ПО АДРЕСУ
ПЛ. КОНСТИТУЦИИ, 18
ROLL CLUB
SUSHI
10:00
23:00
ROLL-CLUB.KH.UA

CHAMBERTIN
Grand Cru
2013
RØDVIN

CHAMPAGNE
&
MUSSERENDE
RØDVIN
GAVEKORT
GIN
&
TONIC
TERRITORIET
VIN & VINYL
Magnus Egerdahl Nørsett
TERRITORIET

Territoriet

OLSSØN BARBIERI created a Futurist identity system and analog sound machine for the Oslo bar.

Founded by two wine lovers with backgrounds in photography and music, Territoriet is a wine bar with a relaxed atmosphere that offers the creations of some of Oslo's best sommeliers. Olssøn Barbieri developed the brand identity inspired by the Futurist artist Luigi Russolo, whose work explored complex sounds generated by machines. The designers built a machine (which also became the bar's logo) that plays special punch cards developed for each type of wine. Brass and oak in the 1920s bar are incorporated into the identity, as well as traditional metal engraving typefaces, which evoke the era of industrial machinery and analog technology.

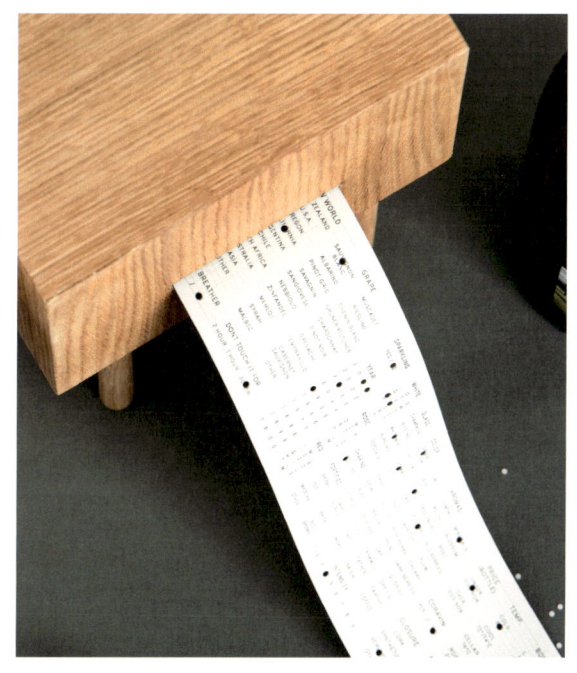

Botanist

GLASFURD & WALKER's visual identity for the Vancouver dining destination plays at the intersection of art and science.

From its decor to its cocktails and cuisine, Botanist in Vancouver reflects the character of the Pacific Northwest. Glasfurd & Walker's branding for the restaurant plays at the intersection of art and science, and it is inspired by gardens and greenhouses in which every plant is chosen for its function and beauty. Each printed piece of the identity incorporates the colors and details of the interior in which it will be used. The menus in the dining room are a mix of soft pastels that complement the femininity of the decor, while the bar menus reference the mixology of cocktails and read more like a botanist's journal, which further underscores the unity of science, art, and enjoyment.

BOTANIST

BAR
COCKTAILS,
WINE, BEER, SPIRITS.

BOTANIST

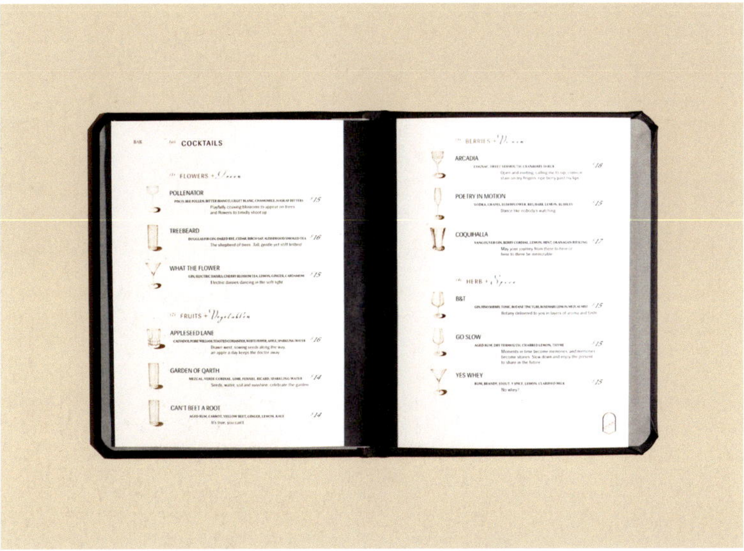
COCKTAILS

BOTANIST MEANS BUSINESS
BOTANIST

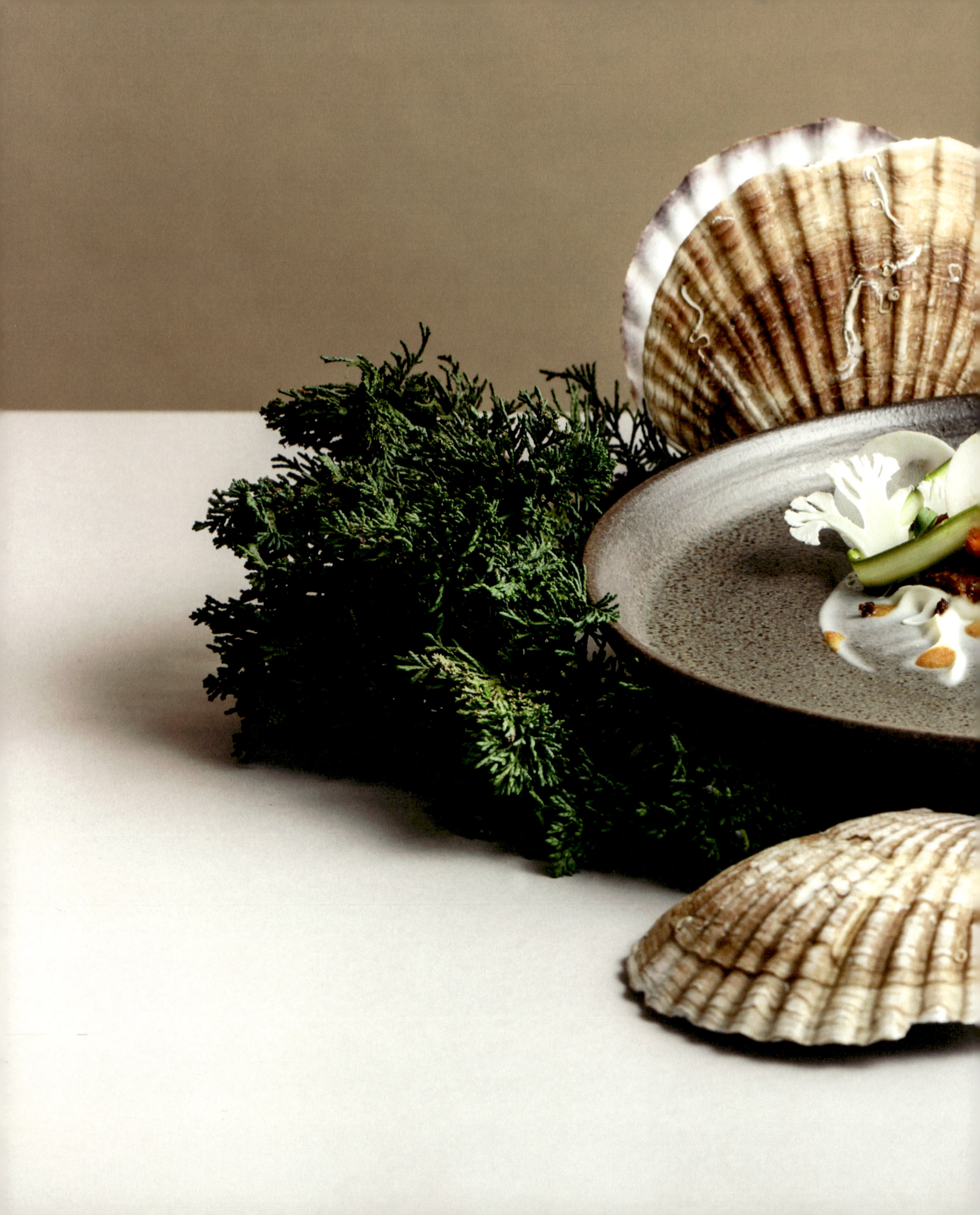

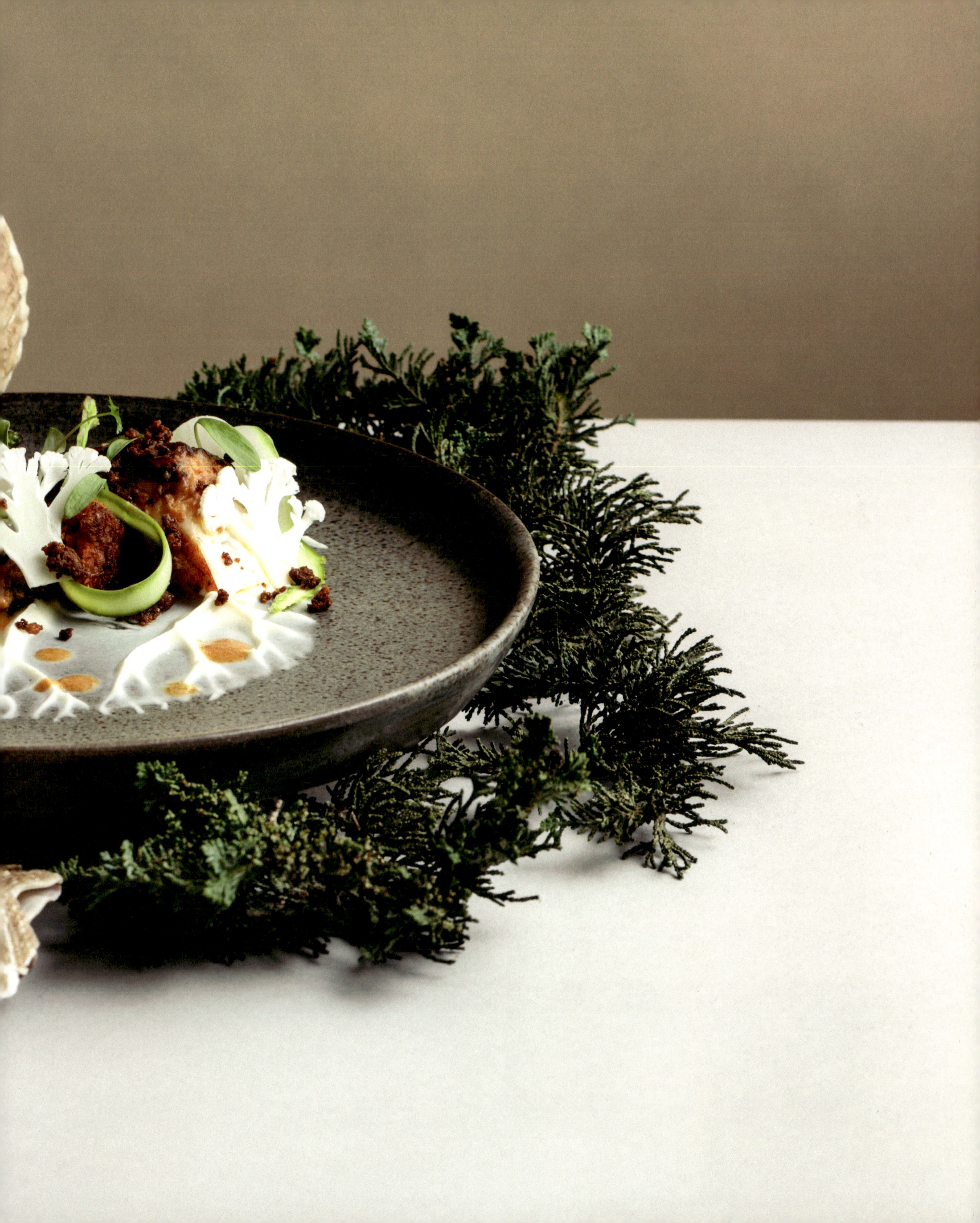

132

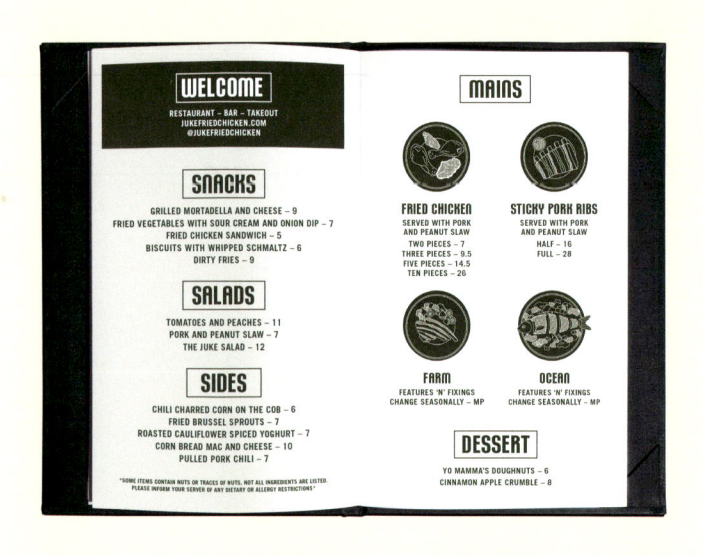

Juke Fried Chicken

GLASFURD & WALKER mixes humorous illustrations and a custom typeface to represent the easy-going atmosphere of the fried chicken restaurant.

Located in Vancouver, Juke Fried Chicken offers fried chicken in addition to a quality selection of cocktails and beer. The restaurant and bar has a fun, loud, and casual atmosphere that derives its inspiration from the 1970s music scene. Glasfurd & Walker designed the visual identity with a custom typeface named Juke Bold, which is inspired by disco records and the graphic design of the era. The logo features dancing chicken legs to reflect the spirit of the venue that doesn't take itself too seriously. Glasfurd & Walker also developed the restaurant's packaging system, including their 'jukeboxes' for takeout food, signage, menus, stationery, and social media animations.

Architecture &
Interior Design studio
SISTER
studio@
SISTER.melbourne

Architecture &
Interior Design studio
SISTER

Architecture &
Interior Design studio
SISTER
Lauren Martin
Architect
+61 418 911 504
lm@
SISTER.melbourne
studio@
SISTER.melbourne

Sister

MILDRED & DUCK's choice of natural papers reflects the architecture and interior design studio's appreciation for using natural materials in their projects.

Melbourne-based architecture and interior design practice Sister wanted a strong brand identity that would position it as a confident new studio in an extremely competitive field. Mildred & Duck's solution strikes a balance between minimalism and warmth using typography to soften the brand's strong wordmark. Sister has an appreciation for using raw materials in their natural state, and requested a tactile element to the design. Mildred & Duck expressed this through the use of uncoated, neutral paper stock and embedded the studio's wordmark into it with a multilevel emboss.

The Broadview Hotel

Branding by BLOK DESIGN for this boutique hotel in Toronto maintains the character of the historic building, while giving it a fresh, no-frills visual voice.

Established in 1891 in Toronto's East End, the Broadview Hotel is one of the city's most recognized architectural landmarks. When setting out to restore the building inside and out, its current owners built upon its lively reputation and gritty roots, and gave it new life as a luxury boutique hotel. Blok Design developed its branding, which marries the old with the new. Historic imagery is juxtaposed with modern type, a geometric motif takes cues from the steel frame and glass structure of the hotel's new floor, and witty phrases add personality. From signage to door hangers, the black-and-white color theme with emerald green tie it all together, creating an identity that feels contemporary, while maintaining the hotel's original character.

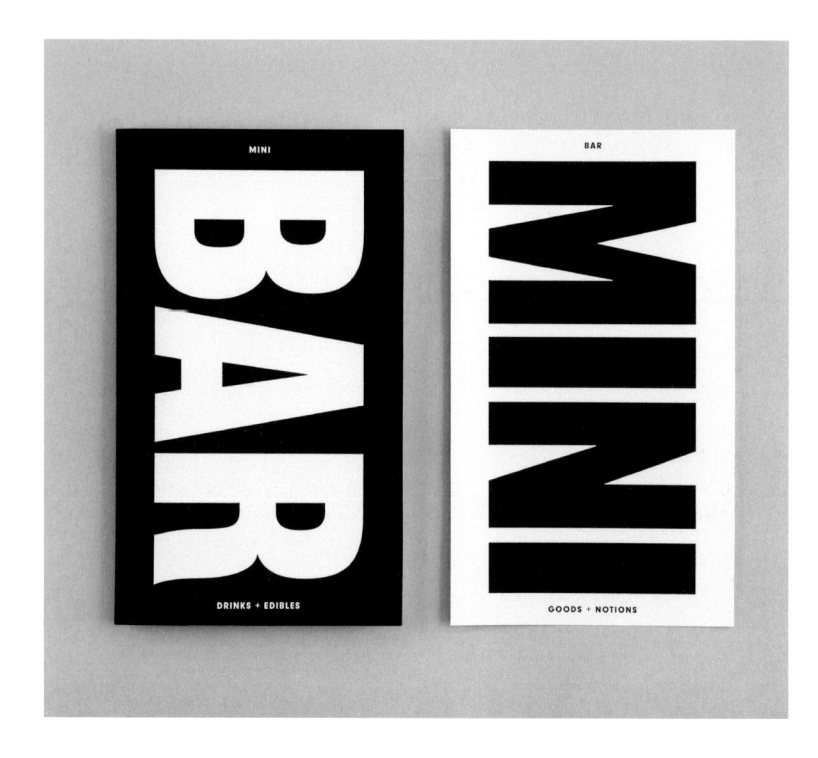

EAST
EAST
EAST

THE BROADVIEW | THE BROADVIEW

THE BROADVIEW | HOTEL

HOTEL

137

138

Liars Bench Beer Co.

HAIGH + MARTINO crosses its fingers with a humorous identity for the New Hampshire brewpub.

Started by two friends with a sense of humor and a passion for beer, Liars Bench Beer Co. is a brewpub with a relaxed and welcoming atmosphere. Its name refers to a place to drink, tell lies, and make undue promises; and the owners asked Haigh + Martino to create an identity that communicated the idea of "talking shit over a beer." Drawing inspiration from the art of conversation, literature, and old Midwest gas stations, they came up with the fingers-crossed logo. The hand gesture commonly symbolizes wishing for luck as well as invalidating a promise. In addition to the company's print collateral, the logo graphic is used on the merchandise and beer bottles.

SAINT LOU'S ASSEMBLY

SAINT LOU'S ASSEMBLY

SAINT LOU'S ASSEMBLY

SAINT LOU'S ASSEMBLY

CASE STUDY: # Saint Lou's Assembly

Saint Lou's Assembly is a Midwestern take on the Southern meat-and-three restaurant, serving seasonal combinations of one meat course plus three side dishes. **DAN BLACKMAN**'s design for the Chicago venue evokes the informal take-your-tray-and-load-up experience that also dominated the old-school diners in the former meatpacking neighborhood. Above all else, the brand pays homage to Lou Finkelman, the owner's grandfather, whose meatpacking factory was located only a few blocks away.

Once the domain of family-owned meatpackers and food wholesalers, Chicago's Fulton Market District has developed into a western extension of the "Loop", the city's central business district. Construction cranes dot the area's building plots, ready to erect more skyscrapers. Tech firms like Google now have offices here, and McDonald's recently opened its brand new HQ. Although a fairly fresh addition to the neighborhood, Saint Lou's Assembly presents itself as a reminder of a quieter time. A time when Bruce Finkelman's grandfather Lou still habitually worked and dined in the area.

"Old Lou owned a meatpacking place right around the corner from our premises," Finkelman recounts. The successful restaurateur had been on the lookout for a property to start a new project with his hospitality collective 16" on Center (16OC). More or less by chance, he found one that he had

"Whenever we start a fresh project, we first look for the space to tell us what should be there. The idea of design should always be aided by what the property gives you, by the story it tells."

known since his childhood. "It was a place my father had taken me many times for lunch," he remembers—a traditional diner, similar to the ones his grandfather had frequented through the '40s and '50s with his workers.

"He died only 14 days after I was born, so I didn't really know him, but a lot about Lou has been passed down from my relatives," Finkelman says. Drawing on old family pictures and anecdotes, he elaborated on the idea of a throwback dining experience that would pay tribute to the departed elder, and condensed much of the information he had into one poetic paragraph: "Lou smoked cigarettes. He drove a Cadillac, had a foul mouth, loved Elvis, hated people from New York City. Loved his wife and kids, hated his neighbors, loved the Bears. He loved red meat and sunshine on his face in the morning. He lived his life the way he pleased, was always fair with others; and to many close to him, Lou was a damn saint." This would set the tone for Saint Lou's Assembly.

"Coming up with the concept, story, and direction is the framework that must be agreed upon before the actual design phase begins, and oftentimes, it is the most fun," says designer Dan Blackman, who worked with Finkelman on the restaurant's branding, and on a series of other prosperous hospitality ventures. This includes Dusek's Board and Beer, a beer-centric restaurant in Chicago's Pilsen neighborhood; The Promontory, a restaurant and bar designed around its brick hearth and named after a close-by peninsula that juts into Lake Michigan; and Moneygun, a discreet cocktail joint located in a former dive bar under Chicago's "L" train.

"Each restaurant, bar, and venue within the collective is a stand-alone business, but 16OC exists to provide support and services to strengthen each and every one," Finkelman and his business partner Craig Golden explain. Like that of Saint Lou's Assembly, their concepts are generally derived from anecdotes, events, or the historical past of their premises: "When we start a fresh project, we first look for the space to tell us what should be there," the restaurateurs share. "The idea of design should always be aided by what the property gives you, by the story it tells."

Recalling his first impression of the location to be turned into Saint Lou's, Dan Blackman describes "an old shitty diner that desperately needed a facelift,"

adding that for both Finkelman and himself, this was "the dream." Bleak and dingy, the place provided the perfect canvas for the revamped but still rather unpolished dining experience they had in mind. As Finkelman puts it, "sometimes letting the history of the project shine through is a better design choice then trying to turn it into Disneyland."

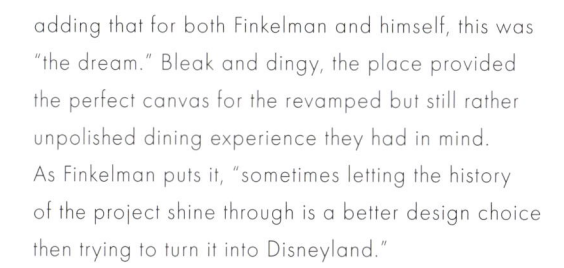

"When we arrived we found an old shitty diner that desperately needed a facelift."

Far from Disneyland indeed, Blackman's design is characterized by a "slightly unfinished" look, with simple primary colors, vintage photography, a typewriter-style font, and the deliberately wonky letterings drawn by hand onto the building by Chicago-based sign painters Right Way Signs. "I wanted it all to feel a bit cheaply made, inspired but not kitschy, nostalgic and fresh at the same time," the designer explains, adding that the resulting no-frills style reflects his idea of old Lou's straight-to-the-chase-mentality: "In my mind, Lou was the kind of guy to choose cheaper materials, do things himself where he can, and do anything to keep his customers happy while saving a buck. The kind of guy that reminded me of what I would think of as a used car salesman from the 50s. A character that was fun to tap into and translate visually."

"It's a pretty surreal experience to see something that personal utilized in a public space. It took a little while for my family to get used to, but I think they're proud of what the space has become."

Besides being named and generally inspired by Lou, the restaurant's graphics and interior are interspersed with old photos from Finkelman's family albums. "It's a pretty surreal experience to see something that personal utilized in such a public space," Finkelman says when asked about the experience of blending a business project with such personal memories and materials. "It took a little while for my family to get used to, but I think they're proud of what the space has become. I feel really lucky to be able to honor my father and grandfather's connection with the area in which Saint Lou's Assembly resides."

They have a saying at 16OC that they don't pick their projects, the projects pick them. Closely intertwined with Finkelman's own family history, one may assume that Saint Lou's is particularly close to his heart, but he dissents. "Everything we do is a really personal project. The idea that life is too short to work on things you're not interested in reality shapes the way 16OC works.

145

LUNCH MEATS		SAINT LOU'S ASSEMBLY	DINNER MEATS	
SLOW ROASTED SALMON	$14	**THREES**	ROTISSERIE HALF CHICKEN	$17
FRIED CHICKEN	$14	BRAISED KALE	MEATLOAF WELLINGTON	$18
MEATLOAF WELLINGTON	$18	MAC & CHEESE	DAILY FISH	$15
CHICKEN POT PIE	$14	GRILLED ASPARAGUS	PRIME RIB	$20
		GREEN BEANS	FRIED CHICKEN	$14
INCLUDES 3 SIDES →		ICEBERG WEDGE SALAD	SPRING VEGETABLE POT PIE	$14
		RATATOUILLE		
5 SIDES	$12	BOK CHOY	← INCLUDES 3 SIDES	
		TABBOULEH	5 SIDES	$12
SERVED UNTIL 3PM		POTATO		

SANDWICHES & SALADS		DRAFTS		BOOZY FLOATS $10	
GYRO	$12	VELTINS PILSNER	$5	BANANA COGNAC	
GRILLED CHEESE	$11	ILLUMINATED BREW WORKS FNORD	$6	RUM & COKE	
PRIME RIB	$16			ROOT BEER	
BUILD A SALAD	$12	HOPEWELL IPA	$6	NOT BOOZY	$5
AVAILABLE ALL DAY INCLUDES 1 SIDE		METROPOLITAN KRANK SHAFT	$6		
DESSERTS				COCKTAIL	$10
BAKER MILLER PIE	$5	SO NONSEQUITOR METAPHOR	$6	LAVENDER GIN LEMONADE	
SOFT SERVE	$2				
WITH BOOZY TOPPINGS	$6			RYE SWEET TEA	
		MEAT N THREE		MARGARITA	

"Everything we do is a really personal project. The idea that life is too short to work on things you're not interested in really shapes the way 16OC works. Without us taking our projects personally, I don't feel we would have reached the level of success that we have."

Without us taking our projects personally, I don't feel we would have reached the level of success that we have."

Before carving out his own prosperous path with his business partner, Finkelman spent some time working for the Hyatt Hotels Corporation, but was, in his own words, "stifled by the big-box corporate mentality," and so he decided to head out on his own. A late-night drive through Chicago's Ukrainian Village would inspire his very first independent venture, a small bar and music venue called The Empty Bottle. Affectionately described as a "cat-ridden hole-in-the-wall," the inaugural project made it into *Rolling Stone*'s hot list of "The Best Clubs in America" in 2013.

Meanwhile running a whole roster of diverse venues under the umbrella of the 16OC collective, Finkelman's love for music and live events still links most of his ventures, Saint Lou's being no exception. Besides serving up food and drinks, the venue hosts regular gatherings, such as a Silent Disco Night, as well as Saint Lou's Farm Share, which brings together farmers from the Chicago area. Its enclosed patio and backyard with a bocce ball court make it a perfect spot for private events, including weddings, birthdays, and corporate gatherings.

According to Finkelman, one of the biggest challenges with comprehensive, multipurpose projects like Saint Lou's Assembly is to keep things cohesive. "We have so many talented folks who work with us that, when we get together and throw out ideas, focusing in on them and going with a single brand concept is often the hardest," he says. Blackman adds that distance can sometimes be an issue too. "I'm based in New York and building a project like Saint Lou's that takes several months in Chicago, I obviously can't be there all the time to oversee every install or brand application." But with several collaborations behind them, he and Finkelman's team have established a relationship of deep mutual trust and creative confidence. "I think Bruce and I both know when to let each other go. Of course we argue, and sometimes let our emotions get to us, but in the end, we always produce stellar work. Not least because we know how to push each other."

Not surprisingly, Blackman's returning client has similarly praising words for the designer. "Besides being an incredibly talented creative, Dan has a good understanding for how something will be perceived by the public. He's great at being collaborative, but not afraid to stand up for his own convictions. He is also very handsome and has great table manners."

His grandfather Lou would have appreciated the down-to-earth atmosphere Blackman achieved in the namesake venue, Finkelman says. "He would have also loved the no-frills bar and the size of the portions served up at Saint Lou's, along with the fact that the food was stick-to-your-ribs good. He would have only hated that he couldn't smoke inside."

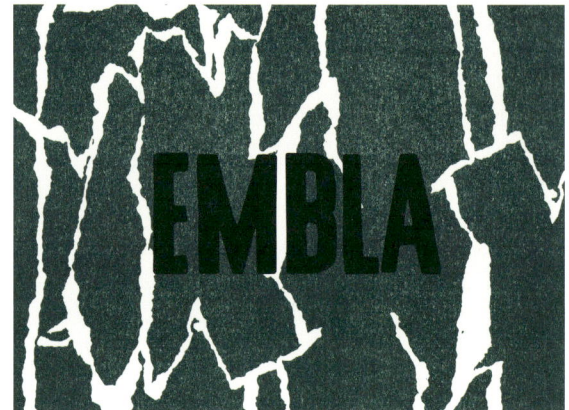

BLACK
ANGUS

OYSTERS

PINOT
GRIGIO

JALAPEÑOS

JUST A GLASS

WHETHER YOU REALLY MEAN IT OR NOT, SOMETIMES YOU DON'T WANT
A WHOLE BOTTLE, OR MAYBE VARIETY IS YOUR THING. SOME OF THESE WINES
WERE MADE JUST FOR US, ARE TOTALLY UNIQUE AND, LIKE A GOOD APRICOT
IN SEASON, SHOULD BE ENJOYED BEFORE THEY RUN OUT.

1

Julia & Navinès Cava Brut NV (Penedès, Spain) / 14
Gentle Folk Pink Fizz 2015 (Adelaide Hills, SA) / 14
Pierre Peters Cuvée de Réserve Blanc de Blancs NV (Champagne, France) / 22

Crawford River Riesling 2014 (Henty, Victoria) / 18
Jo Landron Muscadet Sèvre et Maine La Louvetrie 2014 (Loire, France) / 14
Save our Souls Chardonnay 2013 (Mornington Peninsula, Victoria) / 12
ArFion Fever 2014 (Yarra Valley, Victoria) / 15

Rolet Arbois Rosé Cuvée des Beaux Jours 2014 (Jura, France) / 15

Patrick Sullivan Good Morning Tom Pinot Noir 2014 (Mornington Peninsula, Victoria) / 16
Embla no SO2 Shiraz 2014 (Heathcote, Victoria) / 15
Ampeleia Un Litro 2014 (Tuscany, Italy) / 14
Gentle Folk Vin de Sofa 2015 (Adelaide Hills, SA) / 13

EMBLA

Our sourdough, cultured butter / 3
Anchovy toast / 3.5
Shaved comte, green olive / 11
Terrine / 14
Pickled cucumbers, dill, feta / 7
Goat's curd, broad beans, fennel, mint / 13
Raw beef, lemon, ginger, coastal rocket / 16
Green asparagus, walnut / 8
Creamed corn, creme fraiche, marjoram, dried citrus / 12
Wood roasted broccoli, sunflower seed miso / 8
Calamari, grilled cos, buttermilk, bottarga / 18
Rainbow trout, horseradish, purslane / 26
Spiced lamb neck, watercress, romesco / 30
Black angus bavette, tarragon, green beans / 28

Dried peach rum baba, white chocolate chantilly / 10
Elderflower ice cream, grilled berry compote / 10

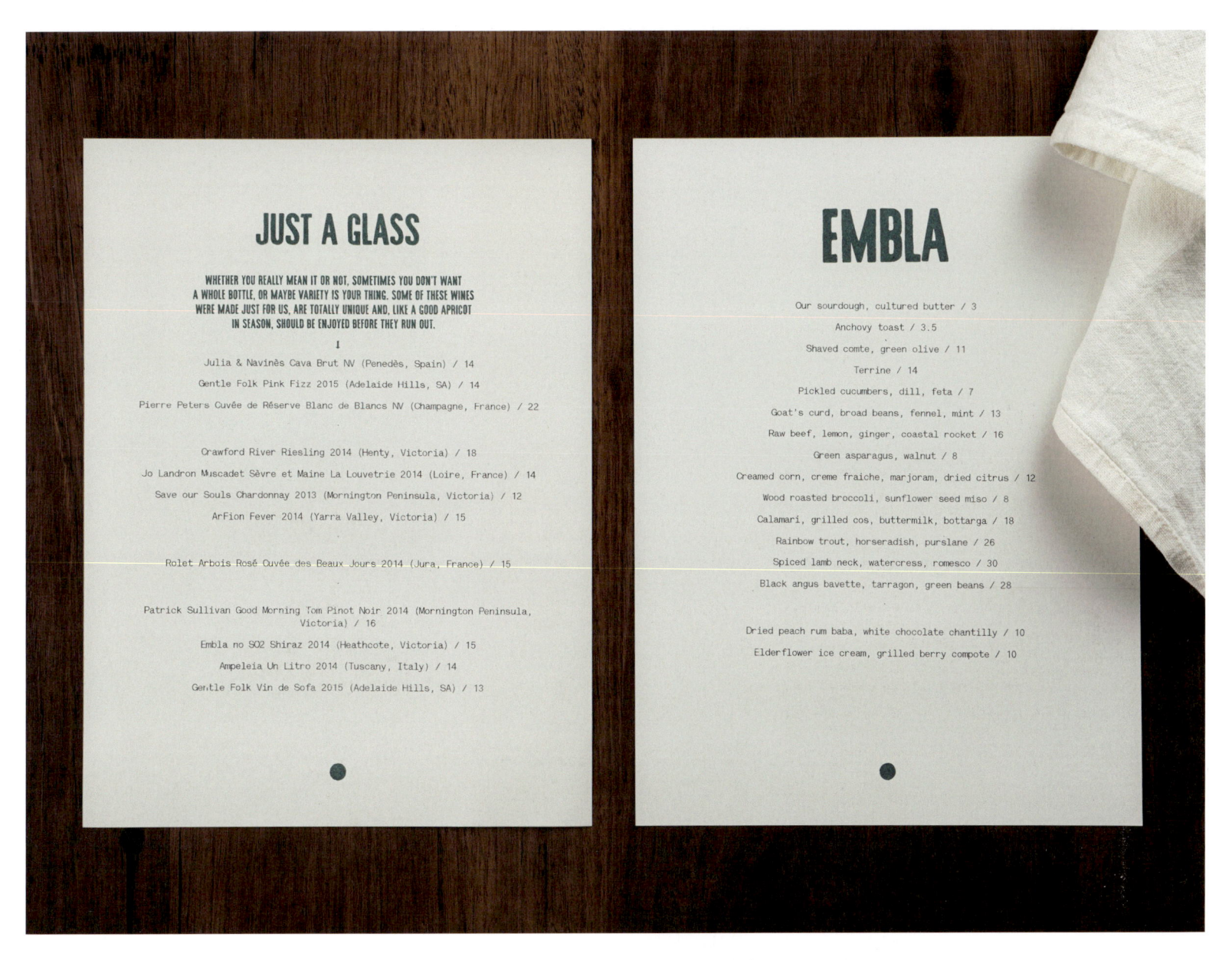

Embla

A FRIEND OF MINE created a custom-made typeface and paper collage pattern to underscore the down-to-earth vibe of this Melbourne-based wine bar.

Melbourne's Embla wine bar has a relaxed atmosphere, an unusual wine list, and a kitchen open from lunch until late. Wanting to emphasize its down-to-earth character and easy-going vibe, A Friend of Mine developed a hand-drawn typeface inspired by vintage signage in the neighborhood. A deep-green paper collage provides a textured background and has an organic feel. This patterning with the typeface is uses across the website and printed collateral to set the tone for Embla's laid-back character. As a finishing touch, the designers created several interior design elements, including a hanging menu frame, in collaboration with a local framer.

Maine Shrimp	FERMENTED HONEY
Cod Skin	DILL, SOURED CREAM
Pig's Blood	ROSEHIP, CLOVES
Bread & Butter	
Peas	ROE, ELDERFLOWER
Scallop	WHEY, SMOKED OIL
Potato	EGG YOLK, HERRING
Skate Wing	NASTURTIUM, RAPESEED OIL
Asparagus	RAMPS, BRONZE FENNEL
Lamb	LAMB LIVER, BLACK CURRANT
Pointed Cabbage	VERBENA
Onions	SWE VINEGAR, FLOWERING DILL
Beef	CURED FAT
Cheese	SMOKED CHEESE, GOOSEBERRIES
Cherries	SPRUCE
Skyr	WOODRUFF OIL

MENU 125 $
WINE PAIRING 75 $
JUICE PAIRING 40 $
ALL PRICES INCL. SERVICE & TAX

aska

aska

ASKANYC.COM
(+1) 929 337 6792

47 SOUTH 5TH STREET
BROOKLYN, NY 11249

INFO@ASKANYC.COM

Aska

Designed by ATHLETICS, this Brooklyn-based restaurant's dark and moody brand identity echoes its unusual ingredient list and presentation methods.

Michelin-starred chef Fredrik Berselius is considered to be one of the world's experts on high-Nordic cuisine. His Brooklyn restaurant Aska specializes in multi-course dinners that include surprising ingredients prepared in unexpected ways, while the more casual Edda Bar serves lighter fare in the basement lounge. Athletics worked closely with Berselius to craft a visual identity for Aska with a high contrast palette, marbleized textures, and moody photography that mirrors the atmosphere of the venue. It has a minimal and organic feel that encompasses the restaurant's distinct spirit but retains the focus on specially sourced ingredients and artistic presentation.

Carlen Parfums

ATHLETICS' bold type and evocative still life photography are designed to speak to the unisex fragrance brand's clientele.

Carlen Parfums creates unisex fragrances that don't adhere to the typical scents associated with each gender. Established in 2014 by the co-founder of fashion house OAK and the creative director of design studio Athletics, the Carlen brand conveys a nonconformist lifestyle in both its product and branding. Athletics created Carlen Parfum's visual identity with the intention of challenging the conventional look of other luxury perfume brands. A bold and minimal design is used across packaging, with evocative campaign photographs that reinforce the brand's commitment to their target audience.

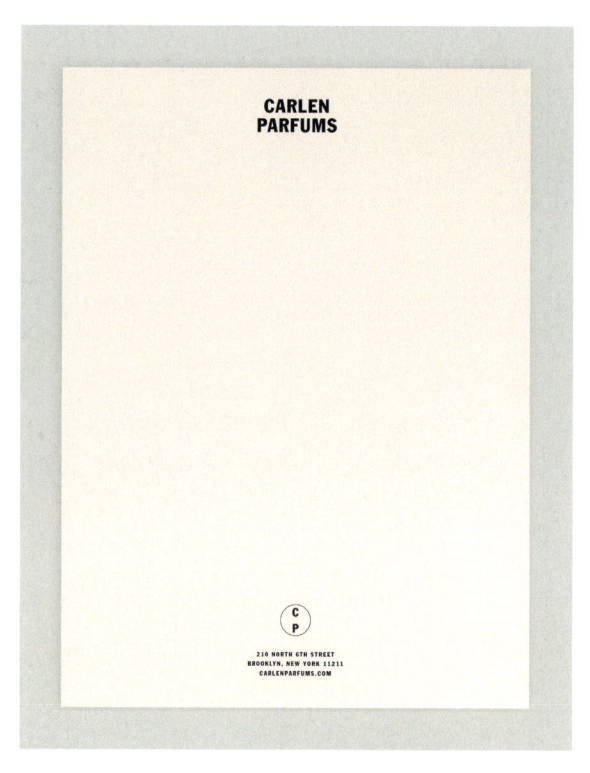

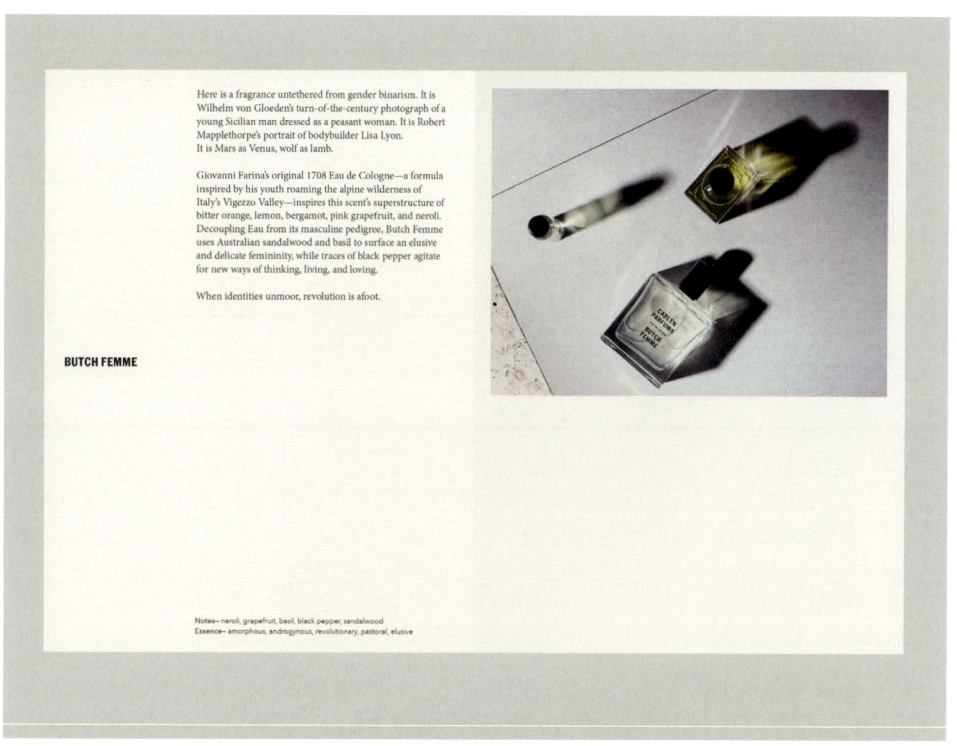

Here is a fragrance untethered from gender binarism. It is Wilhelm von Gloeden's turn-of-the-century photograph of a young Sicilian man dressed as a peasant woman. It is Robert Mapplethorpe's portrait of bodybuilder Lisa Lyon. It is Mars as Venus, wolf as lamb.

Giovanni Farina's original 1708 Eau de Cologne—a formula inspired by his youth roaming the alpine wilderness of Italy's Vigezzo Valley—inspires this scent's superstructure of bitter orange, lemon, bergamot, pink grapefruit, and neroli. Decoupling Eau from its masculine pedigree, Butch Femme uses Australian sandalwood and basil to surface an elusive and delicate femininity, while traces of black pepper agitate for new ways of thinking, living, and loving.

When identities unmoor, revolution is afoot.

BUTCH FEMME

Notes— neroli, grapefruit, basil, black pepper, sandalwood
Essence— amorphous, androgynous, revolutionary, pastoral, elusive

154

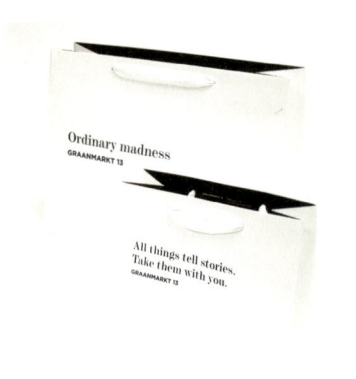

Graanmarkt 13

BASE DESIGN take an adaptable anti-branding approach to the retail and hospitality destination's identity design.

Graanmarkt 13 is an Antwerp destination that incorporates a concept store, restaurant, gallery, and apartment hotel all under one roof. Base Design took an anti-branding approach to the visual identity and presenting the meaningful stories behind the Graanmarkt 13's products and customers. Instead of a fixed logo, the branding emphasizes voice to communicate the brand's stories and personalities, and it can evolve as needed. This includes the slightly mysterious and playful phrases that accompany the fragrance collection and pique customers' curiosity. The new Graanmarkt 13 website reaches people far beyond Antwerp and provides an online home for its stories and product line.

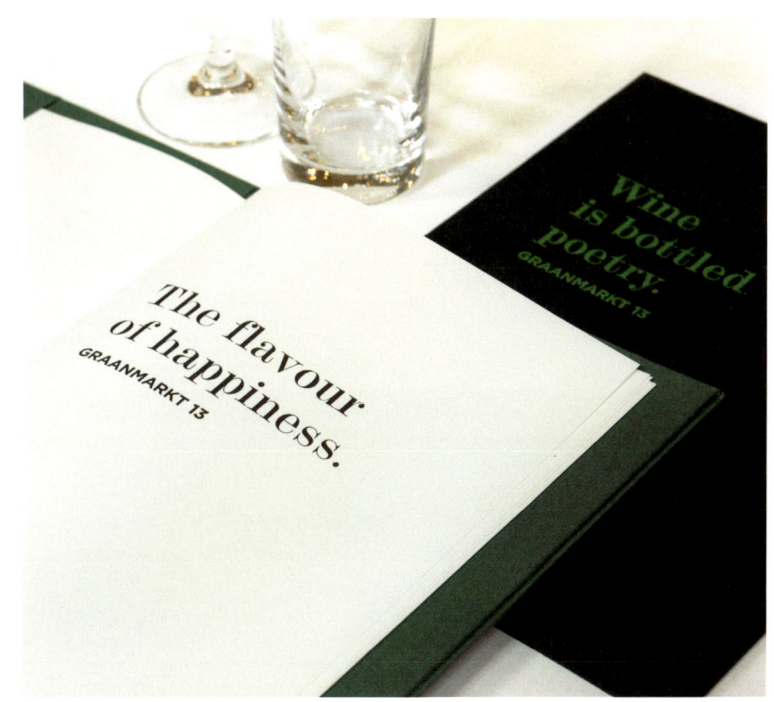

155

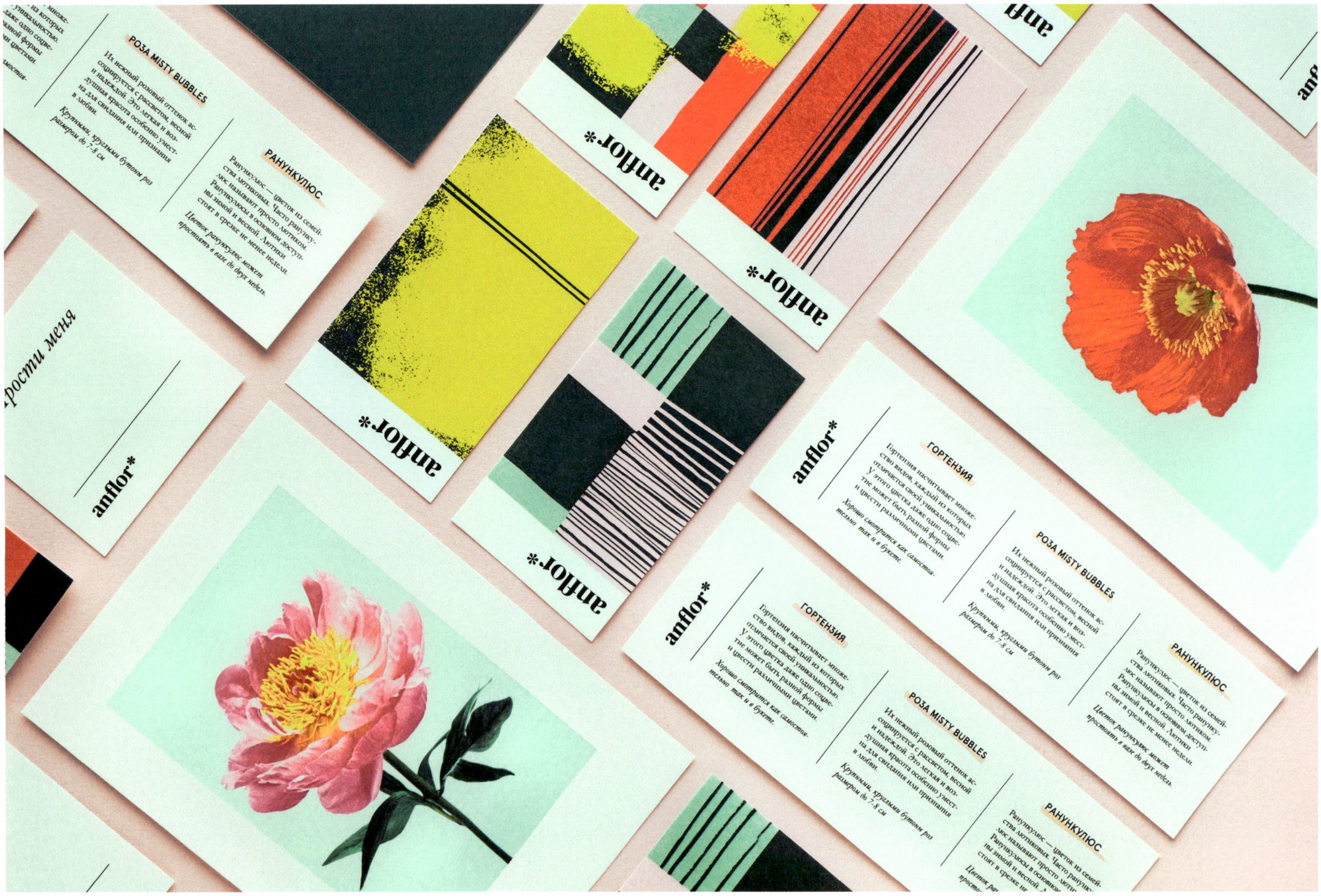
РОЗА MISTY BUBBLES
РАНУНКУЛЮС
ГОРТЕНЗИЯ
anflor*

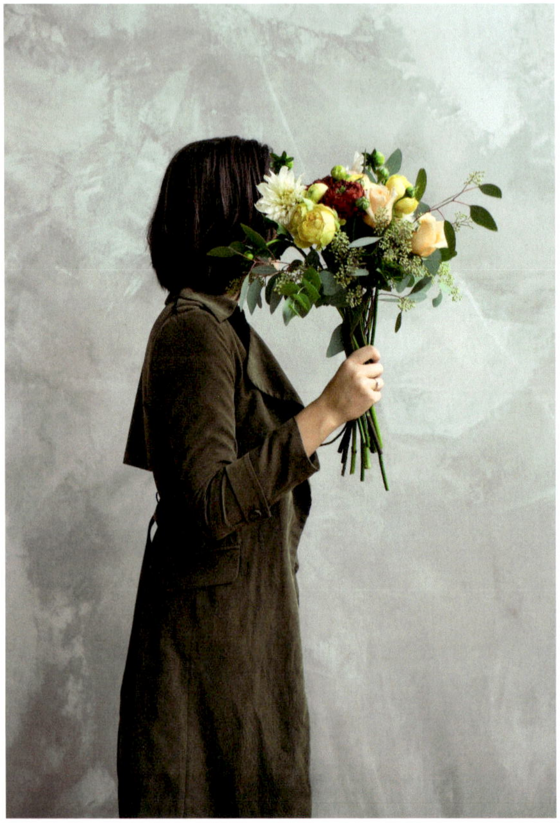

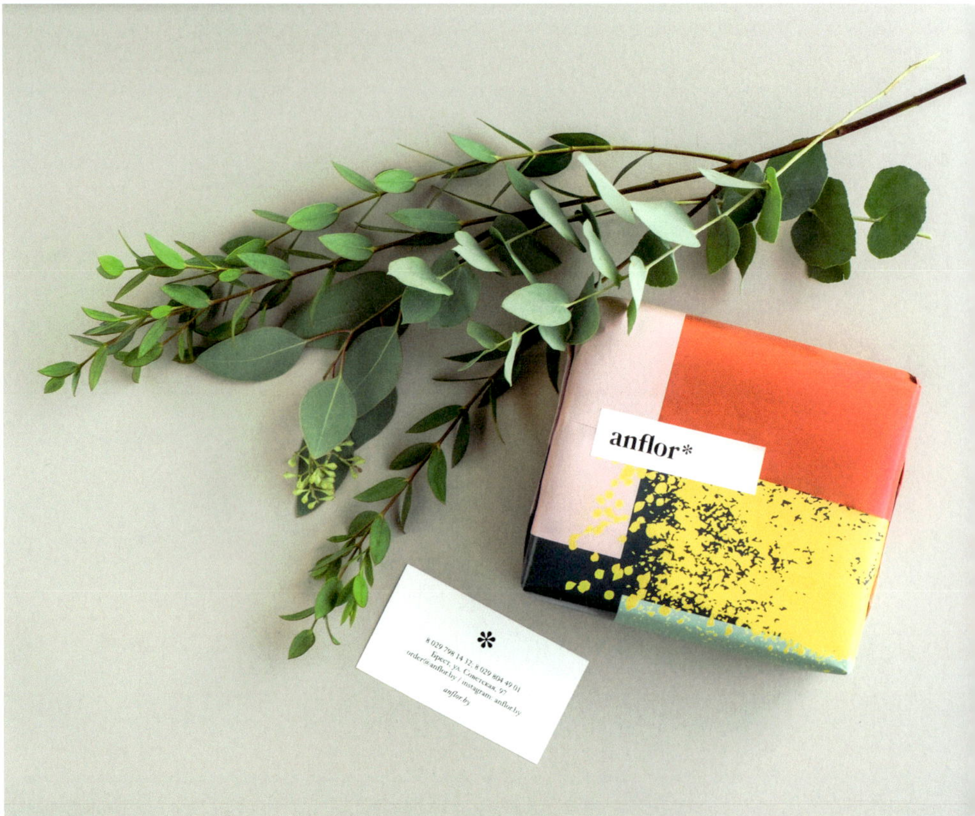
anflor*

Anflor*

<u>ANGELINA PISCHIKOVA</u> uses the asterisk symbol to express the flower studio's business and philosophy.

Flower studio Anflor* believes that, when feelings are complicated, communicating with a bouquet of flowers is the best way to go. The studio carries a wide variety of fresh flowers, and creates bouquets that stand out for their detail and originality. Designer Angelina Pischikova's branding concept for the studio is based on the asterisk symbol—a stylized flower. The symbol indicates there is something more to express, which aligns with Anflor*'s philosophy, "Bouquets are more than words." The cards that accompany each bouquet provide space for writing sentimental notes. Pischikova also emphasizes the beauty and freshness of the flowers through colorful, hand-drawn patterns that evoke endless fields of flowers.

Balholm Handverkcider

OLSSØN BARBIERI's elaborate label designs for the family-owned cider maker underscore the attention given to each of the company's products.

Located inside the Sognefjord on the west coast of Norway, Balholm Handverkcider is a family-owned orchard, distillery, and cider maker. The steep surrounding mountains shield it from the North Sea, making it an ideal place for growing fruit. The deep blue in the color palette is inspired by the Romantic paintings of the area, while the typography expresses the detail and craft that goes into its small-scale production. Each label contains a short description about the cider's specific fruit, taste, and production method, along with an icon depicting the fruit press, and five apples that represent the five generations of family.

159

THE DAYROOMS
THE DAYROOMS

£100
THE DAYROOMS
GIFT VOUCHER
THE DAYROOMS · STAMP OF AUTHENTICITY

THE DAYROOMS

THE DAYROOMS
THE DAYROOMS

212 KENSINGTON PARK RD, LONDON W11 1NR
INFO@THEDAYROOMSCAFE.COM
WWW.THEDAYROOMSCAFE.COM
+44 (0)20 7792 1119
DAYROOMS CAFÉ
·W11·
1 2 3 4
5 6 7 8
THE DAYROOMS

BREAKFAST IN BED
YOUR LOVER'S SET OF KEYS
EARL GREY TEA
THE SMELL OF FRESH FLOWERS
THE DAYROOMS

The Dayrooms Café

A candy-colored identity by *TWO TIMES ELLIOTT* brings laid-back Australian vibes to the busy streets of London.

The Dayrooms Café is the sister project of The Dayrooms, a London-based women's clothing store that specializes in Australian designers. Two Times Elliott uses a beachy, pastel-colored palette mixed with travel photography to communicate the café's connection to Australia as well as to evoke a sense of nostalgia, wanderlust, and faraway places. Snippets of text on the tote bags are inspired by the founders' love of travel, photography, and fashion. Recalling cherished moments, the identity has the narrative quality of a personal journal, blending images and words across cups, bags, cards, and website.

The Laylow

Tropical design by *OMFGCO* riffs on a Hawaiian Modern theme for the small city hotel.

The Laylow is part of Marriott's Autograph Collection in Waikiki. Although OMFGCO originally came on to develop the hotel's concept, name, and brand, the scope of the project grew to include the interior design and hotel's food and beverage labels. Looking to create a brand that appeals to both locals and tourists, the designers celebrated the mid-century style of the building and used a Hawaiian Modern theme to develop a tropical oasis in the middle of the city. The aesthetic permeates all aspects of the brand, including its custom furniture, artwork, signage, and stationery.

HIDEOUT
at the LAYLOW
Ben Buckley
GENERAL MANAGER
2299 KUHIO AVE · HONOLULU, HI · 808 628 3030
CELL 339 927 5054 · BEN@LAYLOWWAIKIKI.COM
HIDEOUT
at the LAYLOW
at the LAYLOW
at the LAYLOW

164

The Faversham

PASSPORT's rebrand of the historic hotel and music hall in Leeds reflects its expansion into a casual restaurant and multi-purpose event space.

The Faversham, also known as The Fav to locals, has been an institution in Leeds since opening in 1947. The venue's pub has attracted many well-known musicians over the years; and today, under new ownership, The Faversham also houses an event space, restaurant, and brewery. Prior to expansion, the new owners engaged Passport to rebrand the business in a way that would continue to appeal to current clientele, predominately students, but also attracting couples looking for a wedding venue. The designers included both the full name and the affectionate nickname on the website and sections of the menu to convey the duality of the brand. The overall look of the identity is fresh but classic with a mint green and red color scheme that appeals to both facets of its business.

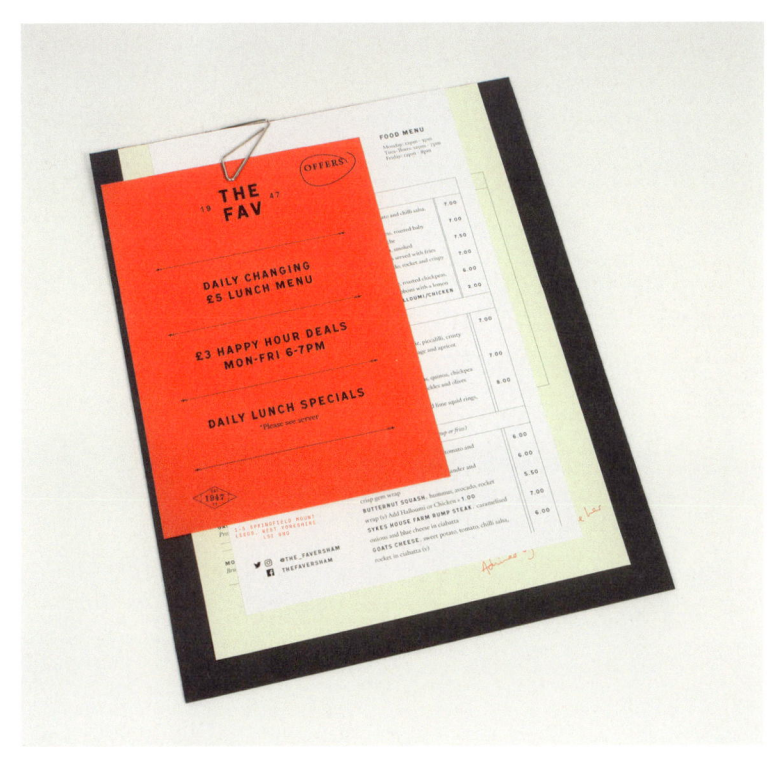

165

… continue

Kisumé

Mesmerizing branding by *FABIO ONGARATO DESIGN* challenges the status quo of fine Japanese dining.

The heads behind the restaurant Kisumé in Melbourne, Australia, asked Fabio Ongarato Design to break convention and develop a new stance on Japanese dining tradition. The result is an aesthetic that interacts with Kisumé's already minimal interior design elements by emphasizing movement and color. In keeping with the experience of dining, the primary language of the design developed by the studio plays with the idea of transformation and the contrast between solid and fluid elements. Accents of vermillion and cobalt on the menus are the only color in the otherwise minimal interior palette. Curated photographs from Nobuyoshi Araki and Polly Borland add atmosphere to the dining experience and complement the graphics.

166

167

Souk

__MILDRED & DUCK__'s design for the Melbourne diner
is a modern take on Middle Eastern culinary culture.

Souk is a Melbourne restaurant that offers a fresh take on Middle Eastern cuisine with dishes from Arabia, North Africa, and Anatolia. Mildred & Duck developed the branding to evoke the sensory overload that is common in the crowded souks of the Middle East. Taking inspiration from the Arabic language, the logo comprises the letters of the restaurant's name arranged from right to left and is featured prominently throughout the space in bright pink neon signage and on custom plates. In addition to the logo, Mildred & Duck created a submark that is a modern version of the traditional evil eye.

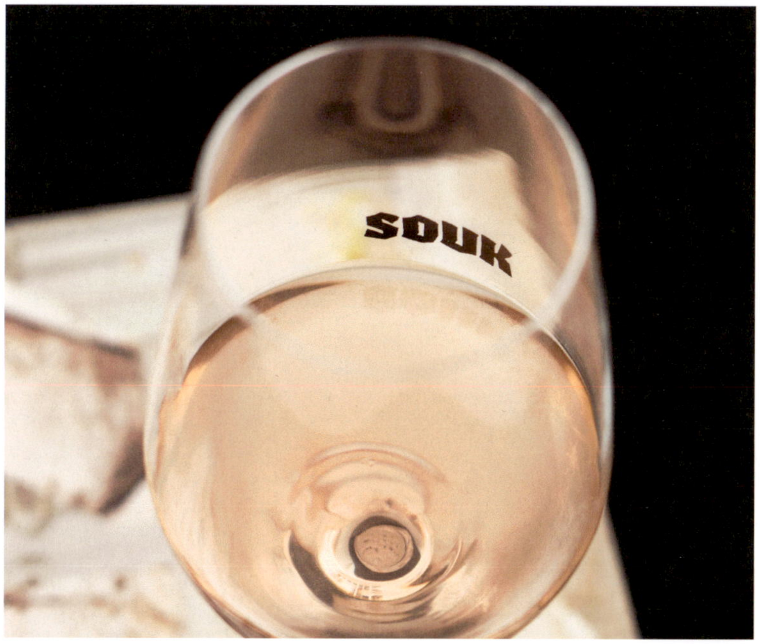
SOUK

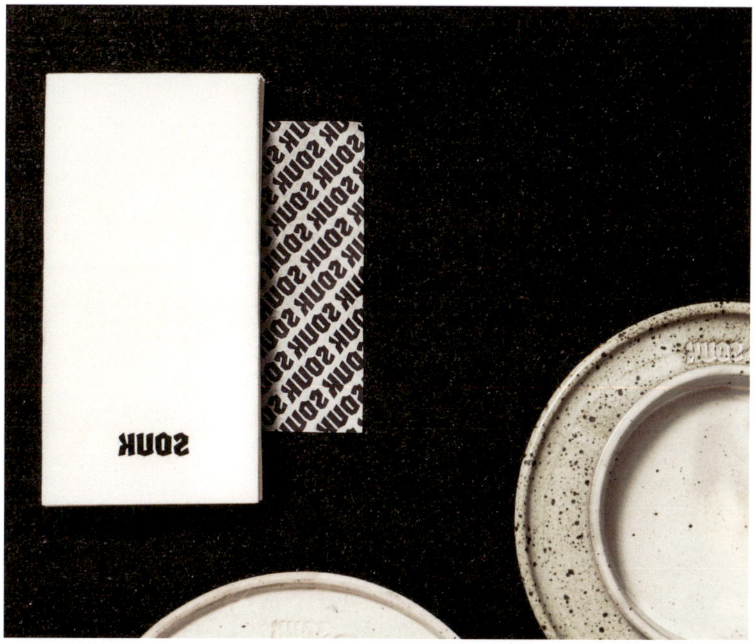
SOUK

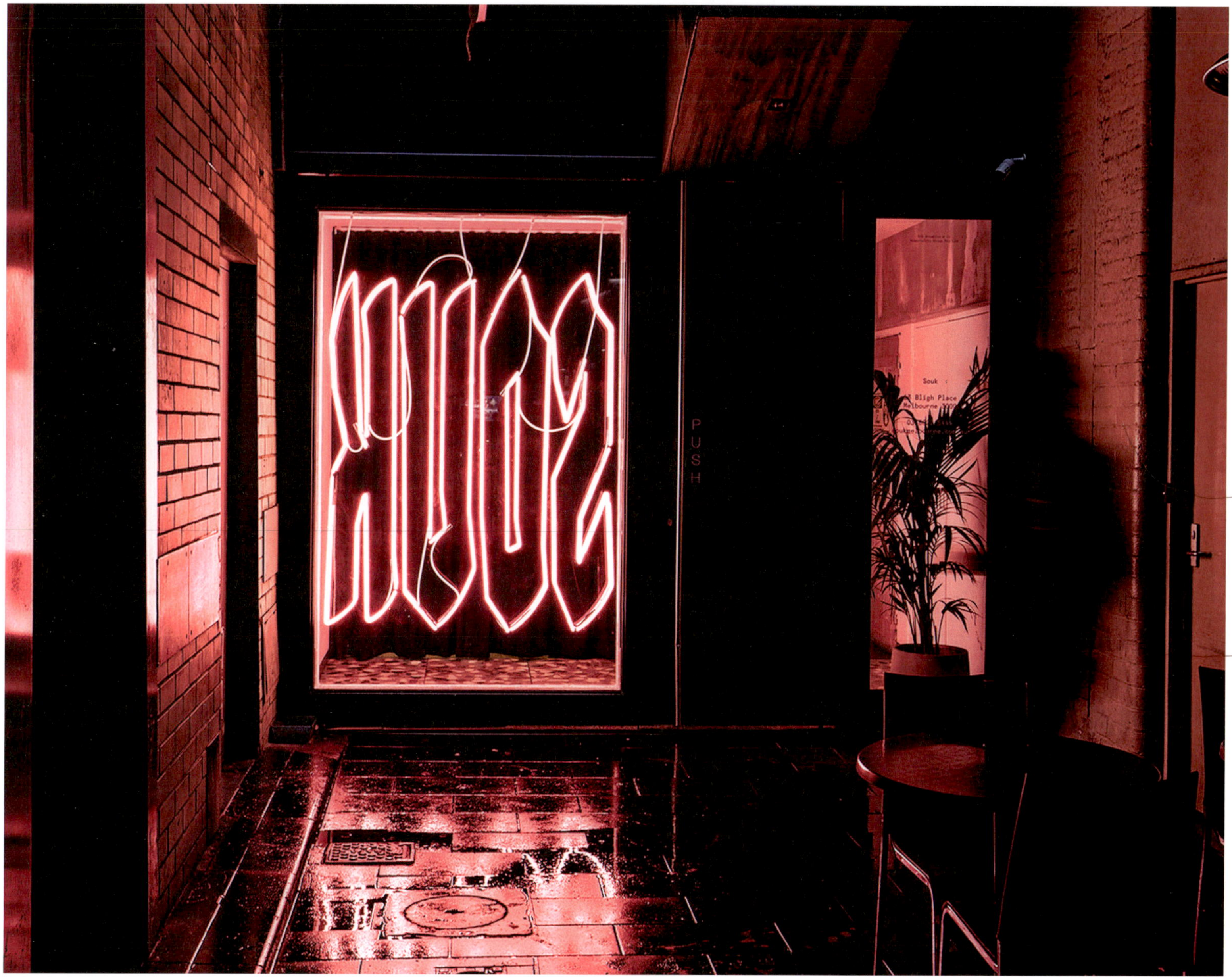
PUSH
Souk

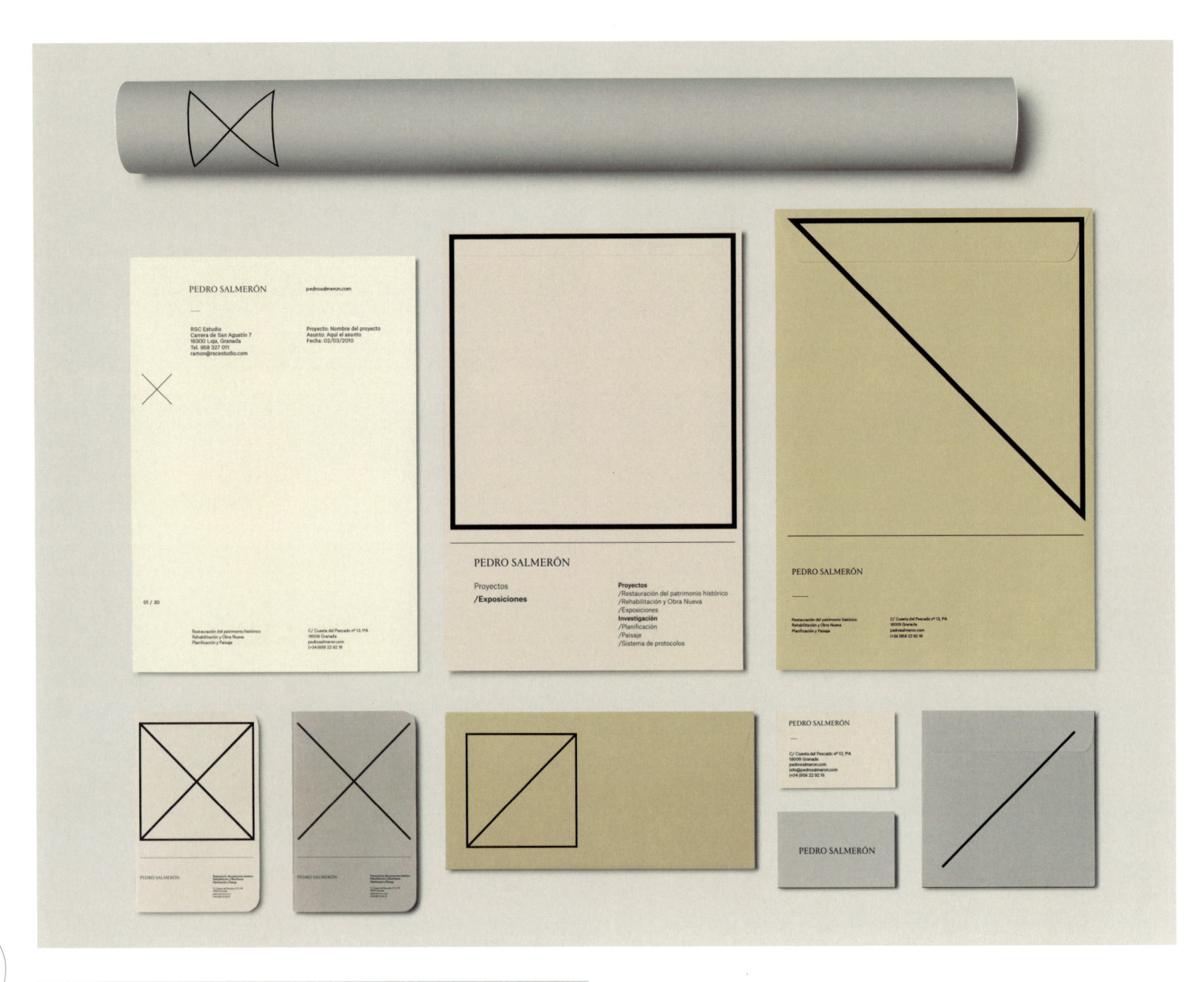

Pedro Salmerón

A rebrand by _BUENAVENTURA_ for the respected architect uses architectural graphic elements that echo the building process.

Spanish architect Pedro Salmerón specializes in historic renovation projects. He commissioned Buenaventura to develop a new brand that would bring all aspects of his practice together. The designers created a flexible and layered identity that communicates a consistent and elegant brand. A visual language of lines and shapes is inspired by elements used in the restoration process, and they can be used alone as graphic elements or combined as a pattern. Collateral is printed on papers with muted tones that recall architecture-related materials. The versatile identity represents the essence of the practice and can be used for all aspects of his business.

171

172

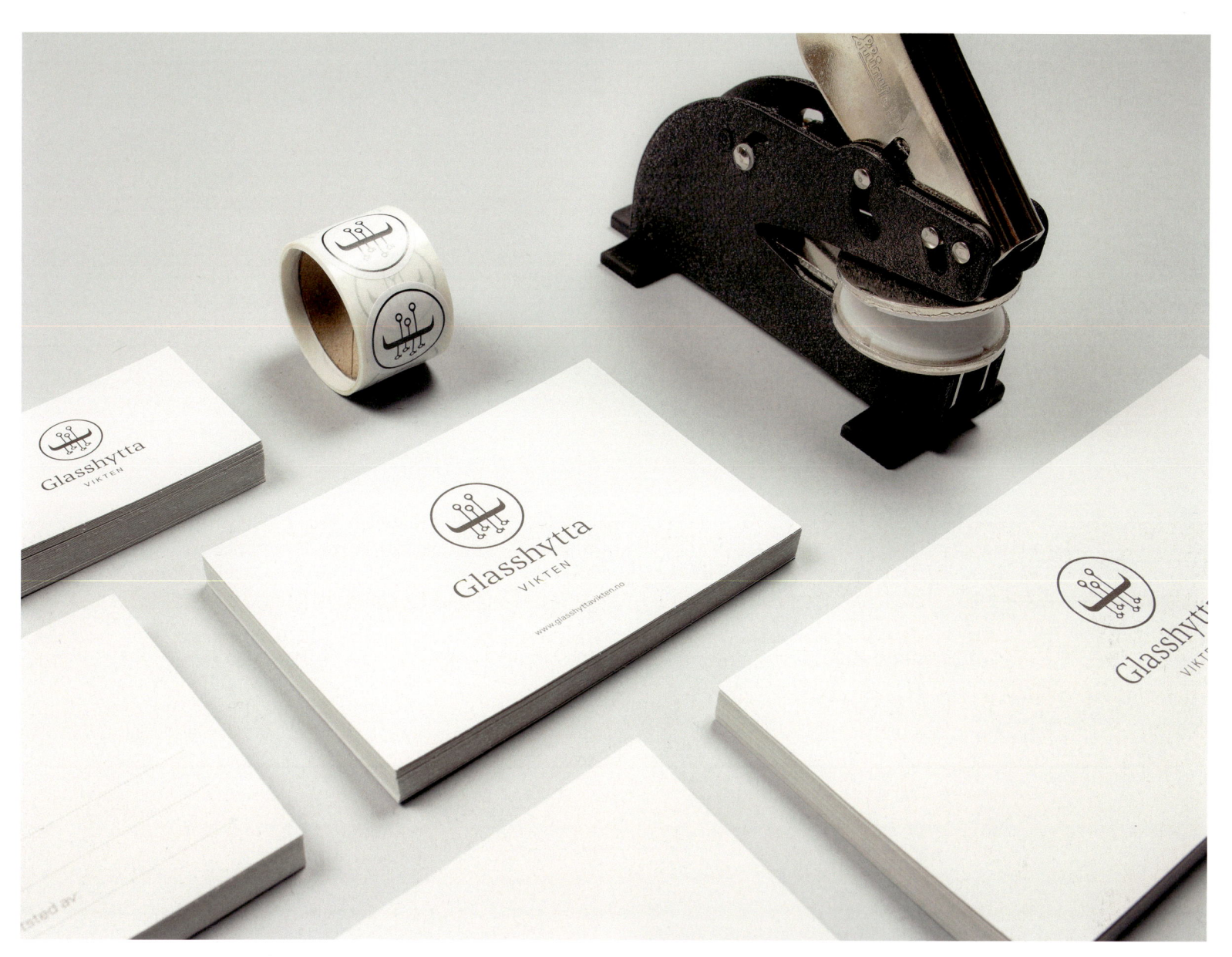

Glasshytta Vikten

BY NORTH™ pays homage to this glass workshop's history by incorporating old and new elements into the rebrand.

In 1976, Åsvar Tangrand opened the first glassblowing workshop in northern Norway. Today the studio is in a beautiful building on the beach at Vikten, Lofoten, and is run by his son, Anders. After 40 years in business, the workshop needed a new visual identity to communicate its activities and products to the thousands of tourists who visit Lofoten each year. By North™ developed an identity that honors Glasshytta Vikten's location and work by focusing on craftsmanship and history. Recycled paper, embossing, and tactile elements help communicate this message. Brand photography shows the process of making blown glass. The designers retained the Lofotruna symbol that Åsvar designed in the early seventies as the logo for the business.

Le Chalet de la Forêt

A minimalist identity system by _CODEFRISKO_ lets the exquisite dining experience speak for itself.

Le Chalet de La Forêt is surrounded by lush gardens and thick tree canopies, despite its location in the center of Brussels. Every day, the staff bake bread, harvest garden vegetables, and smoke a variety of meats to create an exquisite menu for a dining experience that has earned the restaurant a beloved reputation and two Michelin stars. Head chef and owner Pascal Devalkeneer hired Codefrisko to rebrand the establishment by emphasizing the heritage of the house and grounds it occupies. Codefrisko's solution uses a blackletter font for the logo and a black-on-white color scheme across menus, stationery, and signage. The simplicity of the design allows the rich colors of the interiors and grounds to come to the forefront.

175

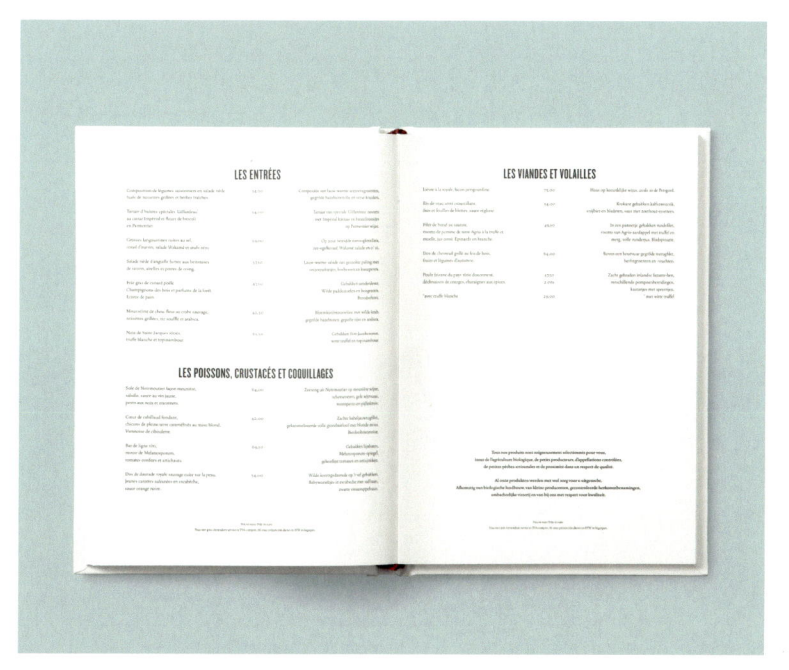

Bon à valoir — Tegoedbo
Date — Datum

SENTEURS D'AILLEURS
HAUTE PARFUMERIE
SENTEURS D'AILLEURS
HAUTE COSMÉTIQUE

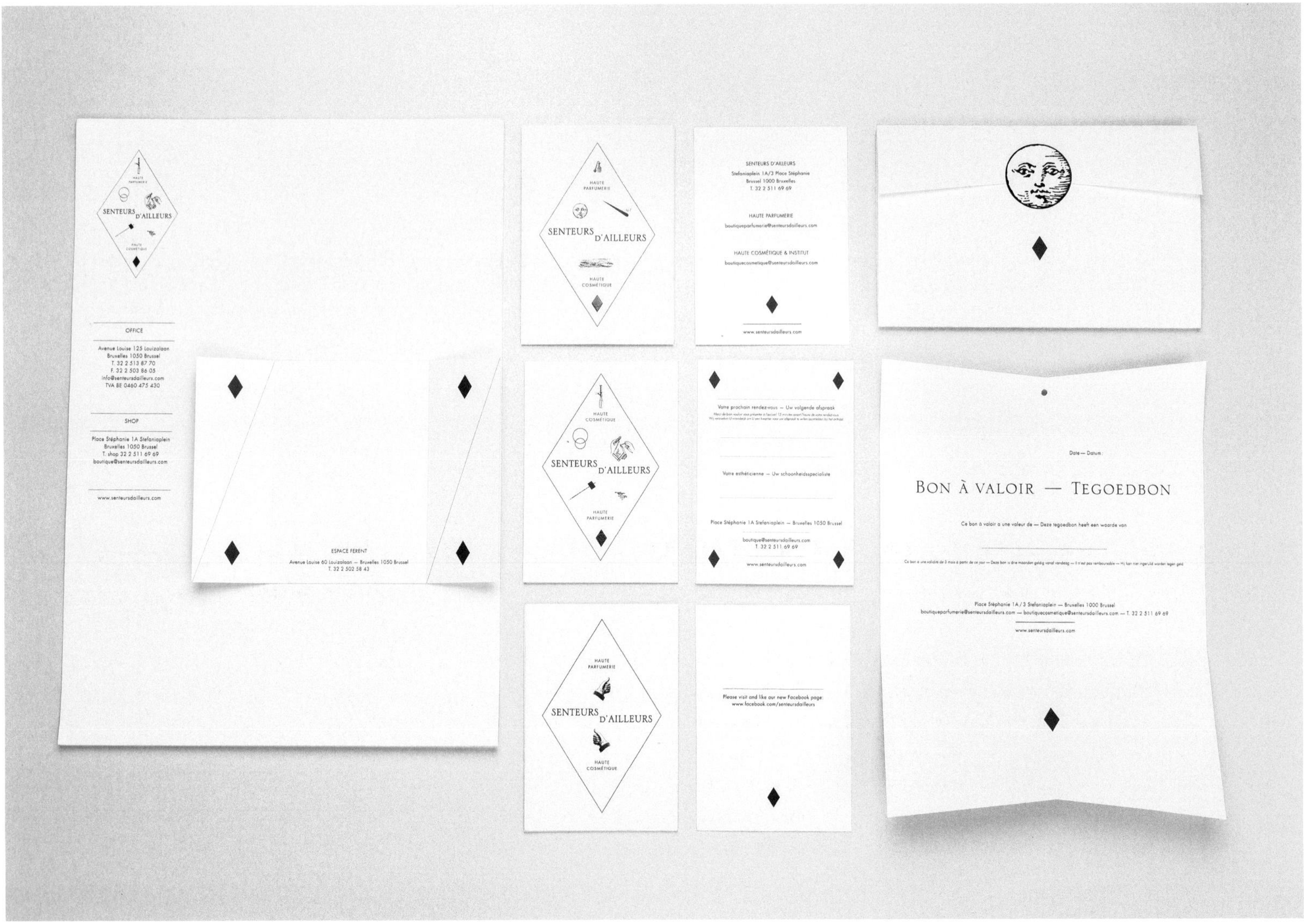
SENTEURS D'AILLEURS
HAUTE PARFUMERIE
HAUTE COSMÉTIQUE
OFFICE
SHOP
Bon à valoir — Tegoedbon
Date — Datum

Senteurs D'Ailleurs

<u>CODEFRISKO</u> developed a set of alchemy-inspired icons as part of the flexible visual language for this high-end perfume and cosmetics store.

For the comprehensive branding for high-end perfume and cosmetics store Senteurs D'Ailleurs, Codefrisko wanted to evoke Old World charm to highlight the alchemy-like practice of mixing rare ingredients to create something magical. The designers developed a set of forms and symbols that can be combined to suggest the components of each product. Inspired by ancient engravings, the icons are based on history and science, as well as referring to more abstract concepts, such as time, exploration, and dreams. They can also be used to vary the logo-mark, when paired with it in different combinations.

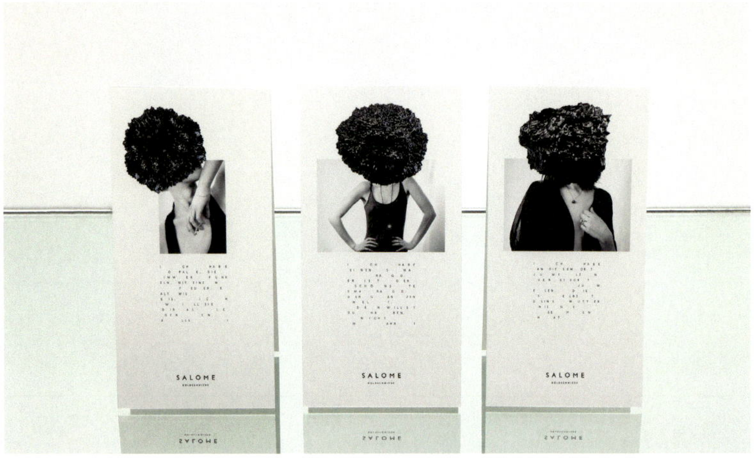
SALOME
SALOME
SALOME

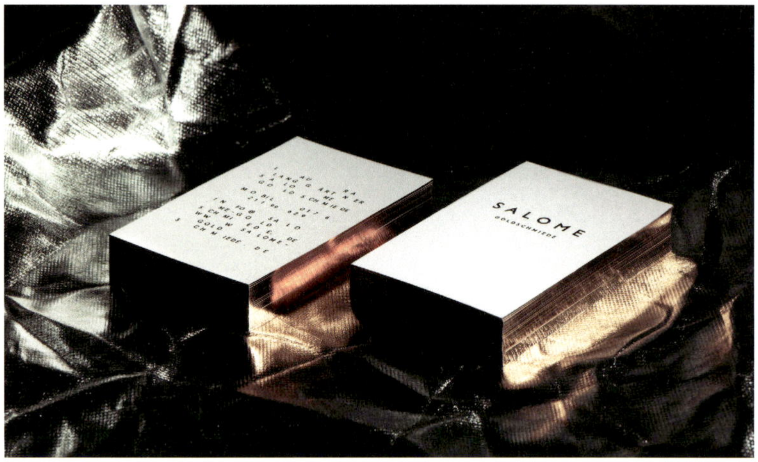
SALOME

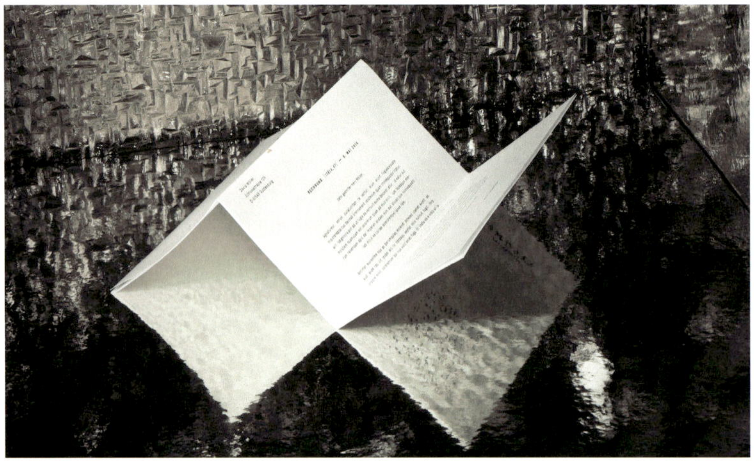

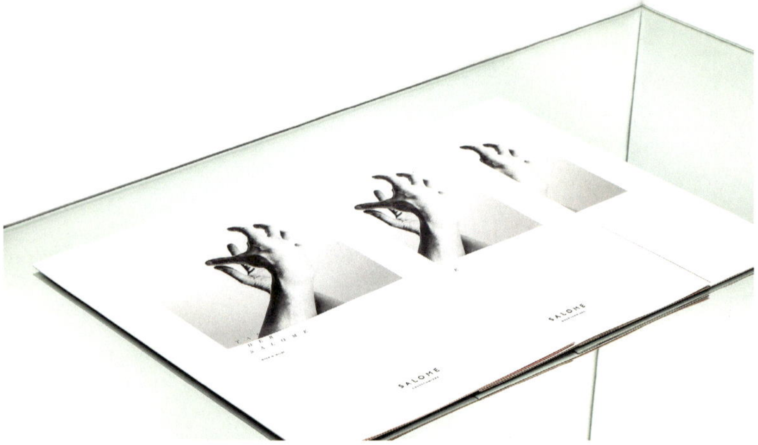
SALOME

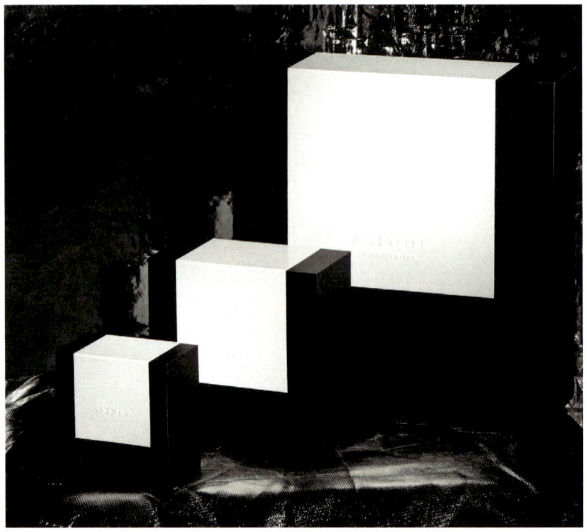

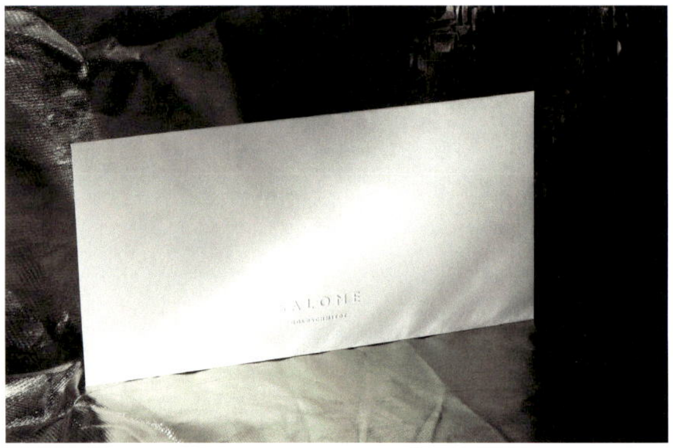

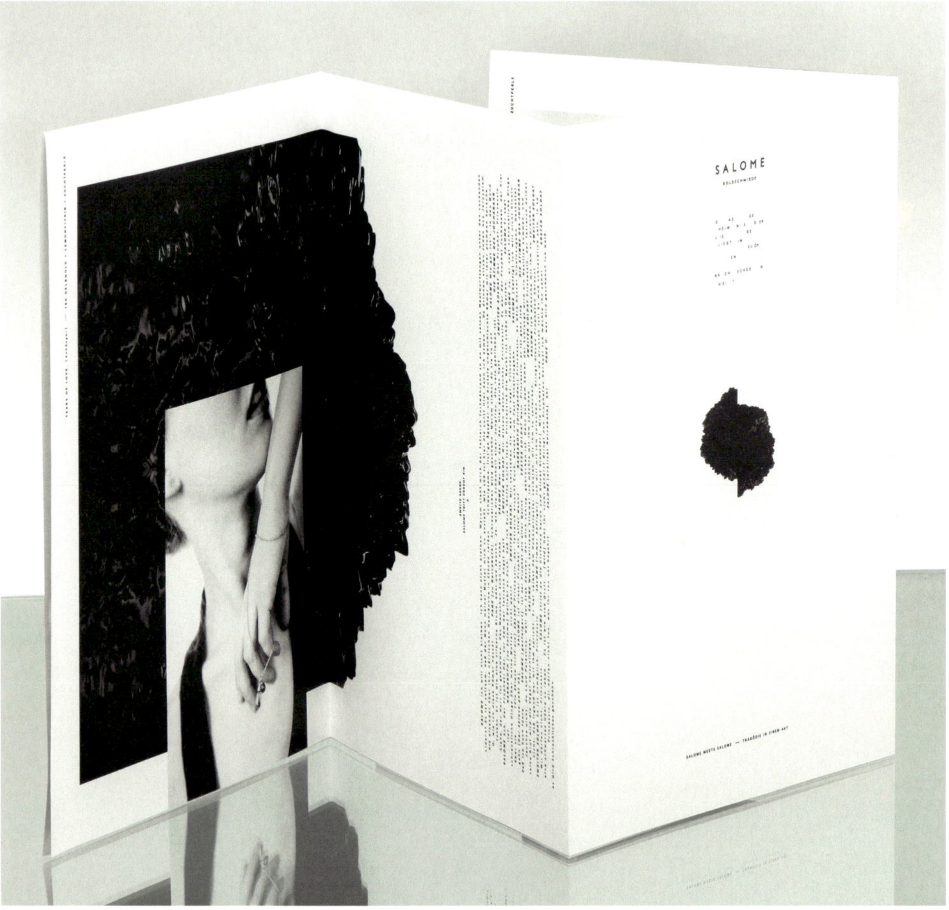
SALOME

Salome

MILCH+HONIG works with conceptual photography to communicate the goldsmith's emphasis on the relationship between her product and customers.

Salome is the middle name of the goldsmith and one of her favorite plays by Oscar Wilde. As the play has themes about emotions in human relationships, Salome seemed like a particularly good name for a jewelry brand. Milch+Honig's design for the visual identity has a scattered typography arrangement across the printed collateral to evoke gold dust particles flying through the air. Instead of focusing on close-up product shots, the black-and-white photography centers on emotion. It juxtaposes an image of a model with the raw materials that Salome uses to show the relationship between the materials and the person wearing them.

CALLEN-LORDE
Caitlin Quigley
Manager of Development
and Communications
CALLEN-LORDE

CALLEN-LORDE
SPLASH

RAINBOW
RUN
CALLEN-LORDE

FAQ
CALLEN-LORDE

Callen-Lorde

Shunning the health care industry's stereotyped visual language, *MOTHER DESIGN* creates a colorful brand inspired by 1980s guerrilla marketing.

Throughout its 50-year history, the New York City-based center Callen-Lorde has been a leader in LGBTQ health care, providing comprehensive services, regardless of the patient's ability to pay. Mother Design created Callen-Lorde's new identity, which celebrates the vibrant spirit of the institution. Inspired by the guerrilla marketing campaigns of the 1980s AIDS crisis, the designers produced a colorful identity that works effectively across stationery, signage, posters, and website. Instead of using conventional branding tactics, the design has a visual language that modernizes the organization's image, while acknowledging the history of the community and its core values.

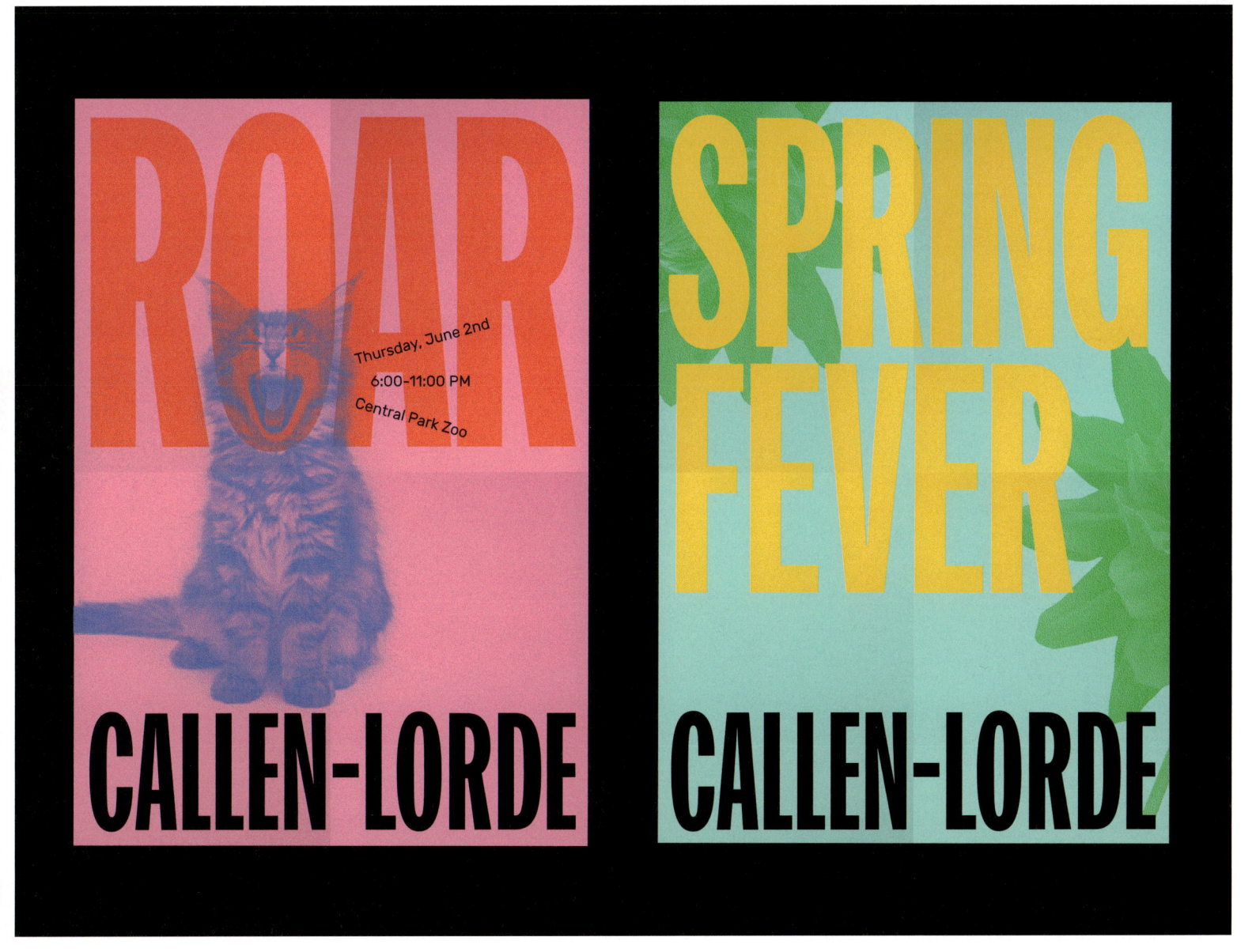

On Rye

Served with a side dish of humor, **PENTAGRAM** updates the familiar design language of the Jewish deli with up-close photography and tongue-in-cheek graphics.

Washington, D.C.-based On Rye serves updated Jewish deli classics along with a few new recipes. In addition to standards like matzo ball soup and egg cream, it offers traditional dishes with a modern twist, such as Wagyu pastrami on gluten-free bread, vegetarian Reubens with smoked beets and portobello mushrooms, and a babka ice cream sandwich. Pentagram's branding highlights On Rye's contemporary take by putting a modern and humorous spin on the utilitarian graphics and photography traditionally used by Jewish delis. The brand captures the heritage of the food the deli serves, while clearly communicating the unique character of its menu.

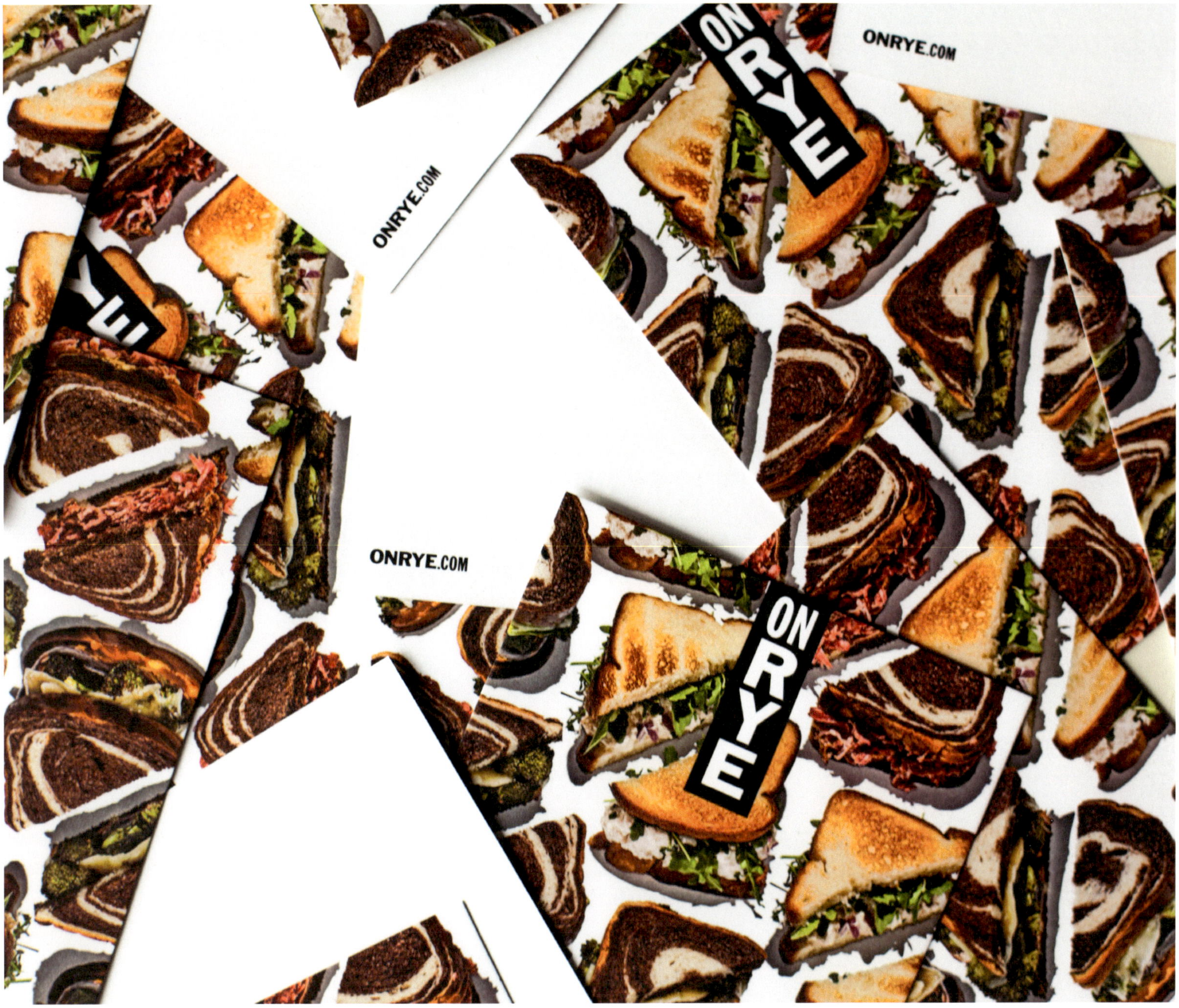
ON RYE
ONRYE.COM

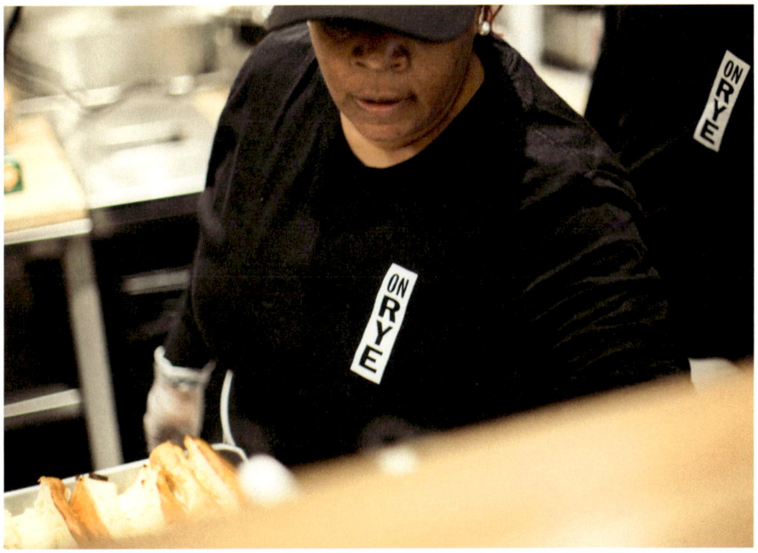
ON RYE

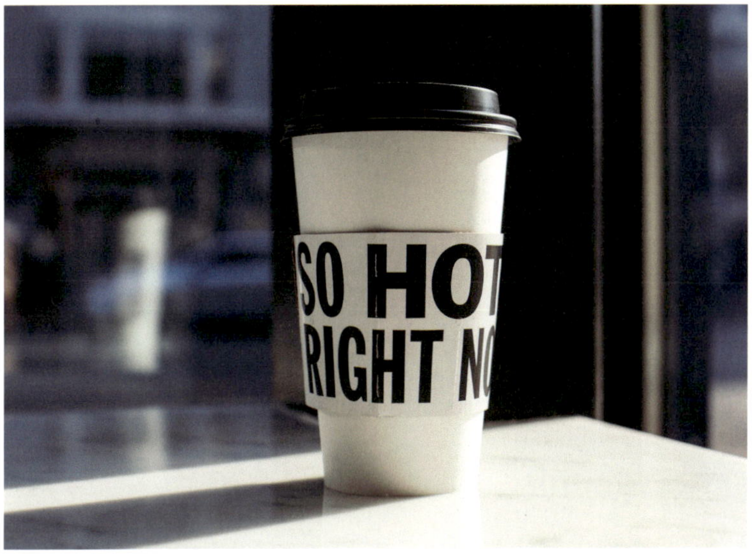
SO HOT
RIGHT NO

Coffee	
Espresso	2.5
Cappuccino	3.5
Latte	4.0
Americano	2.75
Mocha	5.0
Hot Chocolate	3.5
Coffee	2.5
Flash Chilled Coffee	3.0

Etc.	
Tea	MP
Bottled Drinks	MP
Ice	0.0
Almond Milk	0.75
Vanilla Syrup	0.5

Little Wolf
IPSWICH, MA.

Sit.

Little Wolf

Using illustrations of the owner's dog, **PERKY BROS** creates a friendly tone for a coffee roaster and cafe that doesn't take itself too seriously.

Founded by former accountant Chris Gatti and his Husky dog, River, Little Wolf is a small-batch coffee roaster and cafe that makes it pleasant and easy to buy specialty coffee. Perky Bros used an icy-blue color palette for the branding in reference to the eye color of a newborn wolf pup. As the heart and soul of the business, River makes an appearance across all elements of the identity, playfully illustrated as the loyal shopkeeper to remind everyone this is a friendly place where specialty coffee is enjoyed and everyone is welcome.

Ministerstwo Dobrego Mydła

PARIS+HENDZEL CO. establish a pharmacy-like feel for the Warsaw-based fine soap maker.

Founded by two sisters, Ministerstwo Dobrego Mydła produces high-quality soaps and cosmetics made from organic materials. It also caters to customers with special needs and tastes with vegan and scentless product lines. Paris+Hendzel Co. helped craft the soap maker's brand identity, developing everything from packaging to website. With geometric shapes that evoke the straightforward character of old-school pharmacy graphics, the designers created a simple but functional identity that is complemented with photographs of each product's ingredients. The logotype has a reference to the large rock located in the Dziwna channel, from which the name of the town, Kamien Pomorski—the location of Ministerstwo Dobrego Mydła—is taken.

187

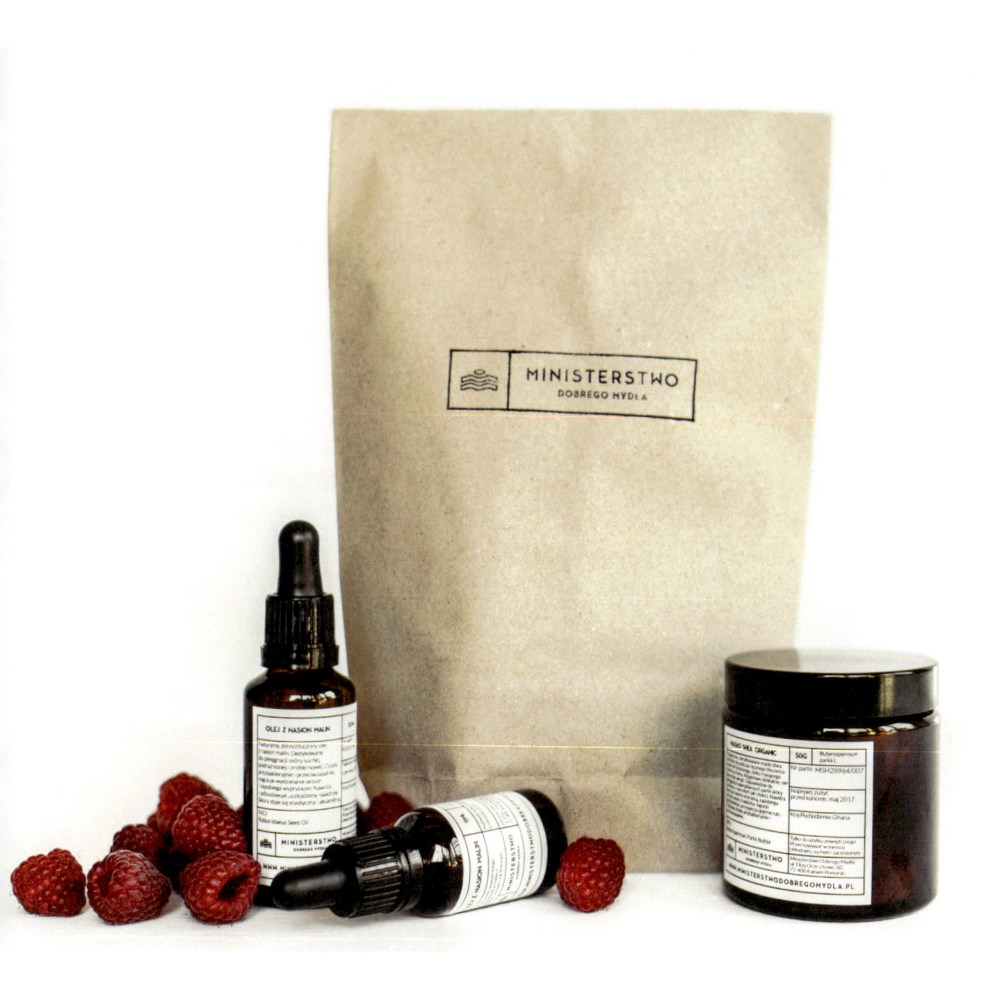

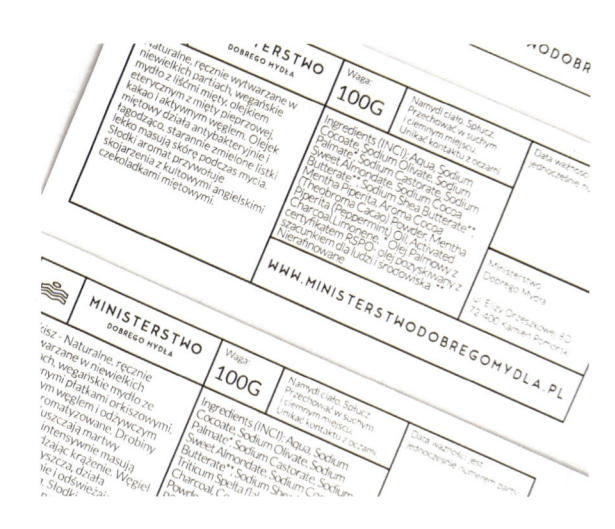

| THE WING | THE WING | THE WING | THE WING |

188

The Wing

PENTAGRAM's branding for the NYC-based women's social club celebrates diversity while referencing suffrage history.

The Wing is a New York social club for women of all backgrounds and professions—a place to work, exchange ideas, or just relax. An all-female team at Pentagram created its visual identity, which is inspired by graphic elements of the women's suffrage movement. They took a flexible, heterogeneous approach to represent The Wing's diverse membership base. The identity uses a series of 30 different Ws for the logo, and the membership cards come in three different styles and can be chosen according to individual taste. The brand's main color, a cool pastel pink, was chosen to reclaim its stereotypical status as female. Working with the founders, the designers developed a smart and humorous voice for the messaging to complement the elegant and scholarly look of the brand.

FRESH
DIPS
DRIZZLES
PICKLES
FREE-RANGE
CHICKEN
SLUSHIES
ICE COLD
SALADS
MADE DAILY
LAFA WRAPS
STONE GROUND FLOUR
HOT
BABA·G
TAKE-AWAY
PICKLED GOODS!
BAGAG.CO.ZA
POST OFFICE CENTRE
ILLOVO
QUARTER / HALF / FULL
DELI

BABA·G

BABA·G
ROTISSE
DELI
SALADS
LAFA WRAPS

S
P

BABA·G

BABA·G
LOYALTY CARD
FULL CHICKENS ONLY ✶ 12TH CHICKEN'S ON US!

Baba G

<u>SHAUN HILL</u> developed patterns inspired by vintage grocery store coupons for this Middle Eastern restaurant.

Named after the Middle Eastern eggplant dish baba ganoush, Baba G is the newest venture from Johannesburg-based Tutto Food Co. The small rotisserie deli focuses on North African and Mediterranean street food. Designer Shaun Hill created the brand identity for the restaurant with the directive to make something contemporary and humorous but that still takes its culinary roots seriously. The design is based on varying arrangements of illustrations and fonts and recalls vintage grocery store coupons. The design incorporates a large assortment of icons for menus and signage, which can also be used across the restaurant's packaging and collateral.

LET'S GET
FRESH
THE
HOTTEST
CHICKENS
ON THE BLOCK
BABA·G
ROTISSERIE & DELI
BABAG.CO.ZA
POST OFFICE CENTRE, ILLOVO
THE
HOTTEST
CHICKENS
ON THE BLOCK
BABA·G
ROTISSERIE & DELI
Hey you beautiful
thang! Not sure if
we've met but let's
get fresh-fresh like
the salads at Baba G.

SHOP 21
POST OFFICE CENTRE
ILLOVO
JHB SOUTH AFRICA
THE HOTTEST CHICKENS ON THE BLOCK
LET'S GET
LIKE THE SALADS AT BABA G
THE
BABA·G
ROTISSERIE & DELI
.CO.ZA
CENTRE, ILLOVO
POST OFFICE CENTRE
ILLOVO
JHB SOUTH AFRICA
SHOP 21
ILLOVO

Fatking

<u>ZÉ STUDIO</u> uses black-and-white photography and drawings of a gold crown to bring a fictional personality to life for the creative production company.

Located in New York and Los Angeles, Fatking is an award-winning production company that works for a range of clients and agencies. Zé Studio developed a fun and playful personification of Fatking as someone who is assertive, yet humble, with a self-deprecating attitude, and it gave the brand a hand-drawn gold crown. As an extension of this idea, the Fatking website promotes the Fatkingdom and its rulers, Zollo and Daniele. It also pays homage to honorary Fatkings such as John Belushi, Jack Nicholson, Jackie Gleason, and Luciano Pavarotti.

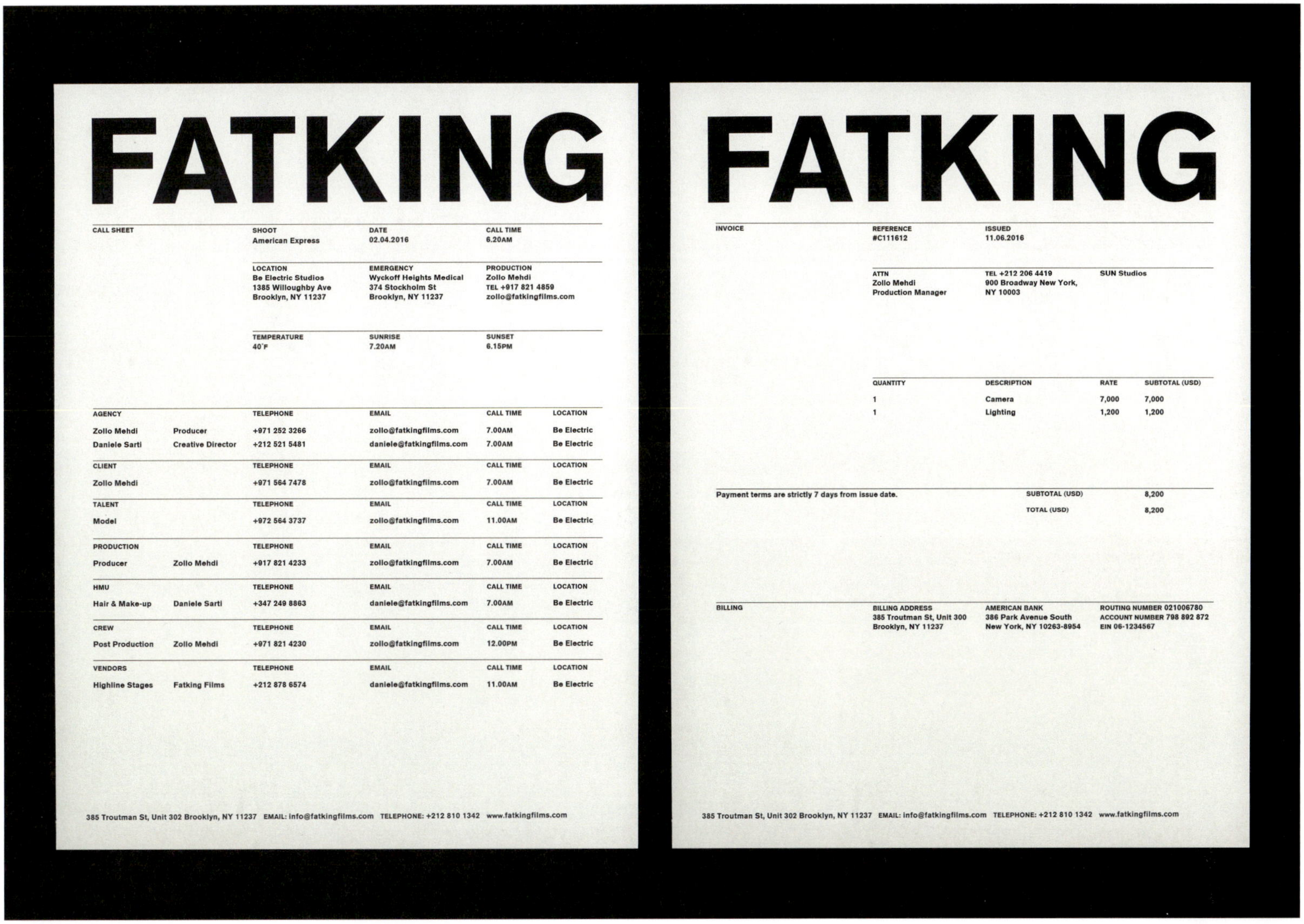
FATKING

CALL SHEET	SHOOT	DATE	CALL TIME
	American Express	02.04.2016	6.20AM
	LOCATION Be Electric Studios 1385 Willoughby Ave Brooklyn, NY 11237	EMERGENCY Wyckoff Heights Medical 374 Stockholm St Brooklyn, NY 11237	PRODUCTION Zollo Mehdi TEL +917 821 4859 zollo@fatkingfilms.com
	TEMPERATURE 40°F	SUNRISE 7.20AM	SUNSET 6.15PM

AGENCY		TELEPHONE	EMAIL	CALL TIME	LOCATION
Zollo Mehdi	Producer	+971 252 3266	zollo@fatkingfilms.com	7.00AM	Be Electric
Daniele Sarti	Creative Director	+212 521 5481	daniele@fatkingfilms.com	7.00AM	Be Electric
CLIENT		TELEPHONE	EMAIL	CALL TIME	LOCATION
Zollo Mehdi		+971 564 7478	zollo@fatkingfilms.com	7.00AM	Be Electric
TALENT		TELEPHONE	EMAIL	CALL TIME	LOCATION
Model		+972 564 3737	zollo@fatkingfilms.com	11.00AM	Be Electric
PRODUCTION		TELEPHONE	EMAIL	CALL TIME	LOCATION
Producer	Zollo Mehdi	+917 821 4233	zollo@fatkingfilms.com	7.00AM	Be Electric
HMU		TELEPHONE	EMAIL	CALL TIME	LOCATION
Hair & Make-up	Daniele Sarti	+347 249 8863	daniele@fatkingfilms.com	7.00AM	Be Electric
CREW		TELEPHONE	EMAIL	CALL TIME	LOCATION
Post Production	Zollo Mehdi	+971 821 4230	zollo@fatkingfilms.com	12.00PM	Be Electric
VENDORS		TELEPHONE	EMAIL	CALL TIME	LOCATION
Highline Stages	Fatking Films	+212 878 6574	daniele@fatkingfilms.com	11.00AM	Be Electric

385 Troutman St, Unit 302 Brooklyn, NY 11237 EMAIL: info@fatkingfilms.com TELEPHONE: +212 810 1342 www.fatkingfilms.com

FATKING

INVOICE	REFERENCE	ISSUED	
	#C111612	11.06.2016	
	ATTN Zollo Mehdi Production Manager	TEL +212 206 4419 900 Broadway New York, NY 10003	SUN Studios

QUANTITY	DESCRIPTION	RATE	SUBTOTAL (USD)
1	Camera	7,000	7,000
1	Lighting	1,200	1,200

Payment terms are strictly 7 days from issue date.

SUBTOTAL (USD) 8,200

TOTAL (USD) 8,200

BILLING	BILLING ADDRESS	AMERICAN BANK	ROUTING NUMBER 021006780
	385 Troutman St, Unit 300 Brooklyn, NY 11237	386 Park Avenue South New York, NY 10263-8954	ACCOUNT NUMBER 798 892 872 EIN 06-1234567

385 Troutman St, Unit 302 Brooklyn, NY 11237 EMAIL: info@fatkingfilms.com TELEPHONE: +212 810 1342 www.fatkingfilms.com

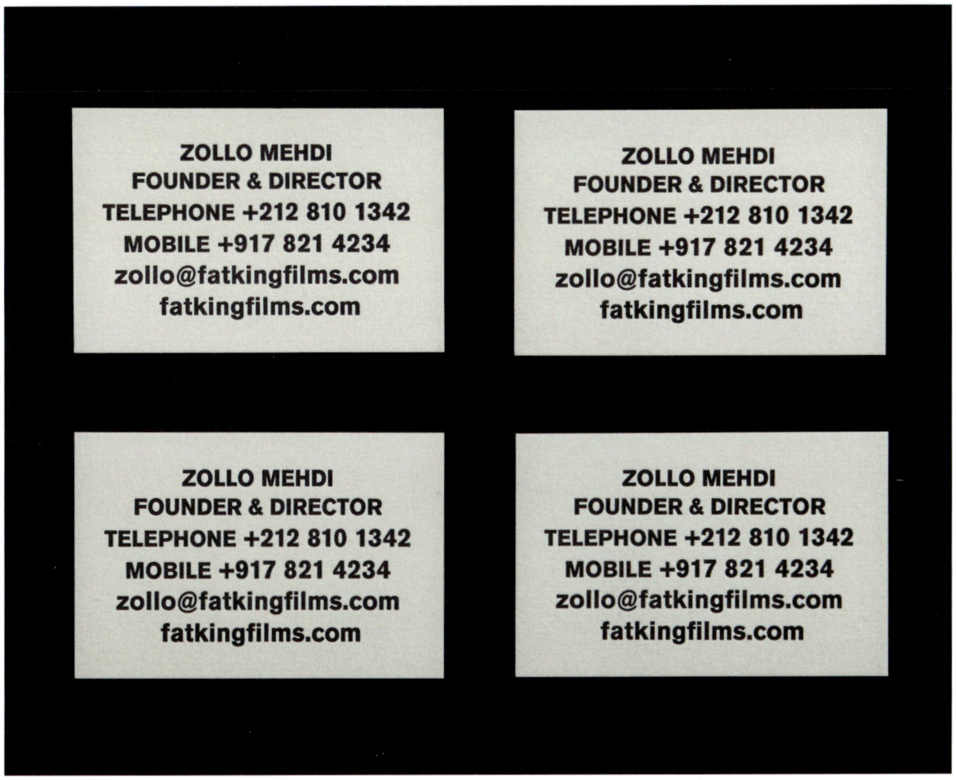

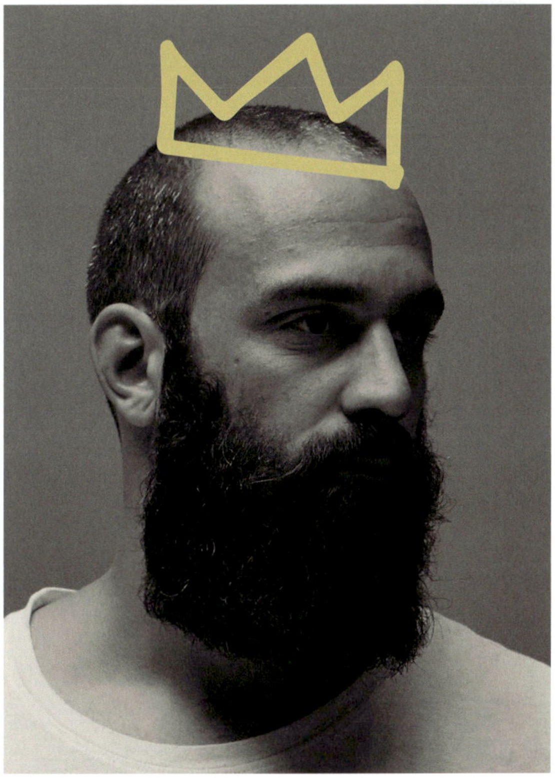

196

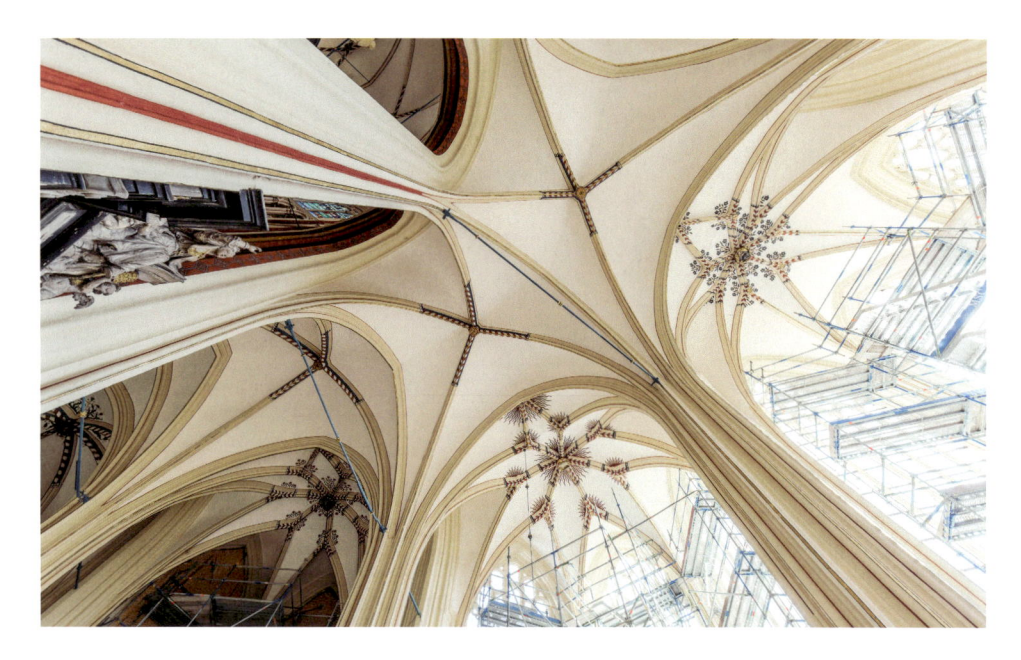

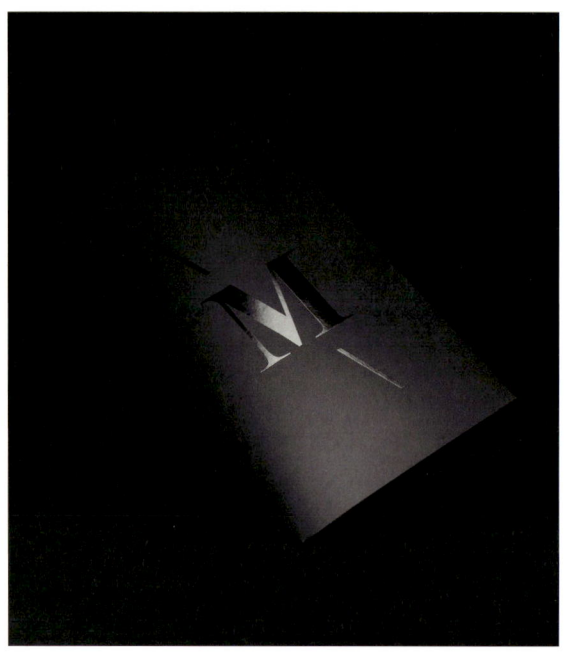

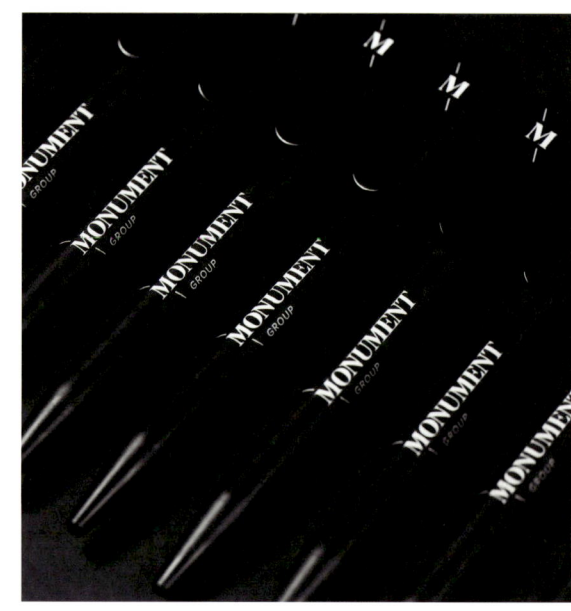

Group Monument

The backslash character conveys the before-and-after aspect of this restoration business in the design concept developed by *SKINN BRANDING AGENCY*.

Group Monument specializes in the restoration of historic buildings and monuments, and has developed a reputation for quality and dependability. The enterprise is structured into 12 subsidiaries that each offer a specific set of services. Skinn Branding Agency rebranded the business by giving each of the 12 companies a uniform identity, using the backslash character to symbolize the before-and-after aspect of each project. The black-and-white color palette lets the actual objects and photography come to the forefront. The typography uses a combination of serif and sans serif fonts—another reference to Group Monument's restoration work. The branding is used on trucks, building equipment, and construction tools.

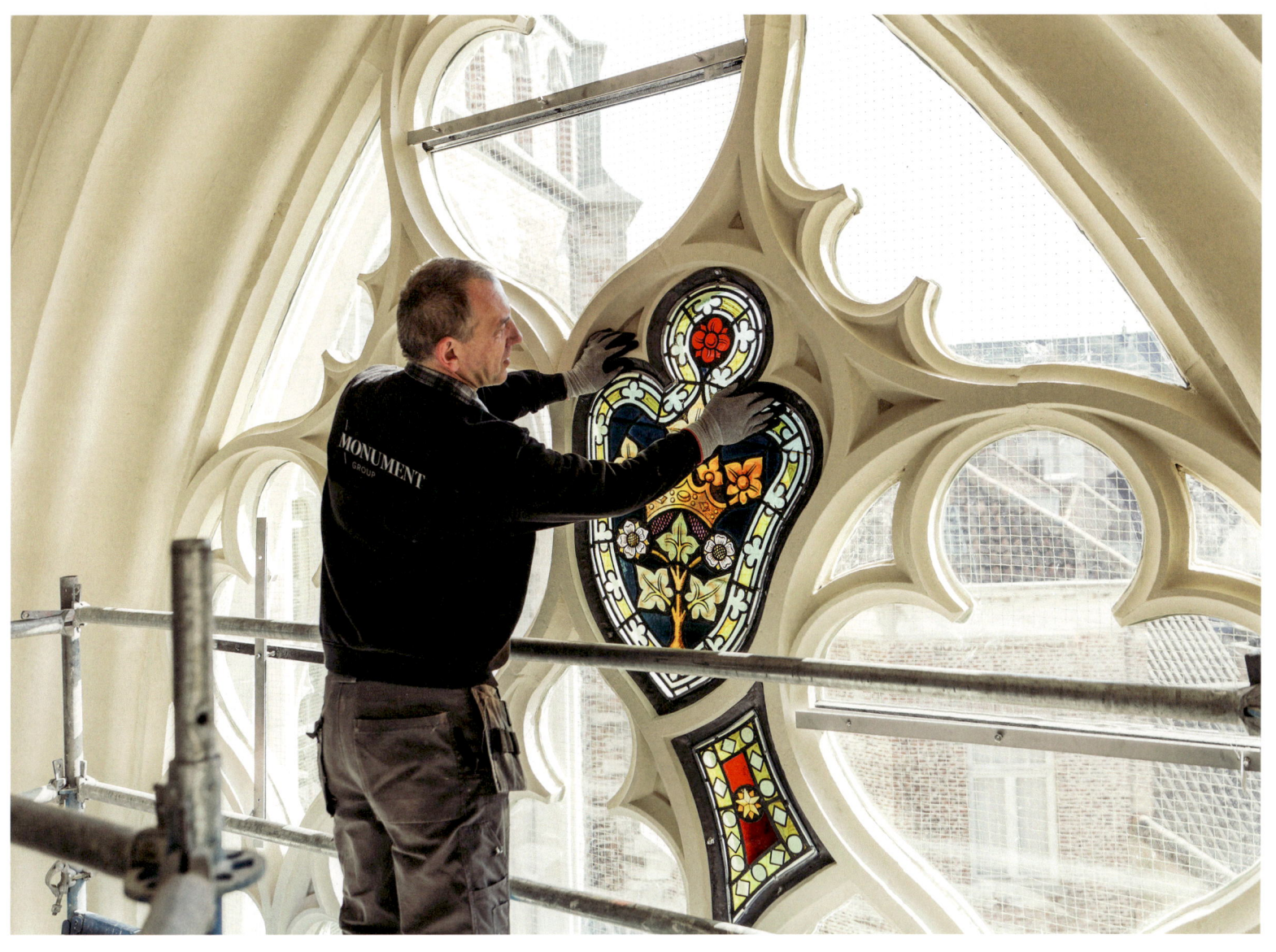

UMAMÌDO
ラーメン
RAMEN SHOP

UMAMÌDO
RAMEN SHOP
Chief Ramen Fanatic
+32 495 27 50 88
umamido.be

UMAMÌDO
RAMEN
SIDES
DRINKS
EXTRA TOPPINGS
TASTES LIKE MORE?
HOW IT WORKS
MENU
WANT MORE?
EXTRA TOPPING
SIDES
DRINKS

Umamido

Branding by _PINKEYE_ for the Belgium ramen shop fuses traditional Japanese themes with bold patterns.

Japanese noodle bar Umamido has locations in Antwerp and Brussels and serves traditional ramen noodles but with a local Belgian accent. Pinkeye created a new visual identity for the restaurant while maintaining continuity with its established brand image. The designers introduced contemporary elements, such as geometric Memphis-style patterns and illustrations, mixed with Japanese themes and iconography. Printed in high-contrast black and white, the visual language blends traditional elements with playful surprises.

HELVETIMART

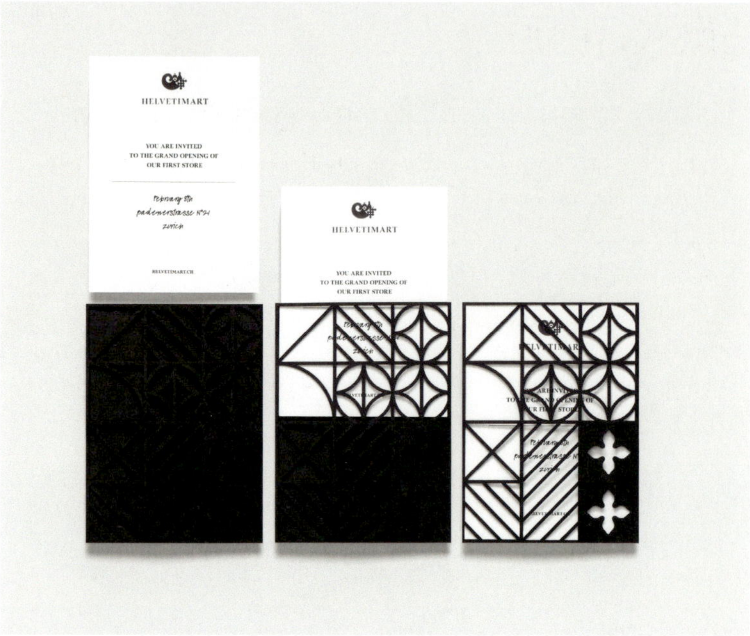
HELVETIMART
YOU ARE INVITED
TO THE GRAND OPENING OF
OUR FIRST STORE
HELVETIMART
YOU ARE INVITED
TO THE GRAND OPENING OF
OUR FIRST STORE

HELVETIMART

HELVETIMART
HELVETIMART
HELVETIMART

Helvetimart

Inspired by Swiss minimalism, ANAGRAMA's design for the specialty food store defines the country's distinctive regions.

Switzerland's culinary heritage is more than just chocolate and cheese, despite what many outsiders might think. At Lausanne-based specialty store Helvetimart, visitors can explore Switzerland via its food and sample culinary delights from each of the country's cantons. Anagrama developed a visual system based on each state's coat of arms, which it then simplified into flags for easy reference. The flags are used on packaging and stationery to further unify the brand. The store's cornucopia icon symbolizes abundance and references the wide selection available in the market. The clean, geometric look of the identity reflects the minimal design aesthetic for which Switzerland is known.

202

Harp Lane Deli

BURGESS STUDIO's identity for this British delicatessen incorporates the shape of its historic home.

Located in a historic building that is three stories high, but only 12 feet wide, Harp Lane Deli offers sandwiches, cheeses, salads, and drinks to the town of Ludlow in Shropshire. The branding by Burgess Studio incorporates multiple elements of the deli's inventory, including the shape of the building, which inspired its logo. The striking yellow color references the shop's cheese selection and makes a memorable impression, alongside the die-cut business and coffee cards, as well as its branded tote and product bags. It's a warm and inviting system, and a perfect message for a little shop that wants to provide high-quality local food and hospitality to residents and visitors.

Big Fernand

VIOLAINE & JEREMY create vintage-inspired visual language for the French burger company.

Big Fernand serves artisanal burgers with a French spirit. For its expansion into the international market, including new restaurants in Dubai, Hong-Kong, and London, the company aspired to create a stronger brand that would reflect its personality and values. Violaine & Jérémy developed a visual language with vintage-style illustrations of objects, such as newspaper, stamps, and trays. The designers wanted the branding to communicate a humorous but elegant image, and they inserted jokes throughout the design, which is inspired by old encyclopedias and pharmaceutical products. The designers also developed bespoke fonts and illustrations for Archibald Fernand, the company's ice cream and beverage brand.

205

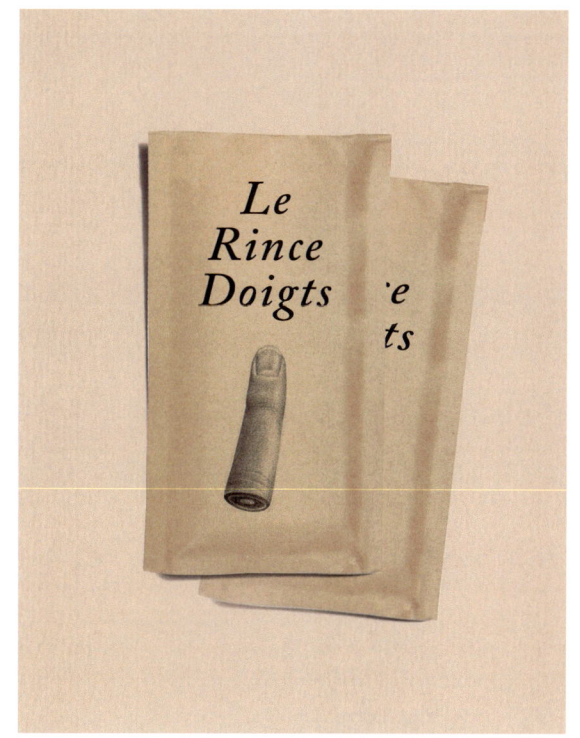

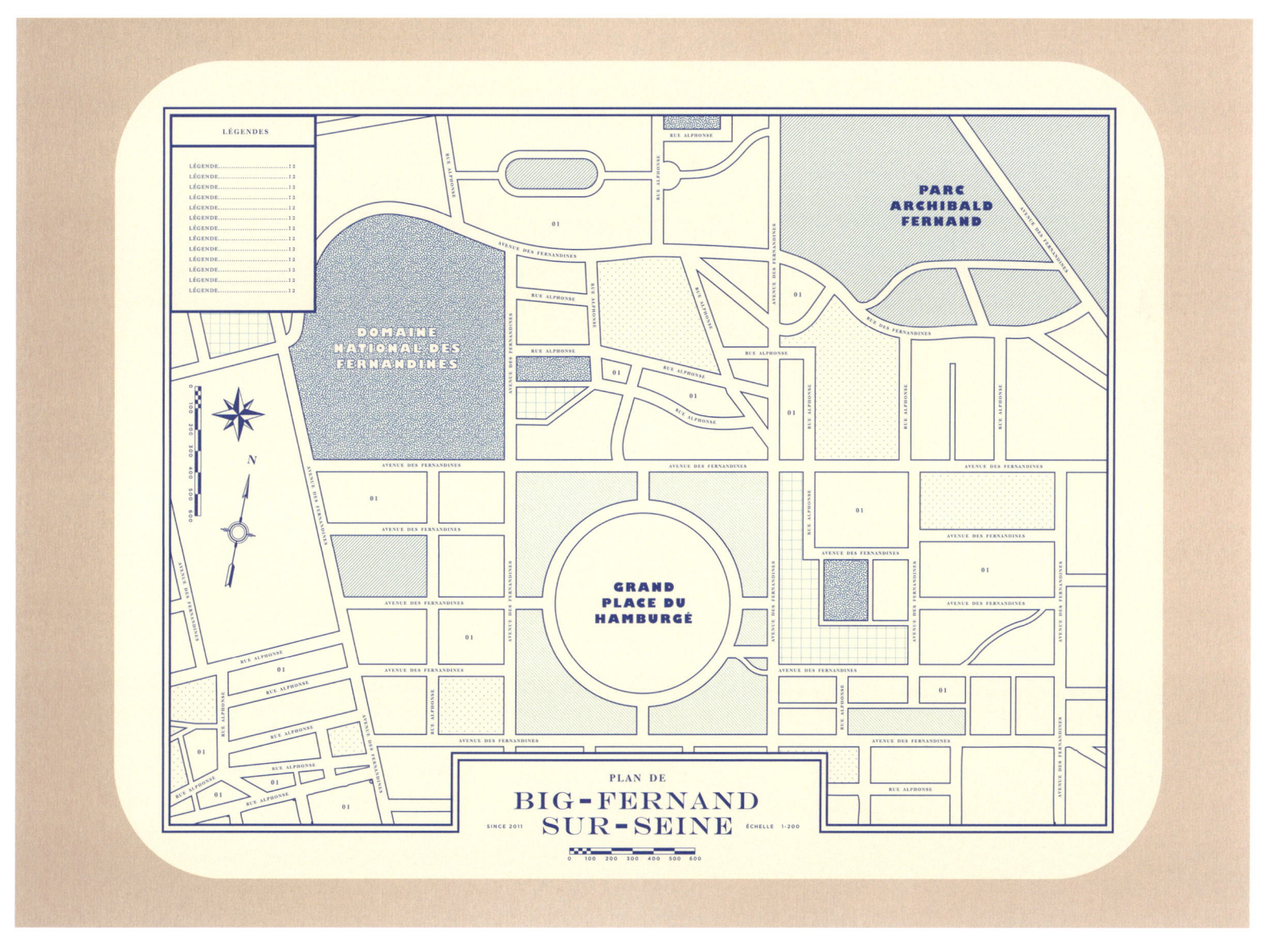

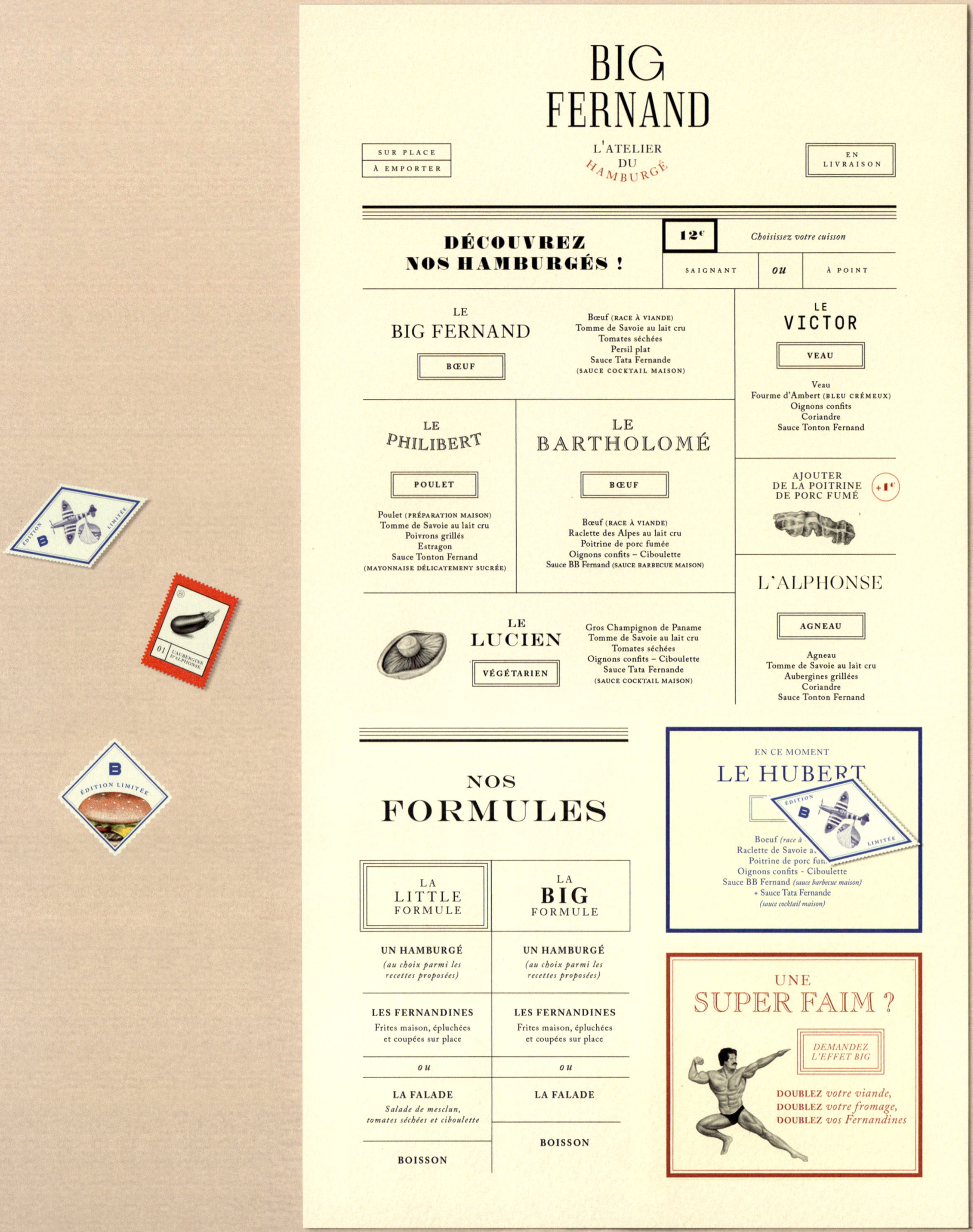

BIG FERNAND

L'ATELIER DU HAMBURGÉ

| SUR PLACE À EMPORTER | | EN LIVRAISON |

DÉCOUVREZ NOS HAMBURGÉS !

12€ — *Choisissez votre cuisson*

| SAIGNANT | *OU* | À POINT |

LE BIG FERNAND
BŒUF

Bœuf (RACE À VIANDE)
Tomme de Savoie au lait cru
Tomates séchées
Persil plat
Sauce Tata Fernande
(SAUCE COCKTAIL MAISON)

LE VICTOR
VEAU

Veau
Fourme d'Ambert (BLEU CRÉMEUX)
Oignons confits
Coriandre
Sauce Tonton Fernand

LE PHILIBERT
POULET

Poulet (PRÉPARATION MAISON)
Tomme de Savoie au lait cru
Poivrons grillés
Estragon
Sauce Tonton Fernand
(MAYONNAISE DÉLICATEMENT SUCRÉE)

LE BARTHOLOMÉ
BŒUF

Bœuf (RACE À VIANDE)
Raclette des Alpes au lait cru
Poitrine de porc fumée
Oignons confits – Ciboulette
Sauce BB Fernand (SAUCE BARBECUE MAISON)

AJOUTER DE LA POITRINE DE PORC FUMÉ +1€

L'ALPHONSE
AGNEAU

Agneau
Tomme de Savoie au lait cru
Aubergines grillées
Coriandre
Sauce Tonton Fernand

LE LUCIEN
VÉGÉTARIEN

Gros Champignon de Paname
Tomme de Savoie au lait cru
Tomates séchées
Oignons confits – Ciboulette
Sauce Tata Fernande
(SAUCE COCKTAIL MAISON)

NOS FORMULES

LA LITTLE FORMULE	LA BIG FORMULE
UN HAMBURGÉ *(au choix parmi les recettes proposées)*	UN HAMBURGÉ *(au choix parmi les recettes proposées)*
LES FERNANDINES Frites maison, épluchées et coupées sur place	LES FERNANDINES Frites maison, épluchées et coupées sur place
ou	*ou*
LA FALADE *Salade de mesclun, tomates séchées et ciboulette*	LA FALADE
BOISSON	BOISSON

EN CE MOMENT
LE HUBERT

Bœuf *(race à viande)*
Raclette de Savoie au lait cru
Poitrine de porc fumée
Oignons confits - Ciboulette
Sauce BB Fernand *(sauce barbecue maison)*
+ Sauce Tata Fernande *(sauce cocktail maison)*

UNE SUPER FAIM ?

DEMANDEZ L'EFFET BIG

DOUBLEZ votre viande,
DOUBLEZ votre fromage,
DOUBLEZ vos Fernandines

COMPOSEZ VOUS-MÊME

VOTRE HAMBURGÉ

N°1
VOTRE BARBAQUE
D'ORIGINE FRANÇAISE

Bœuf (race à viande)
Poulet (préparation maison)
Veau
Agneau

N°2
VOTRE LÉGUME
GRILLÉ

Aubergines grillées
Poivrons grillés
Tomates séchées – Oignons confits
Gros Champignon de Paname

N°3
VOTRE FROMAGE
D'ORIGINE FRANÇAISE

Raclette des Alpes au lait cru
Tomme de Savoie au lait cru
Fourme d'Ambert
(BLEU CRÉMEUX)

AJOUTER DE LA POITRINE DE PORC FUMÉ
+ 1€

N°4
VOTRE SAUCE
PRÉPARÉE SUR PLACE PAR NOS SOINS

Tonton Fernand
(MAYONNAISE DÉLICATEMENT SUCRÉE)
Tata Fernande
(LA SAUCE COCKTAIL)
BB Fernand
(LA SAUCE BARBECUE)

N°5
VOTRE HERBE FRAÎCHE
CISELÉE AVANT LE SERVICE

Persil plat – Ciboulette
Coriandre – Estragon

VOTRE ACCOMPAGNEMENT
3€

LES FERNANDINES
Frites maison, épluchées et coupées sur place
ASSAISONNEMENT AU CHOIX :
HERBES DE PROVENCE
OU PAPRIKA AIL

LA FALADE
Salade de mesclun, tomates séchées et ciboulette

NOS BOISSONS	NOS DESSERTS	NOTRE CAVE
LES ÉLIXIRS D'ARCHIBALD FERNAND *(Nos limonades artisanales)* – 33 cl • Esculence de citronnier • Flaveur pomme, citron et larme de réglisse • Succulence de grenadine, menthe poivrée, citron	**LES CRÈMES FIGÉES D'ARCHIBALD FERNAND** • Chocolat Noisette avec pépites de meringue • Madeleine • Sorbet Framboise avec pépites de chocolat	**AOP CÔTES-DU-RHÔNE** Notes de fruits rouges et d'agrumes Domaine Chapoutier *(rosé)* • 13,5 % – 12,5 cl *(au verre)* 5€ • 13,5 % – 75 cl 19€ / **AOP CROZES HERMITAGE** Fin et fruité Domaine Chapoutier *(rouge)* • 13,5 % – 37,5 cl 14€ • 13,5 % – 75 cl 25€
NOS GAZEUX 33 cl Canada Dry • Liptonic • Coca-Cola / Zéro **NOS EAUX** • Evian citron, fleur de sureau 37 cl • Evian rose, raisin 37 cl	**NOS BIÈRES** • Ch'ti *(Venue des confins du Nord)* 6,4% 25 cl +1€ • Gallia Pression *(Bière blonde)* 5% 25 cl +1€ • Gallia Pression *(Bière blonde)* 5% 50 cl +3€	**LES GODETS MOUSSE** Oréo • Spéculoos framboise **LA FALADE DE FRUITS ROUGES** Grenade, framboises, fraises, coulis de fruits	**UNE SUPER FAIM ?** *DEMANDEZ L'EFFET BIG* Doublez votre viande, votre fromage, et vos Fernandines + 4€

208

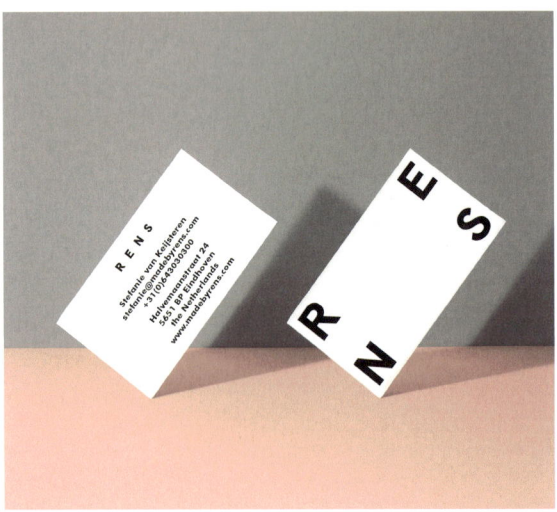

RENS

An adaptive identity design by *STUDIO &* creates the framework for the design studio's portfolio.

Renee Mennen and Stefanie van Keijsteren commissioned Studio& to develop a new visual identity and website for their research-based design studio RENS. Studio&'s concept is based on a podium—something upon which RENS can experiment, create, and present work. Although the logo has a strong presence, it is also adaptive and can be increased in size or rearranged as needed. In addition to designing the studio's business cards, packaging, and signage, Studio& also created the website, where the letters of RENS change position according to user navigation.

209

ZÓLDI

cute. but devilish
inside.

ZÓLDI

zóldi jewels

ZÓLDI

cute. but devilish inside.

Zóldi

F61 WORK ROOM use a gold, bubblegum-pink, and jet-black color palette to show off the minimalistic products of this Dubai-based jewelery business.

Based in Dubai, the innovative jewelry brand Zóldi partners with expert manufacturers to create silver and 18-karat gold jewelry. Zóldi embodies the philosophy that successful women know who they are, and strives to create accessories that fit each woman's soul, rather than just her body. In creating Zóldi's brand identity, F61 Work Room chose a bubblegum-pink color palette with accents of gold to represent its main material. The jet-black color in the interiors of its boxes provides contrast to the pink and offsets the fine products each package contains. Its destinctive brand photography sticks to a decidedly feminine palette to let Zóldi's little gems shine.

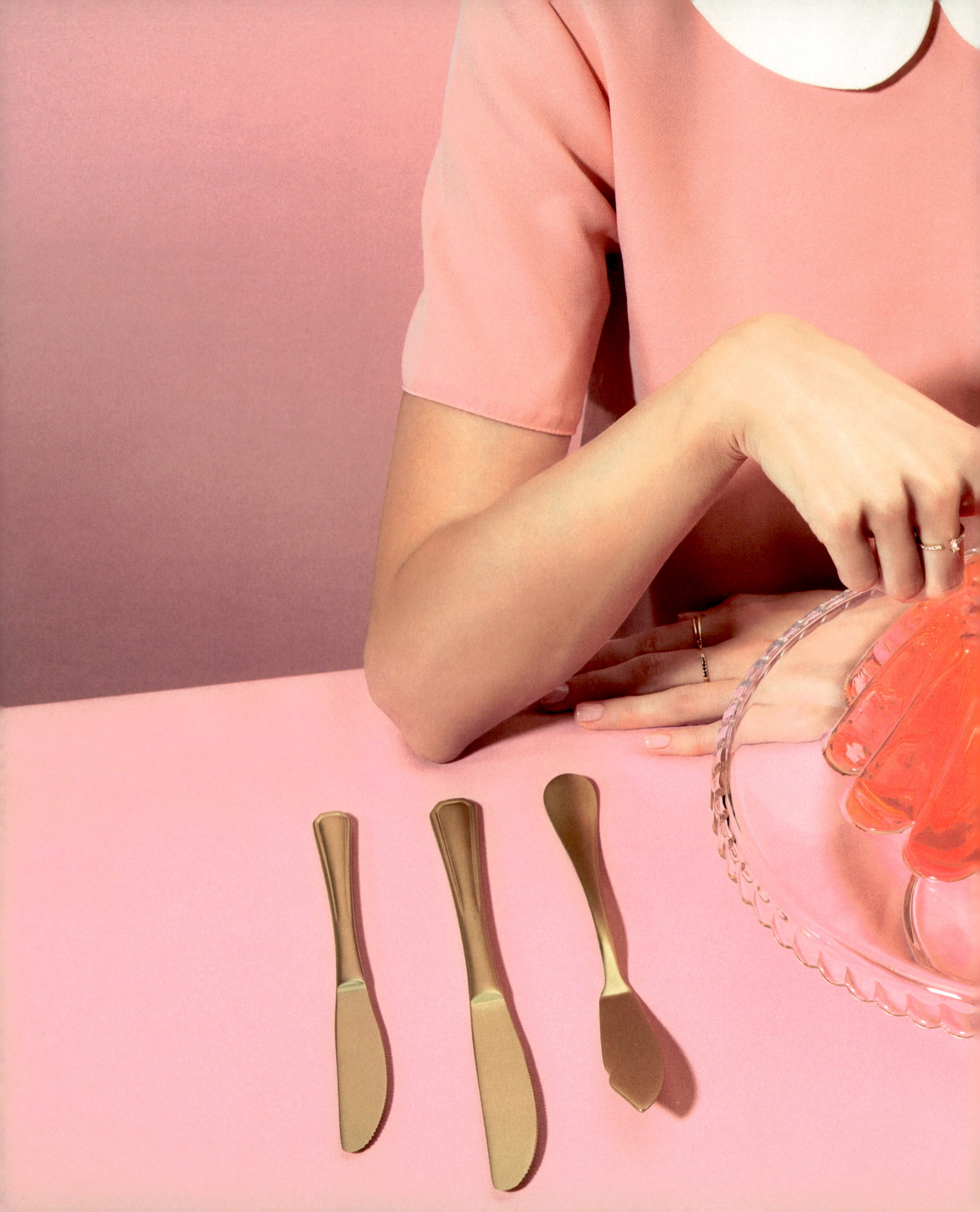

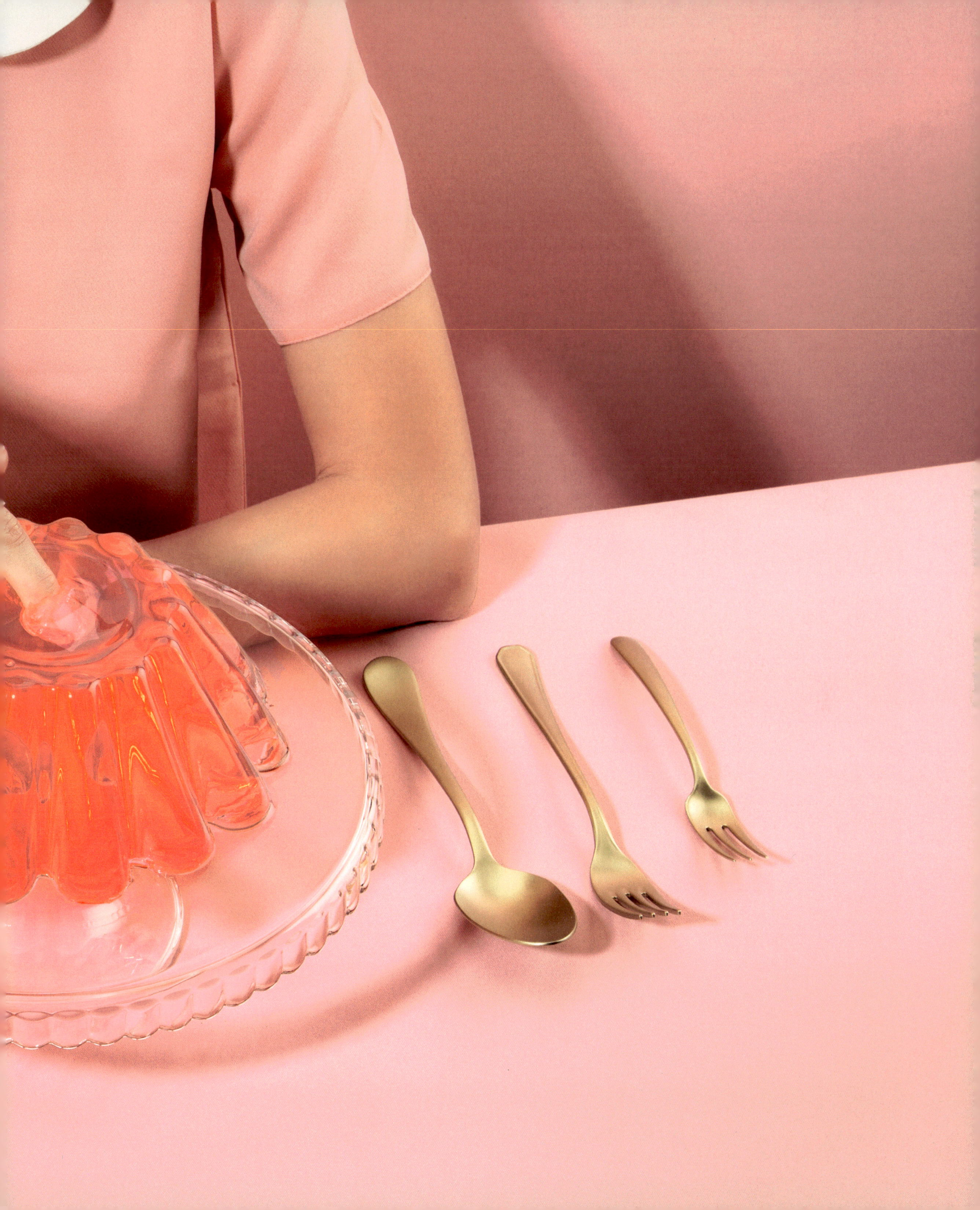

Shana Teugels

VRINTS-KOLSTEREN's minimal branding allows the jeweler's bold work to come to the fore.

Contemporary jewelry artist Shana Teugels's practice is based on the relationships between jewelry, objects, and kitsch. Teugels's work is anything but subtle, which led Vrints-Kolsteren to create a visual identity that gives her pieces a voice. The designers have achieved this with an understated design that incorporates photography and accentuates the rich colors and textures that characterize Teugels's work.

Shana Teugels
(Contemporary Jewelry and Art)

shanateugels@info.com
tel. +32 (0) 499 108 554
www.shanateugels.com

Material Desire, *3 of 7 (Aqueous Diamond)*
Brooch, 2010, 13,5 × 19 × 15 cm.

Shana Teugels *(Contemporary jewelry and Art)*

Idols are always beautiful, *3 of 4 (Vitreous Lustre)*, Object, 2012, 31 × 32 × 35 cm.

Shana Teugels　　　*(Contemporary jewelry and Art)*

216

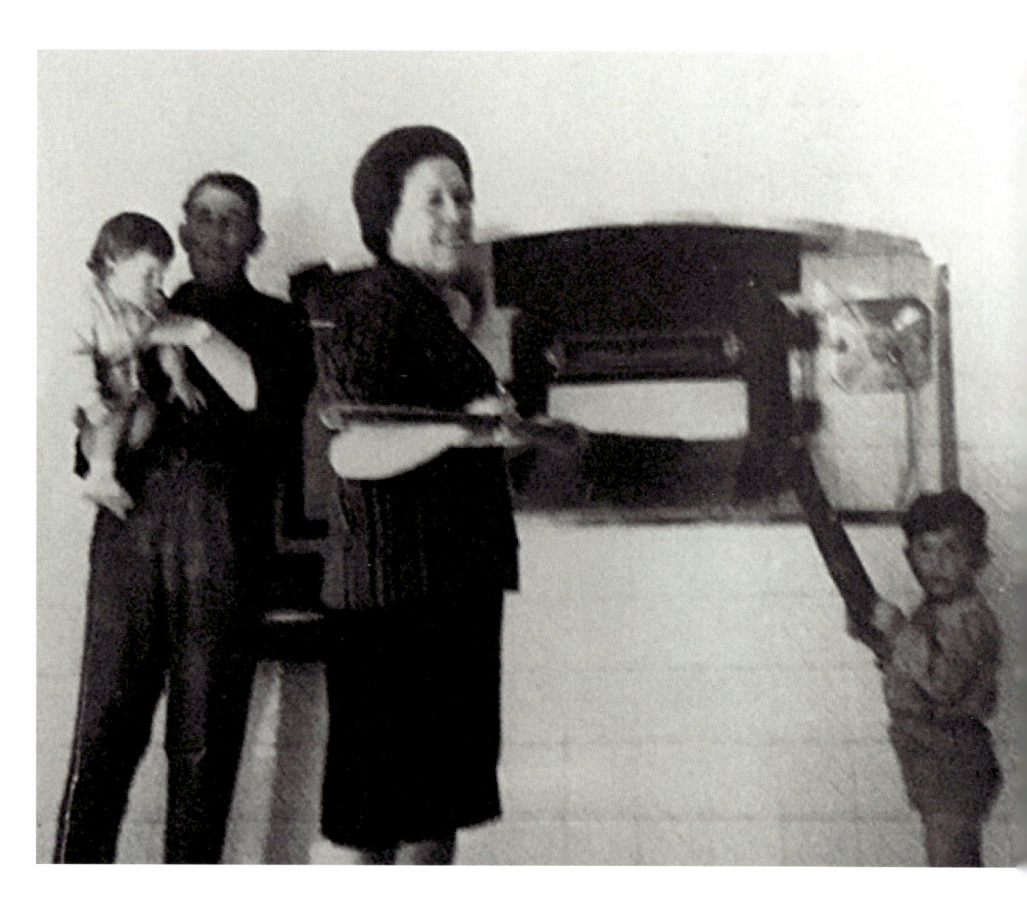

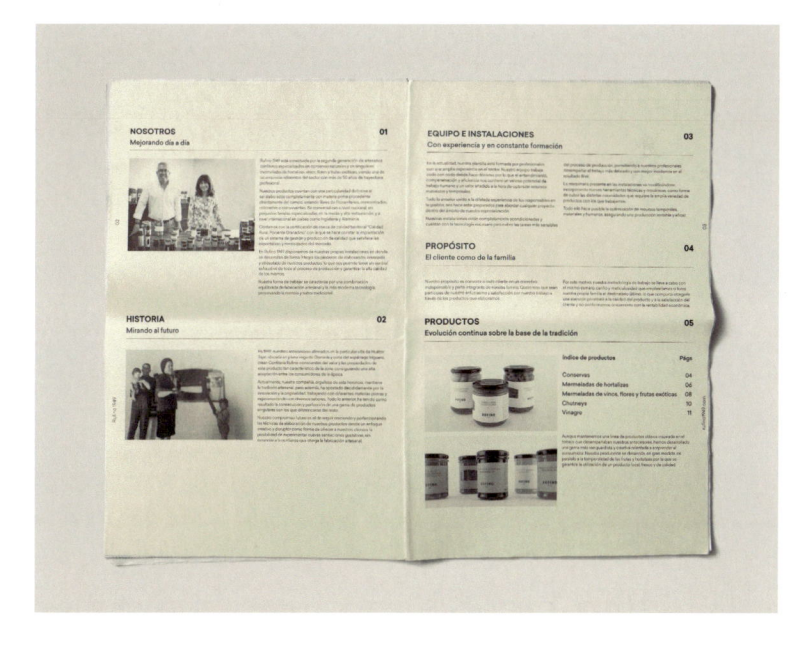

Rufino 1949

BUENAVENTURA's rebrand for the family food company highlights the natural colors of its produce.

For almost 70 years, Rufino 1949 has manufactured its products using traditional methods. Originally a bakery, the family-owned company also makes jams, chutneys, vinegars, and preserves. Buenaventura's rebranding of the business and its product lines captured the traditions of Rufino 1949's artisanal process, while highlighting its contemporary take on modern flavors and gastronomic trends. The shape of the oven door from the original bakery is used across packaging to indicate the origin of the business; cut out of the labels on the jars it allows the product to be visible. Vivid colors reflect the freshness of the fruits that the company's products are made of.

217

Koub

Traditional construction techniques and a simple graphic approach by <u>AKAONI</u> create a welcoming atmosphere for the Japanese bakery shop.

The owners of Koub, a small independent bakery in northern Japan, tasked Akaoni with creating their business' identity, including the exterior and interior design of the Koub shop. The solution involved integrating traditional Japanese elements and building techniques with a contemporary feel. A specially trained craftsman, known as a sakan-shokunin, did the plaster on the exterior walls. The shop's countertop was made using a technique called kamado and the earthen tataki-doma floor is common in traditional Japanese homes. The space looks and feels simple yet has impact, and the handmade construction techniques create a human touch that is warm and welcoming.

BREAD
IS
LIFE!
BREAD
IS
LIFE!

CLOSE
OPEN.10:00-19:00
{SAT&SUN.9:00-19:00}
CLOSED.TUESDAY

OPEN.10:00-19:00
{SAT&SUN.9:00-19:00}
CLOSED.TUESDAY

OPEN
OPEN.10:00-19:00
{SAT&SUN.9:00-19:00}
CLOSED.TUESDAY

BREAD
IS
LIFE!

KOUB
2-8-11
NARISAWA-NISHI
YAMAGATA
TEL.023(665)1188
www.koub.jp

KOUB

Blind Butcher

Classic butcher shop branding by _TRACTORBEAM_ for the meat-centric restobar in Dallas.

Located in Dallas's eclectic East Side, Blind Butcher offers fine dining in a casual pub setting. Its ever-changing menu is locally sourced, seasonal, and anchored by a wide variety of cured meats and sausages, as well as fresh cocktails and an extensive beer and wine list. Tractorbeam helped brand the restaurant by developing its name and a custom typeface for its classic logomark. Inspired by the typography and design associated with vintage butcher shops, the designers created a menu system that echoes their inspiration. The restaurant is located in a 1920s building and, thanks to local workshop 44 Build, maintains many of the structure's original architectural details. While retaining its art deco style, the designers infused the space with a modern industrial look and feel.

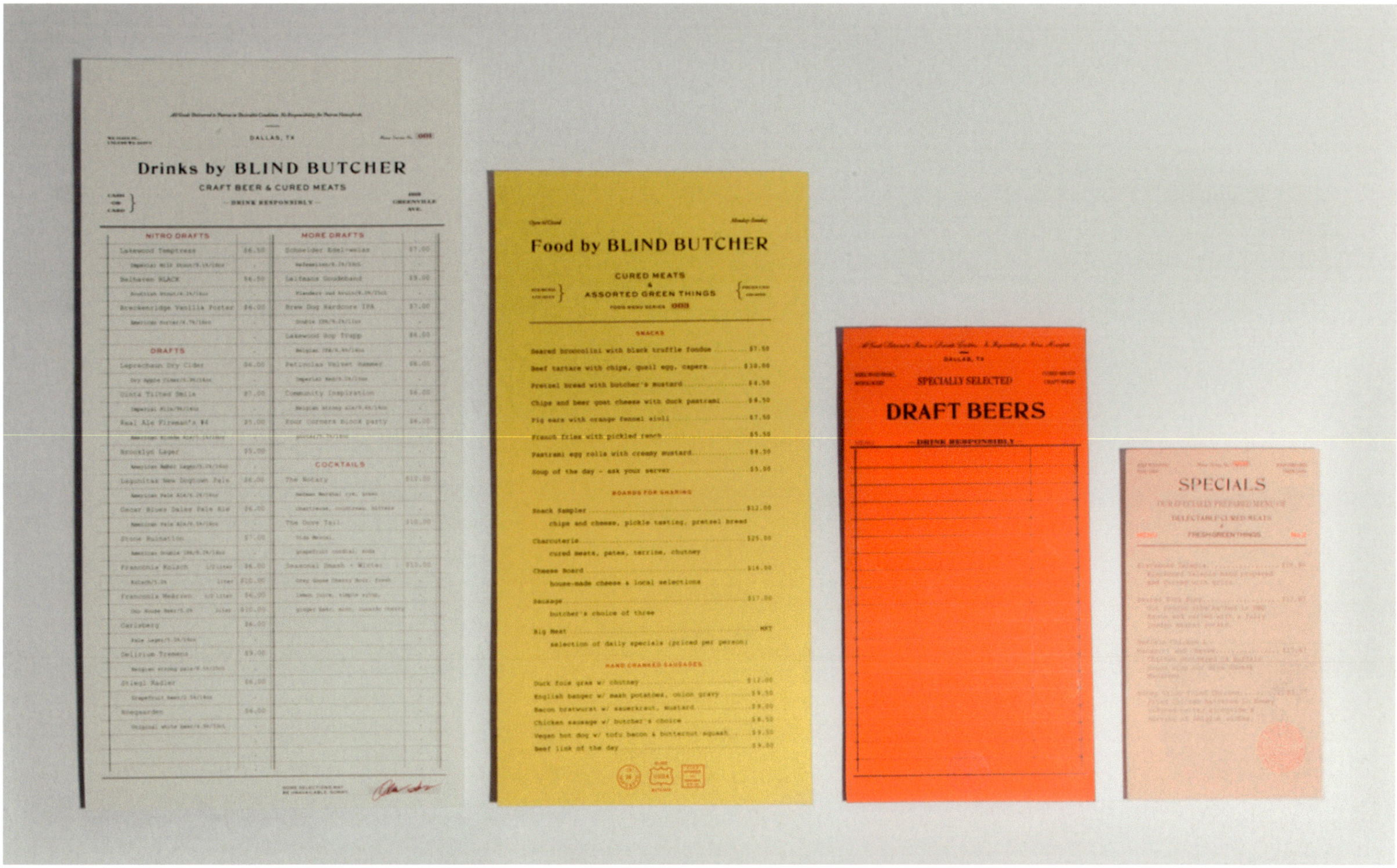

NO ONE LIKES A KNOW IT ALL.

CURED MEAT **BLIND BUTCHER** CRAFT BEER

1919 GREENVILLE AVE.

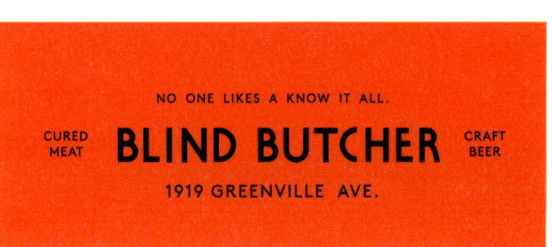

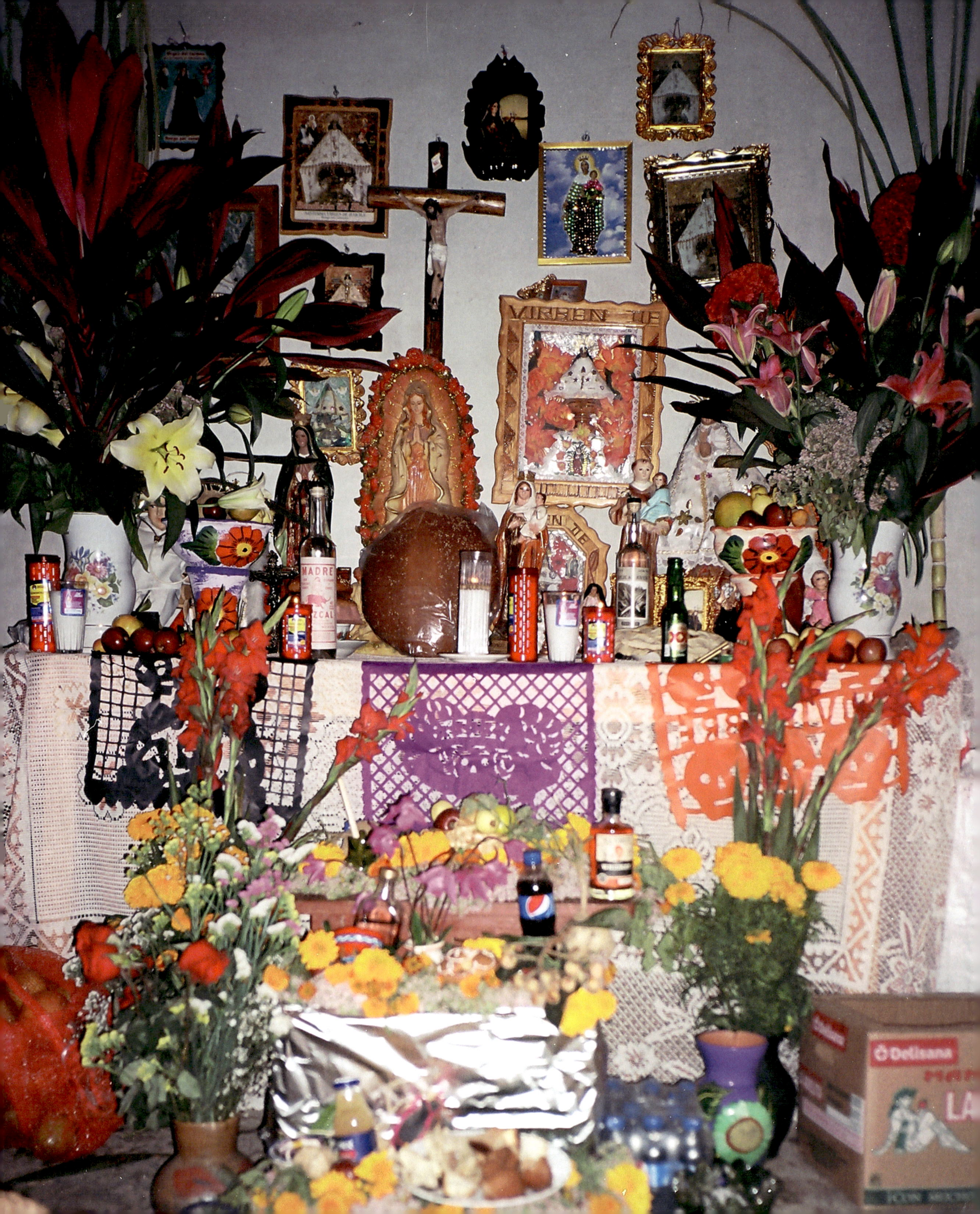
VIRGEN DE
MADRE
Delisana

CASE STUDY: **Madre Mezcal**

Madre Mezcal is distilled in the dusty hills of San Dionisio, southeast of Oaxaca City. The family recipe is based on centuries of mezcal wisdom. The agave from which it is made is stone-ground by horse, and the spirit itself is smoked in the earth. The branding aesthetic reflects that earthiness, paying tribute to the simple techniques mezcal makers have used for generations. "There are no bells and whistles to the brand. Madre just is," the designers and creative partners at <u>LAND</u> say. A closer look reveals that it is, in fact, much more than a brand.

Several years ago, an artist and anthropologist from New York travelled through Southeastern Mexico to investigate native shamanism. He eventually landed in the mystical mountain town of Huautla, where magic mushrooms grow wild, and a history of psychedelics spills into the streets. It was here that he met a man working with mezcal as medicine. The glossy-eyed elder told the visitor about the "mezcal mother" that gives this elixir from the earth, and regaled him with a bottle of his favorite type from Oaxaca.

A few months later, the creative explorer, Tony Farfalla, began searching for the origin of the mezcal he had tasted in Huautla, for it had been the best he had ever tasted. After getting lost in the deserts and mountains of Oaxaca, he found Jose Ines Garcia Morales and his family. For the next few years,

Farfalla smuggled small batches of Garcia Morales's mezcal back home, stocking select bars, and sharing the wonderful spirit with friends.

One random day in Montauk, New York, Farfalla ran into Stefan Wiegand, an old childhood friend who happened to work in brand development and photography now. Back in Colorado, the two had grown up watching surf films in Wiegand's basement, but had lost touch long ago. Nearly 15 years after their last encounter, they found each other surfing the same break in Montauk and finished the day with Farfalla's contraband mezcal. Agreeing that it should be shared with more people, they decided to try their hand at starting a business: Madre Mezcal was born.

Caleb Owen Everitt and Ryan Rhodes of LAND soon came on board as creative partners. They all spent some time in Oaxaca together on the Morales ranch, getting to know the family and their way of working on the homemade palenque. Helping out with production, cutting agave, cooking, and fermenting, the visitors

"The design hallmarks of the Madre Meszcal brand are simplicity and honesty mixed with mystery."

became immersed in the hands-on process. There was no doubt that this artisan spirit would need to be at the heart of everything Madre.

"The design hallmarks of the brand are simplicity and honesty mixed with mystery," Everitt and Rhodes describe. "The label design has been created by placing each letter, one at a time. The illustration is hand drawn." In the illegal days of Madre, they stamped and applied each label by hand, but had to create efficiencies once sales were official. Madre's labels are still applied by hand, but are now printed with flexography, "the closest method of industrial printing to a hand stamp while remaining modestly affordable," the designers explain. Madre's bottles are handblown, and the business cards manually composed and letterpressed.

Notwithstanding the brand's artisanal feel, one finds a whole multimedia world spun around Madre Mezcal. There is *Madre Journal*, which brims with distinctive photography; there are social media accounts; Madre bandanas, available for purchase on the website; and even *Madre Radio*, in the form of curated Spotify playlists.

"There is a great ability to facilitate discussion and education—to even spawn creativity and adventure—through a thoughtful and sincere brand identity."

"We want to offer a platform and tell stories that people can relate to and involve themselves with. Not just through narratives, but also imagery, music, and experience," Farfalla and Wiegand explain. "The mezcal tradition and appreciation really lends itself to this idea, and sits nicely among the concepts we are exploring. There is a great ability to facilitate discussion and education—to even spawn creativity and adventure—through a thoughtful and sincere brand identity."

Farfalla refers back to the deep connection he found with mezcal and everything surrounding its production. "It's a truly magical and sincere spirit that was clearly meant to be a part of my life, and I want to share this experience—an experience that is far greater than just a drink. So, Madre tries to offer a more holistic presentation of it." Ideally, their customers do not merely taste the mezcal, but feel it. "We want them to feel the labor and effort that goes into it, but also the heritage and ritual that shows through in the recipe," Wiegand says.

"We look at Madre as more of an art brand than a manufacturer of mezcal," Rhodes and Everitt say.

"We always try to push progressive thoughts into client work, but most times there is a sense of 'playing it safe' that we have to keep in mind for a client. With Madre, we can run a bit wilder."

Compared with other branding projects they have worked on, both are keen to stress that Madre is particularly close to their hearts. "As partners, we are a part of it, we are the clients, in a way. That is the dream. We always try to push progressive thoughts into client work, but most times there is a sense of 'playing it safe' that we have to keep in mind for a client. With Madre, we can run a bit wilder."

While daily business on the Morales ranch has not changed much since the Madre crew came along, the collaboration has enabled the family to finally focus on production full-time. "Oaxaca is one of the poorest states in Mexico, and like most men in his town, Jose used to spend a lot of time working in the U.S. to earn a decent wage to send home for his family," Farfalla explains. With the new interest in mezcal, and the Madre brand boosting the product, Morales can now rely upon a fairly stable income and provide jobs for his family too.

There may be a flipside to the potation's newfangled popularity, for artisan mezcaleros like Jose. "Looking back at the path tequila took, one may indeed be concerned that similar things happen here: an industrialization of the product, outsourcing small producers, and an overconsumption of agaves. It depends on the direction the Mezcal industry will take in the future," say Wiegand and Farfalla, who are doing their bit to put it on

MADRE
CALEB EVERITT
CALEB@
512 626 3946
MADREMEZCAL.COM
MEZCAL

MADRE
MEZCAL
OAXACA
MEXICO
100 Percent Maguey Joven
Espadin y Cuishe
JOSE GARCIA MORALES Y FAMILIA

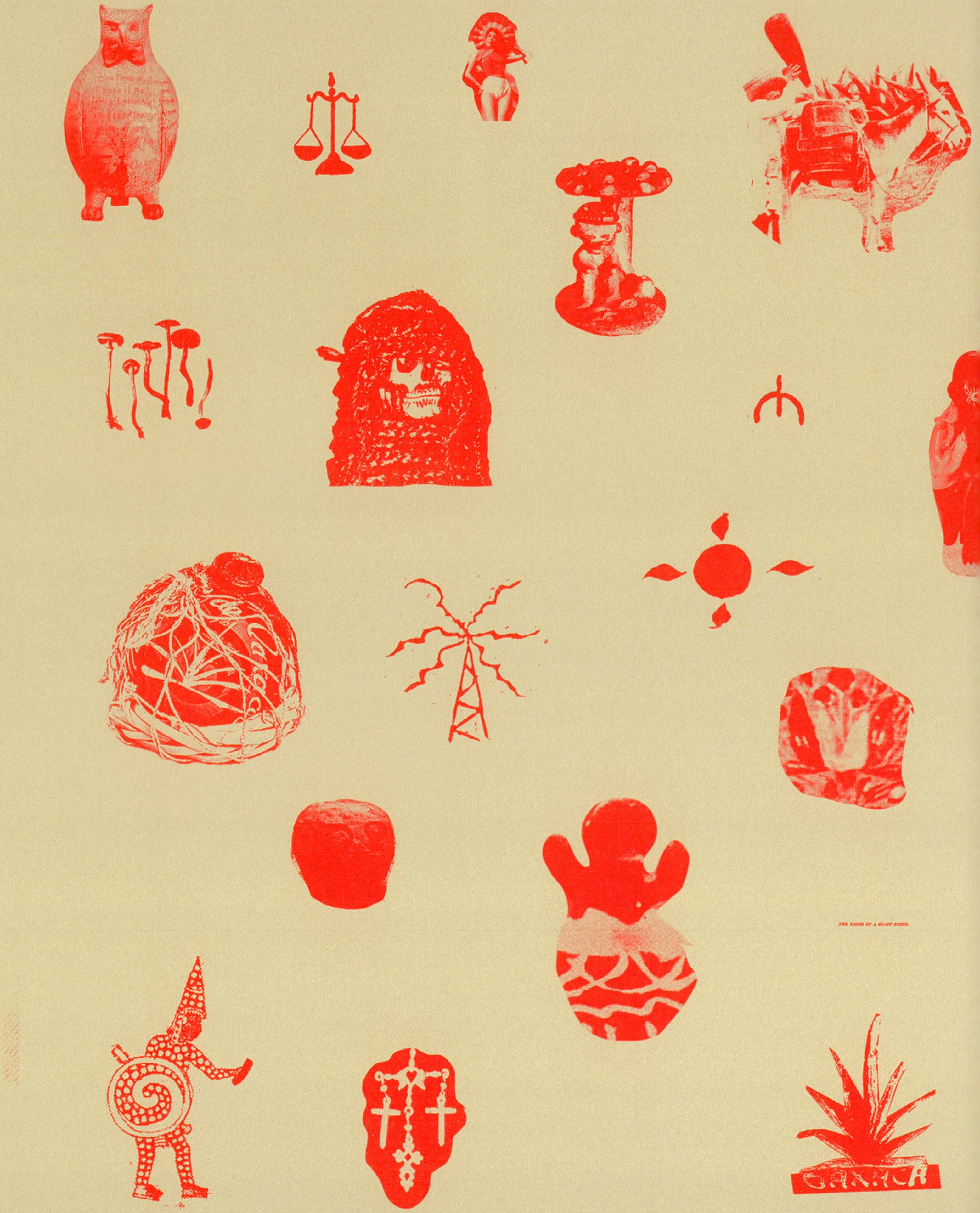
THE BONES OF A GIANT FOUND.
OAXACA

MEXICO
OAXACA

That last day does not bring extinction to us, but change of place.

230

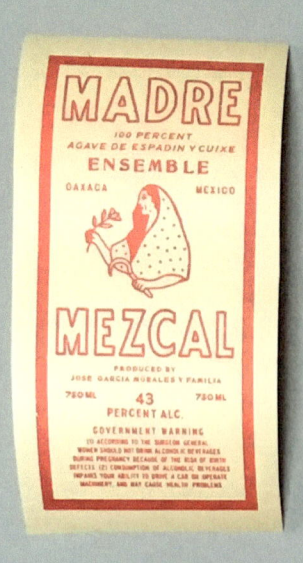

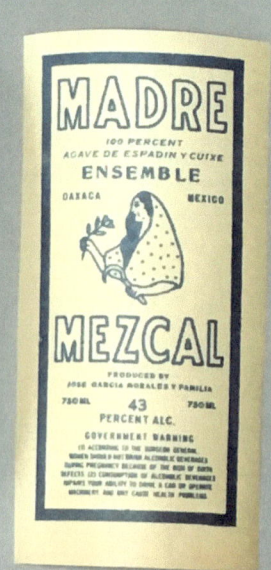

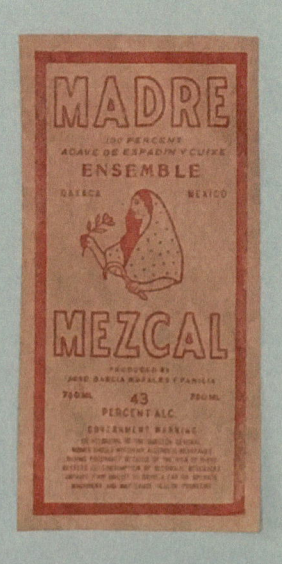

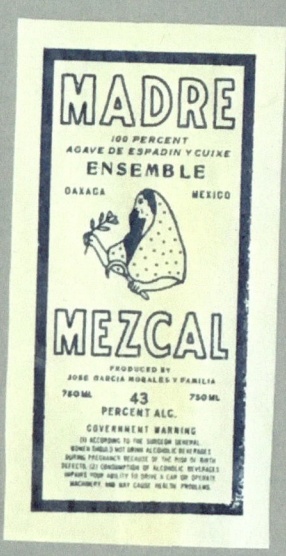

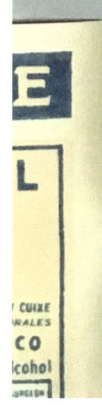

"We create brands that reflect our humanness. That involves imperfections, shifts in color, and constant change in a brand's appearance."

the right track, with Madre's sustainability program, for example, which promotes biodiversity in agave cultivation.

"While the staple agave of mezcal production (agave espadín) has been cultivated for many years, the other 'wild' varieties have only recently been introduced to cultivation," the entrepreneurs explain. "A big problem with cultivating wild agaves is the plant's inability to grow in well-maintained rows on flat, arid soil. By planting these wild agaves in conditions similar to their native wild habitats, such as hillsides, where they sit amongst other native plants, their ability to grow is dramatically increased." Madre's cultivation program is based on these ideas. "We are currently growing all agave types used in our recipe," Farfalla says. "When we harvest wild agaves from our mezcalero's land, we adhere to harvesting principles that always leave flowering plants to reseed, and we plant a new agave for each one we harvest."

As Rhodes and Everitt point out, Madre's ecological mission is pursued in the brand's communications:

"Keeping the packaging stripped down to a two-color label helps to keep the coverage of ink to a minimum. A single label saves on paper instead of having the waste that comes with top and back labels. The case boxes have a single label, instead of printing all over the box, which again cuts down on ink and costs. Keeping the overall packaging stripped down not only saves on money and waste, but doesn't stray far from the original spirit of Madre."

Aside from LAND, Farfalla and Wiegand work with two consulting partners, who advise them on all the business things they themselves "aren't so keen on." Above all, they consider Madre to be their passion project, they say, but even as they both continue to work on other jobs to pay their bills, that project continues to grow. "For now, we mainly sell in the larger Los Angeles region, but business is expanding. This summer we will be launching in New York, and a few other states within the U.S. soon after. We would love to share Madre internationally too, but this all depends on production capacities, and our ability to maintain control over the brand's identity and quality."

The designers and partners at LAND agree: "Madre has to grow organically so that we remain true to how the Morales family operates. A lot of mezcal and tequila brands start small, but jump into a big plant production and potentially sacrifice the original spirit that excited them in the first place." They say that the biggest challenge in developing identities for small businesses is to stay flexible and resist stagnation. "We create brands that reflect our humanness. That involves imperfections, shifts in color, and constant change in a brand's appearance." Madre is a prime example of this. "It can be a challenge at times to work with a humble budget, but we like to stay rooted closely to the earth."

Takahashi Beef Farm

AKAONI reinforces the local beef farmer's relationship to its animals and customers with a figurative logomark.

Japanese beef wholesaler Takahashi Beef Farm is involved in all aspects of bringing quality beef to its customers, breeding, raising, processing, and retailing all of the beef it sells. Akaoni redesigned the logomark by transforming the original abstract geometric logomark into a recognizable image of a steer that it easy for customers to identify and associate with the brand. The new look is more in line with the spirit of Takahashi Beef Farm, as a proud producer of local and high-quality beef that places a high priority on transparency and the relationship between the farmer and consumer.

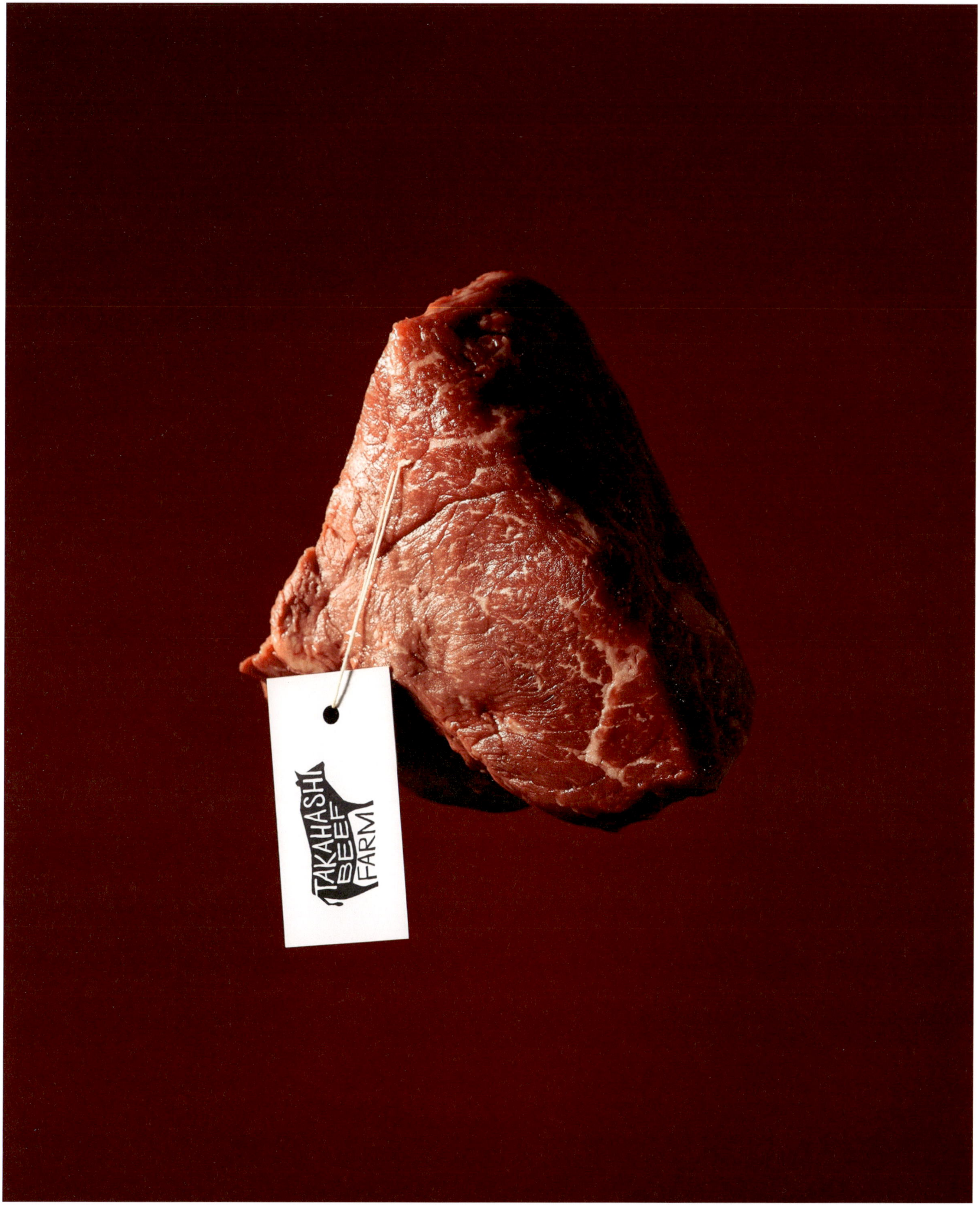
TAKAHASHI
BEEF
FARM

234

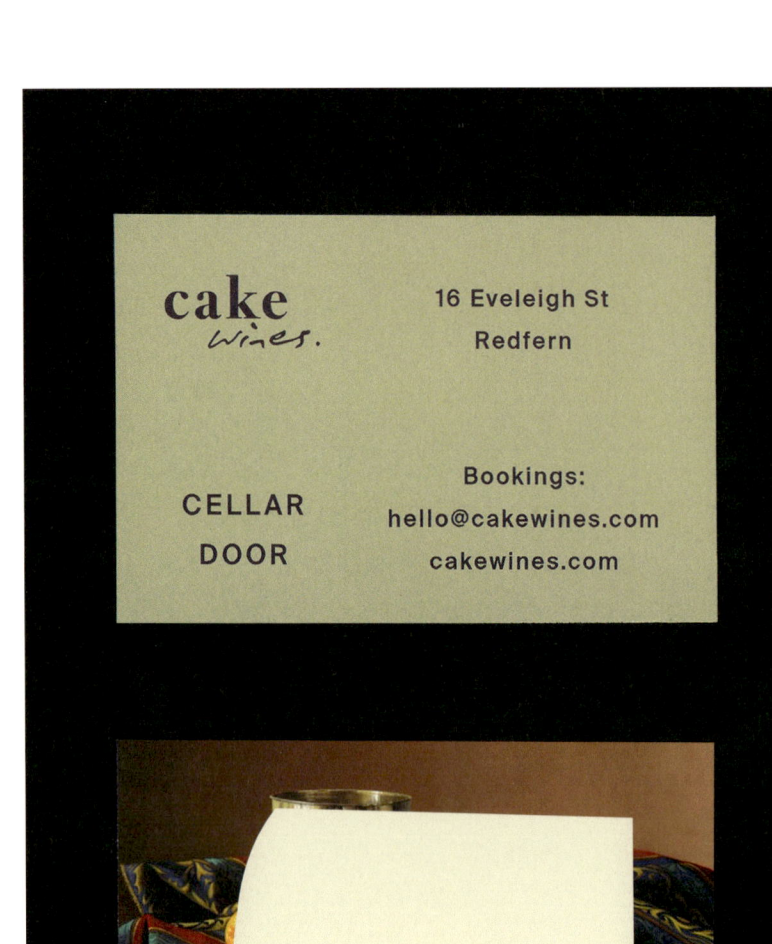

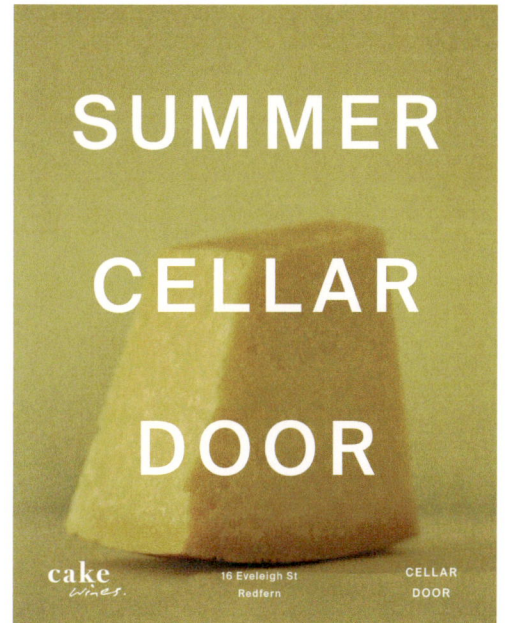

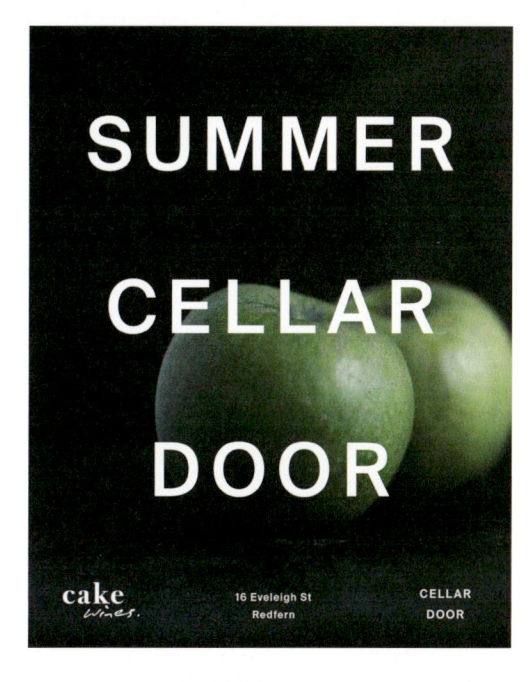

Cake Wines Cellar Door

<u>ZÉ STUDIO</u> marries the language of classic still lifes and contemporary art to highlight the winemaker's traditional methods and modern approach.

Cake Wines founders Glen Cassidy and Sarah Burial started their business out of the back of a truck; and it grew in size and popularity to eventually become a restaurant, Cake Wines Cellar Door. Zé Studio created the visual identity, which plays with the genre of still life paintings and the interplay of shapes found in contemporary art, as a metaphor for Cake Wines's working approach, which mixes traditional methods with a modern approach. The studio worked with photographer Traianos Pakioufakis to make a collection of still life photographs for a summer campaign promoting a series of events celebrating music, food, and culture.

235

236

Era Ceramics

<u>MENTA</u> mixes a sleek monogram with natural papers to promote handmade ceramic goods.

Era Ceramics produces handmade dinnerware and home décor. Each form is thrown on the wheel and glazed by hand, ensuring that each piece is unique. Era Ceramics produces work that is simple and pared down with a quiet, natural beauty. Menta's visual identity is a modern take on the studio's earthy look, using off-white paper that gives the product photography and letterhead a muted, slightly weathered look to enhance the textures and natural tones of its products. The monogram, which connects the E and C as basic circular shapes, is printed in copper foil.

Common Lot
info@commonlot.com
973 467 0494 —t
973 379 5847 —f
27 Main Street
Millburn NJ 07041
commonlot.com

Dinner

COMMON LOT

broccolini, barley, burrata, chilli, cumin, carrots, cabbage, collard greens, cauliflower, brussel sprouts, kohlrabi, onion, radish, beans, lentils, parsnips, honey, vanilla

Common Lot

PERKY BROS takes a lighthearted approach to seriously good cuisine for the communal diner.

Created by Ehren Ryan, the Common Lot draws on its chef's globally diverse culinary background. The open kitchen and shared tables encourage communal dining; and the relaxed atmosphere allows family and friends to share an evening of conversation over a meal. Inspired by Ryan's serious attitude towards food, and his lighthearted attitude towards life, Perky Bros created a visual identity using the ideas of common space, shared plates, and lost sheep. The logotype plays with the Os in Common Lot, and scatters abstract drawings of sheep across the collateral, which is printed on natural papers. The result is unpredictable and thoughtful—a true reflection of the owner.

239

Ricky & Pinky

<u>ROUND</u>'s lucky-cat logomark riffs on a classic Chinese dining aesthetic for this modern hotel restaurant in Melbourne.

Builders Arms Hotel is a Melbourne institution that has remained a beloved corner pub, despite its decades of reinvention. For its most recent addition—a Hong Kong-style Chinese restaurant—owner Andrew McConnell wanted a bold new design that still honored the venue's history. In close collaboration with Sibling Architecture, Round orchestrated a cultural collision between the hotel and the restaurant with lazy Susans, fish tanks, and giant fortune cookies. The designers developed a relatable personality for the brand by creating a riff on the classic Chinese restaurant aesthetic. Ricky & Pinky's color palette is dominated by red and gold; a line drawing of a waving cat serves as a playful logomark.

241

Barbearia Porto

OSCAR MAIA highlights the Portuguese barber shop's historical legacy with a vintage-inspired look produced with traditional printing techniques.

Founded in 1946, Barbearia Porto underwent a number of reinventions throughout its many generations of owners, while its quality services remained unchanged. Following the barber shop's change in ownership in 2015, Oscar Maia redesigned the visual identity by exploring the shop's rich heritage. The typography and layout not only have a vintage look, but were also produced using traditional techniques. The window signage is hand-painted with the rare technique of gold-leaf glass gilding, and the letterpress-printed stationery further highlights the barber's commitment to tradition. The result speaks to the modern urban gentleman who appreciates a haircut and shave accompanied by the kind of service that comes from decades of experience.

243

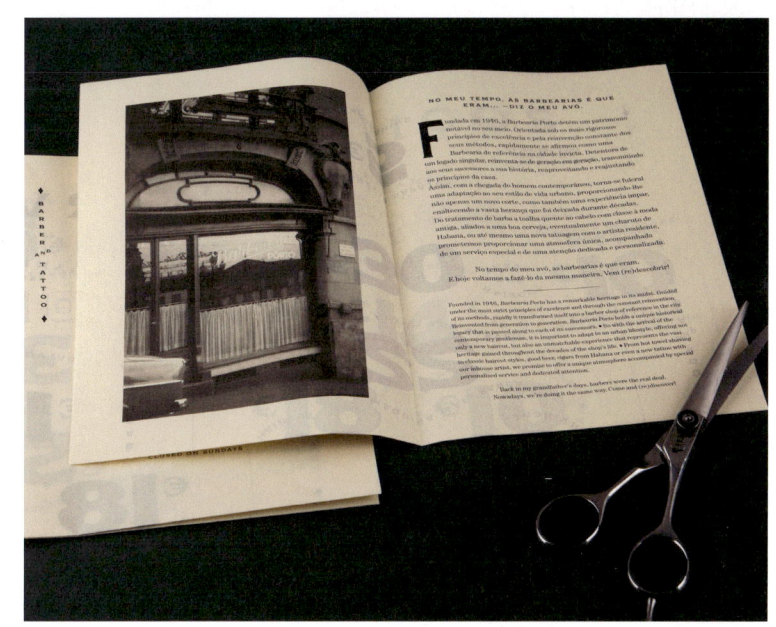

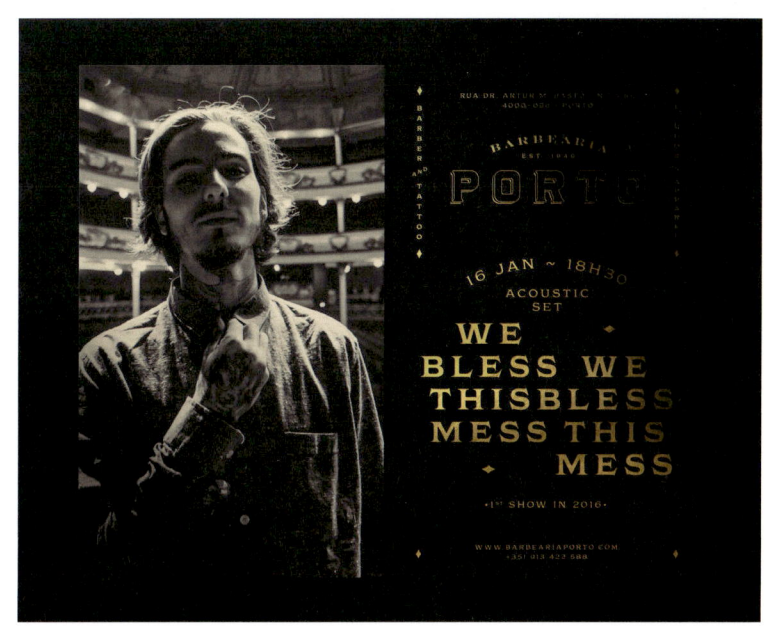

BARBEARIA
EST. 1946
PORTO
+351 913 422
BARBER AND TATTOO
LIQUOR AND APPAREL
RUA DR. MAGALHÃES • N.º 6 RC
4000~096 • PORTO
BARBEARIA
EST. 1946
RUA DR. MAGALHÃES • N.º 6
4000~096 • PORTO

BARBEARIA
EST. 1946
PORTO
WWW.BARBEARIAPORTO.COM
+351 913 422 588

RUA DR. MAGALHÃES · N.º 6 RC
4000~096 · PORTO

BARBER AND TATTOO

LIQUOR AND APPAREL

246

The Moneygun

Fresh branding for an old dive bar turned cocktail lounge. Designed by _DAN BLACKMAN_ with a dash of nostalgia.

Located under Chicago's "L" train, Moneygun is a former dive bar with red vinyl seats and smoke-stained ceilings. Since reopening in 2016, it has gained a reputation as one of the city's best cocktail bars, while continuing to stay true to its roots. Dan Blackman developed the bar's brand direction, which recalls an era of cheap cocktails and barflies. Choosing Moneygun's name was the first part of the process, followed by creating a contemporary visual system with notes of nostalgia. The design balances a sense of timelessness and something new, with a distinctive identity that is stylish and unpretentious.

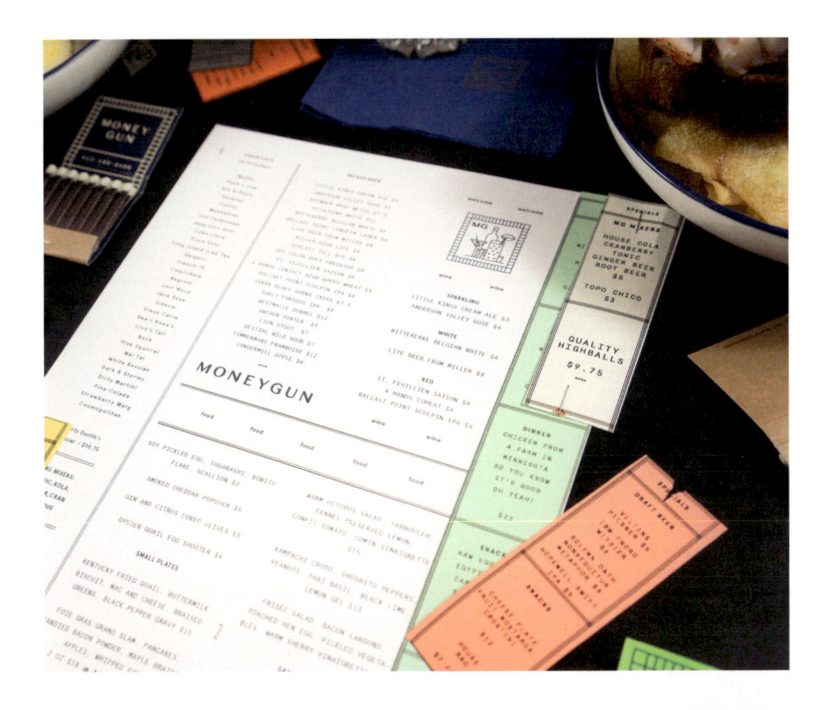

248

Heritage Pizza and Taproom

TRACTORBEAM's 1950s-inspired typography and illustrations for the eatery evoke the heyday of the American pizza parlor without being kitsch.

Heritage Pizza and Taproom is a classic American pizza parlor that specializes in sourcing locally grown ingredients and pouring beers from local breweries. The owners asked Tractorbeam to develop a visual identity that captured a sense of nostalgia for yesteryear without resorting to a kitsch, retro, or vintage look. The designers researched the roots of the brand—pizzerias from the 1950s—and created an identity that casts it within a modern context. The branding uses a variety of typefaces that subtly recall the time period, yet retain a contemporary feel. An illustrated mascot of a rabbit wearing a varsity jacket appears on bottles, beer cans, menus, and other marketing collateral.

Delicious! BEER ON TAP — GROWLERS TO GO ★

BREW	ABV	IBU	13oz	16oz	32oz	64oz
1. Collective Brewing – Petite Golden Sour	4.5%		$3	$3	$5	$10
2. Austin Eastciders – Texas Honey Cider	5%		$4	$4	$6	$14
3. Bishop Cider – Suicider	6.9%		$3	$3	$5	$15
4. Bitter Sisters – Busy Body	5.92%		$4	$4	$7	$15
5. Avery Brewing – White Rascal	5.6%		$4	$4	$7	$15
6. Manhattan Project – Half Life	6.2%	33	$5	$5	$8	$20
7. Revolver – Blood & Honey	7%	20	$2	$2	$5	$10
8. Martin House – Bockslider	5.6%	18	$3			
9. Peticolas – Golden Opportunity	4.6%	27	$5			
10. Southern Star – Blonde Bombshell Ale	5.25%	20	$6			
11. Noble Rey – Off The Leash	6%	22	$5			
12. Four Corners – Super Bee	8%	23	$2			
13. Goose Island – Green Line	5.4%	30	$2			
14. Audacity – Repercussion	5%	23	$2			
15. Karbach – Weekend Warrior	5.5%	45	$2			
16. OHB – Freaky Deaky	10%	45	$2			
17. Blue Owl – Van Dayum!	6.3%	29	$4			
18. 903 – Land of Milk and Honey	6.5%		$4			
19. T.A.P. – Fire Ant Funeral	6%	32	$3			
20. Founders All Day IPA	4.7%	42	$5			
21. Oskar Blues – Dales Pale Ale	6.5%	65	$3	$3	$5	$10
22. Peticolas – Velvet Hammer	9%	85	$4	$4	$6	$14
23. Green Flash – Soul Style	6.5%	75	$3	$3	$5	$15
24. Firestone Walker – Luponic Distortion	5.9%	59	$4	$4	$7	$15
25. Ballast Point – Sculpin	7%	70	$4	$4	$7	$15
26. Lone Pint – Yellow Rose	6.8%	62	$5	$5	$8	$20
27. Stone – Delicious IPA	7.7%	75	$2	$2	$5	$10

★ DRINK • COLD • BEER •

HOW·TO·PLAY TEXAS·HOLD'EM

EVERY PLAYER IS DEALT TWO CARDS FACE DOWN. THESE ARE YOUR 'HOLE CARDS'. THEN THERE IS A ROUND OF BETTING WHERE YOU CAN CHECK, BET OR FOLD, KNOWN AS PRE-FLOP AND WHAT YOU SHOULD DO IS DEPENDS ON THOSE HOLE CARDS, OR STARTING HAND.

APPETIZERS

PIZZA PAN CHEESE BREAD 5
Garlic Butter • Mozzarella • Parmesan

SPICY BLACK BEAN HUMMUS 8
Fresh Lime • Feta • Corn Relish

CHICKEN BITES 9
Boneless Wings • Moonshine BBQ • Celery
Summer Camp Ranch

CLASSIC ITALIAN MEATBALLS 9
Grandma's Marinara • Herbed Ricotta
Shaved Asiago

PRETZELS & BEER CHEESE FONDUTA 7
Pretzel Dough • Sea Salt
New Belgium Cheddar

STUFFED MUSHROOMS 9
Local TX Sausage • Goat Cheese
Breadcrumbs • Garlic Parmesan • Alfredo

MOZZARELLA BRUSCHETTA 8
Tomato • Artisan Mozzarella
Balsamic • Fresh Basil • Red Onion
Olive Oil Crostini • Red Onion

BAKED PASTAS
*Chicken, Sausage, Veggies (+3)

BAKED BUCATINI CARBONARA 12
Thick-Cut Bacon • White Wine • Garlic
Egg Yolk • Peppercorn Cream • Parmesan

BAKED RIGATONI & RICOTTA 11
Grandma's Marinara • Herbed Ricotta
Chili Flake • Mozzarella

SMOKED BRISKET MAC & CHEESE 12
Garlic Parmesan Alfredo • Sharp Cheddar
HAMM'S Chopped Brisket

FRESH SALADS

HERITAGE RANCH 4
Black Olive • Cucumber • Sharp Cheddar
Croutons • Tomato • Summer Camp Ranch

SEASONAL HARVEST 8
Arugula • Spinach • Seasonal Fruit
Candied Pecans • Red Onion • Gorgonzola
Shaken Vinaigrette

MEXICAN CAESAR 8
Shredded Pepper Jack • Tortilla Strips
Crispy Bacon • Spicy Creamy Caesar

ITALIAN CHOPPED 9
Red Onion • Kalamata Olive • Mushroom
Ham • Pepperoni • Salami • Pepperoncini
Fontina • Tomato Vinaigrette

SOUTHWESTERN COBB 9
Tomato • Red Bell Pepper • Roasted Corn
Bacon • Avocado • Hard Boiled Egg
Tortilla Strips • Sharp Cheddar
BBQ Summer Camp Ranch

ADD CHICKEN or VEGGIES (+$3)

HOT SANDWICHES
Served with Kettle Chips
Substitute Heritage Salad (+$2)

SOUTHSIDE 12
Slow Smoked Beef • Peppercorn Cream
Hot Peppers • Provolone • Turano Bun

ALL AMERICAN GRILLED CHEESE 11
Havarti • Sharp Cheddar • Thick-Cut Bacon
Tomato • Beer Braised Onions • TX Toast

SPICY MEATBALL GRINDER 12
Sliced Meatballs • TX Sausage • Provolone
Mozzarella • Grandma's Marinara
Turano Bun

WEST COAST BLT 12
Thick-Cut Bacon • Fried Egg • Avocado
Lettuce • Tomato • Garlic Aioli • TX Toast

A Real Treat!

Homemade Milkshake 5
Chocolate or Vanilla

Candy Bar Brownie 4
Crushed Candy Bar
Homemade Brownie

Ice Cream Sandwich 4
House Baked Cookies
Henry's Ice Cream

HERITAGE
PIZZA • TAPROOM

EAT DELICIOUS PIZZA
DRINK COLD
214.396.7333   INFO@H...

DRINK • COLD • BEER • DRINK • COLD • BEER

GROWLER
PROGRAM

DRINK • COLD • BEER • DRINK • COLD • BEER

GROWLERS TO-GO, PINTS TO STAY, PIZZA ALL DAY

HERITAGE
PIZZA AND TAPROOM

THE FINEST AMERICAN PIZZA IN TOWN • COLD BEER

ZA PIES
Two Sizes ★ BIG GUY: 14" Little Guy: 10" Only Minimal Substitutions Available

	10"	14"
...za Cheese • Feta • Garlic Olive Oil • Tomato ...kan • Baby Spinach	12	16
...Ham • Chicken • TX Bacon ...lack Pepper	13	17
...ES ^ ...essata • Fresh Mozzarella	12	16
...za Cheese • Canadian Bacon • Pepperoni ...Mushroom • Red Onion • Black Olive ...ckled Jalapeño *	13	17
...OAF ...memade Meatloaf	11	15
...ESE STEAK ...e • Slow Smoked Beef ...ns • Bell Pepper • Provolone	13	17
...E KALE ...shroom • Tomato • Baby Kale ...Goat Cheese	12	16
...A ...Bacon • Pineapple • Salted Cashews ...Cheddar	12	16
...CRITA ...Mozzarella • Fresh Basil • Shaved Asiago	11	15
...s Wings • Bacon • Blue Cheese ...mer Camp Ranch	11	15
...labrian Chili • Sopresatta • Genoa Salami	13	17
...Garlic • Roasted Corn • Black Beans ...House Pickled Jalapeno • Cilantro	12	16

BUILD YOUR OWN
↓ PIZZA ↓

Little Guy (10")	Big Guy (14")
8	**11**

Each custom pie comes with Classic Red Sauce & House Blend Cheese

SAUCES

Classic Red • Garlic Parmesan Alfredo
Moonshine BBQ • Summer Camp Ranch
Cashew Pesto • Buffalo
Spicy Red Sauce

CHEESES $1 | $2

Asiago • Feta • Cheddar
Gorgonzola • Fresh Mozzarella
Ricotta • Fontina

MEATS $1.5 | $2.5

Italian Sausage • Chicken
Pepperoni • Canadian Bacon • TX Bacon
Meatballs • Genoa Salami • Anchovies

VEGGIES & SUCH $1 | $2

Artichokes • Garlic • Mushrooms
Tomatoes • Red Onions • Bell Peppers
Carmelized Onions • Roasted Corn
Kalamata Olives • Baby Spinach
Black Olives • Cashews
Pepperoncinis

PREMIUM TOPPINGS $2 | $3

Sopresatta • Slow Smoked Beef
HAMM'S Chopped Brisket
Calabrian Chili • Goat Cheese

EAT DELICIOUS PIZZA
DRINK COLD BEER
H.P.Co   ★

A

A FRIEND OF MINE

afom.com.au; Australia

> pp. 148–149: **Embla**
> CLIENT: Embla
> CLIENT WEBSITE: embla.com.au
> PHOTOS: Courtesy of A Friend of Mine
> PHOTOGRAPHER: Sarah Anderson
> ADDITIONAL CREDITS: The signage was a collaboration with United Measures, produced by Decently Exposed. The tilt frame is by United Measures.

A PRACTICE FOR EVERYDAY LIFE

apracticeforeverydaylife.com; United Kingdom

> pp. 90–91: **Librairie Marian Goodman**
> CLIENT: Marian Goodman Gallery
> CLIENT WEBSITE: mariangoodman.com
> PHOTOS: Courtesy of A Practice for Everyday Life/Installation photography by Max Creasy
> ARCHITECTURE: OMMX

AKAONI DESIGN

akaoni.org; Japan

> pp. 218–219: **Koub**
> CLIENT: Koub
> CLIENT WEBSITE: bread-lab.com
> DESIGNER: Motoki Koitabashi
> PHOTOS: Kohei Shikama

> pp. 232–233: **Takahashi Beef Farm**
> CLIENT: Takahashi Beef Farm
> CLIENT WEBSITE: takahashi-beef.jp
> DESIGNER: Motoki Koitabashi
> PHOTOS: Isao Negishi
> COPYWRITER: Mikio Soramame
> WEB DESIGNER: Nobu Goto
> DESIGNER: Yugo Sato

ANAGRAMA

anagrama.com; Mexico

> pp. 14–17: **Sally Beauty Supply**
> CLIENT: Sally Beauty
> CLIENT WEBSITE: sallybeauty.com
> PHOTOS: Caroga Foto/carogafoto.com

> pp. 200–201: **Helvetimart**
> CLIENT: Helvetimart
> CLIENT WEBSITE: helvetimart.ch
> PHOTOS: Caroga Foto/carogafoto.com

ANGELINA PISCHIKOVA

behance.net/angelinapi1626; Belarus

> pp. 156–157: **Anflor***
> CLIENT: AIDA Pioneer
> CLIENT WEBSITE: aidapioneer.by
> DESIGN, ART DIRECTION: Angelina Pischikova
> PHOTOS: Karina Zhukovskaya
> COPYWRITER: Vladimir Varava

ANJE JAGER

anjejager.com; Germany

> pp. 28–29: **And the Friet**
> CLIENT: Kenji Onozawa
> CLIENT WEBSITE: andthefriet.com
> ILLUSTRATOR: Anje Jager
> ART DIRECTION: Naomi Hirabayashi
> DESIGN: Naomi Hirabayashi, Kumiko Hoshino
> PHOTOS: Courtesy of Anje Jager

ATHLETICS

athleticsnyc.com
United States

> pp. 150–151: **Aska**
> CLIENT: Aska
> CLIENT WEBSITE: askanyc.com
> DESIGNER: Malcolm Buick
> PHOTOS: Courtesy of Athletics (p. 150 left middle, right top, right bottom, p. 151 right top), Charlie Bennet (p. 150 left top, left bottom, p. 151 right bottom, right middle), Tuukka Koski (p. 151 left top)
> ADDITIONAL CREDITS: Carl von Arbin

> pp. 152–153: **Carlen Parfums**
> CLIENT: Carlen Parfums
> CLIENT WEBSITE: carlenparfums.com
> DESIGNER: Jason Gnewikow
> PHOTOS: Pippa Drummond, Pippa Drummond & Zander Abranowicz (p. 153 right top)

ATLAS

designbyatlas.com; Spain

> pp. 12–13: **Eolo**
> CLIENT: Eolo Hotel and Restaurant
> CLIENT WEBSITE: eolopatagonia.com
> PHOTOS: José Hevia (p. 12 left bottom, p. 13 right top, right middle, left bottom, right bottom), Borja Bellvé (p. 12 top, right bottom, p. 13 left middle)
> CREATIVE DIRECTION: Astrid Stavro, Pablo Martín (Atlas)

B

BASE DESIGN

basedesign.com; Belgium

> pp. 154–155: **Graanmarkt 13**
> CLIENT: Graanmarkt 13
> CLIENT WEBSITE: graanmarkt13.com
> DESIGN: Lara Berg, Fumi Congan, Thomas Byttebier, Jasmine De Bruycker
> PHOTOS: Courtesy of Base Design, Filip Vanzieleghem (p. 155 top), Jesse Willems (p. 154 right top)

BIENAL COMUNICACIÓN

bienal.mx; Mexico

> pp. 40–41: **La Valise**
> CLIENT: La Valise Hotels CDMX
> CLIENT WEBSITE: lavalise.com
> CREATIVE DIRECTOR: Carlos Martínez Trujillo
> DESIGNER: Juventino Vázquez
> PHOTOS: Courtesy of Bienal, Fernanda Linage (p. 40 right top), Eugenia Díaz (p. 40 left top, p. 40 bottom, p. 41 top)

BLOK DESIGN

blokdesign.com; Canada

> pp. 42–43: **Summerhill Market**
> CLIENT: Summerhill Market
> CLIENT WEBSITE: summerhillmarket.com
> DESIGNER: Vanessa Eckstein, Jaclyn Hudson, Steven Tachauer
> PHOTOS: Courtesy of Blok Design
> CREATIVE DIRECTORS: Vanessa Eckstein, Marta Cutler
> COPYWRITING: Marta Cutler
> ILLUSTRATOR: Flavia Lopez

> pp. 136–137: **The Broadview Hotel**
> CLIENT: The Broadview Hotel
> CLIENT WEBSITE: thebroadviewhotel.ca
> DESIGNER: Vanessa Eckstein, Jaclyn Hudson, Steven Tachauer
> PHOTOS: Courtesy of Blok Design
> CREATIVE DIRECTION: Vanessa Eckstein, Marta Cutler
> COPYWRITING: Marta Cutler

BRAVO CREATIVE

bravo.rocks; Singapore

> pp. 44–45: **Full of Luck Club**
> CLIENT: The Allied Folks
> CLIENT WEBSITE: fullofluck.com
> CREATIVE DIRECTOR: Edwin Tan
> GRAPHIC DESIGNER: Zheng FangTing
> PHOTOS: Courtesy of Bravo Creative Pte
> INTERIOR DESIGN: FARM

BUENAVENTURA

buenaventura.pro; Spain

> pp. 170–171: **Pedro Salmerón**
> CLIENT: Pedro Salmerón
> CLIENT WEBSITE: pedrosalmeron.com
> PHOTOS: Courtesy of Buenaventura Studio

> pp. 216–217: **Rufino 1949**
> CLIENT: Rufino 1949
> CLIENT WEBSITE: rufino1949.com
> PHOTOS: Marietta Arco

BUREAU COLLECTIVE

bureaucollective.ch; Switzerland

> pp. 56–57: **Einholz**
> CLIENT: Einholz
> CLIENT WEBSITE: einholz.ch
> DESIGN: Ollie Schaich, Ruedi Zürcher
> PHOTOS: Courtesy of Bureau Collective

> pp. 58–59: **Kafi Franz**
> CLIENT: Kafi Franz
> CLIENT WEBSITE: kafifranz.ch
> DESIGN: Ollie Schaich, Ruedi Zürcher
> PHOTOS: Courtesy of Bureau Collective

BURGESS STUDIO

burgess-studio.co.uk; United Kingdom

> pp. 202–203: **Harp Lane Deli**
> CLIENT: Harp Lane Deli
> CLIENT WEBSITE: harplane.com
> PHOTOS: Courtesy of Burgess Studio

BY NORTH

bynorth.no; Norway

> pp. 172–173: **Glasshytta Vikten**
> CLIENT: Glasshytta Vikten
> CLIENT WEBSITE: glasshyttavikten.no
> PHOTOS: Morten Iveland, by north

C

CANAPÉ AGENCY

canape.ua; Ukraine

> pp. 122–125: **Roll Club**
> CLIENT: Roll Club
> CLIENT WEBSITE: roll-club.kh.ua
> PHOTOS: Courtesy of Canapé Agency

CODEFRISKO

codefrisko.com; Belgium

> pp. 174–175: **Le Chalet de La Forét**
> CLIENT: Pascal Devalkeneer
> CLIENT WEBSITE: lechaletdelaforet.be
> DESIGN: Audrey Schayes
> PHOTOS: Courtesy of Codefrisko, Oskar (p. 175 top), Xavier Harcq, Big Book (p. 174 left bottom, p. 175 left bottom) Xavier Harcq (p. 175 right bottom)

> pp. 176–177: **Senteurs d'Ailleurs**
> CLIENT: Senteurs d'Ailleurs
> CLIENT WEBSITE: senteursdailleurs.com
> DESIGN: Audrey Schayes
> PHOTOS: Courtesy of Codefrisko, Christophe Coënon

COMMISSION STUDIO

commission.studio; United Kingdom

> pp. 88–89: **Institute**
> CLIENT: Nathaniel Brown, INSTITUTE
> CLIENT WEBSITE: studio.institute
> PHOTOS: Luke Evans

COMMUNAL

communal.mx; Mexico

> pp. 6–7: **Salón Sociedad**
> CLIENT: Heineken México
> PHOTOS: Courtesy of Communal

D

DAN BLACKMAN

danblackman.com; USA

> pp. 140–147: **Saint Lou's Assembly**
> CLIENT: 16" on Center (16OC)
> CLIENT WEBSITE: saintlouschicago.com
> PHOTOS: Courtesy of Dan Blackman

> pp. 246–247: **The Moneygun**
> CLIENT: 16" on Center (16OC)
> CLIENT WEBSITE: moneygunchicago.com
> PHOTOS: Courtesy of Dan Blackman

DEUTSCHE & JAPANER

deutscheundjapaner.com; Germany

> pp. 38–39: **Bonechina**
> CLIENT: Bonechina Bar
> CLIENT WEBSITE: bonechinabar.com
> PHOTOS: Courtesy of Deutsche und Japaner

> pp. 106–107: **Opaak**
> CLIENT: Opaak
> CLIENT WEBSITE: opaak.de
> PHOTOS: Eva Baales

F

F61 WORK ROOM

f61room.com; Russian Federation

> pp. 210–213: **Zoldi**
> CLIENT: Zoldi
> CLIENT WEBSITE: zoldijewels.com
> DESIGN: Svetlana Lomakina, Alan Bur
> PHOTOS: Anatoly Vasiliev
> WEB DEVELOPMENT: Viktor Shkidina

FABIO ONGARATO DESIGN

fabioongaratodesign.com.au; Australia

> pp. 166–167: **Kisumé**
> CLIENT: The Lucas Group
> CLIENT WEBSITE: kisume.com.au
> PHOTOS: Mark Roper
> ARCHITECTURE: Wood Marsh Architecture.
> ARTISTS: Nobuyoshi Araki & Polly Borland

FÖDA STUDIO

fodastudio.com; USA

> pp. 96–97: **Hewn**
> CLIENT: Hewn
> CLIENT WEBSITE: hewnaustin.com
> DESIGN: Jett Butler, Tom Ahn, Dale Wallain
> PHOTOS: Nick Simonite

FUTURA

byfutura.com; Mexico

> pp. 20–21: **Remoto House**
> CLIENT: Remoto
> PHOTOS: Rodrigo Chapa

G

GLASFURD & WALKER

glasfurdandwalker.com; Canada

> pp. 128–131: **Botanist**
> CLIENT: Fairmont Pacific Rim
> CLIENT WEBSITE: www.fairmont.com
> PHOTOS: Concept photography by Ian Lanternman, Interior photography by Ema Peters
> INTERIOR DESIGN: Ste Marie Design

> pp. 132–133: **Juke Fried Chicken**
> CLIENT: Juke Fried Chicken
> CLIENT WEBSITE: jukefriedchicken.com
> PHOTOS: Courtesy of Glasfurd & Walker

H

HAIGH + MARTINO

haighandmartino.com; USA

> pp. 138–139: **Liars Bench Beer Co**
> CLIENT: Liars Bench Beer Co
> CLIENT WEBSITE: liarsbenchbeer.com
> PHOTOS: Courtesy of Haigh + Martino

HIGH TIDE

hightidenyc.com; USA

> pp. 26–27: **Dig Inn**
> CLIENT: Dig Inn
> CLIENT WEBSITE: diginn.com
> PHOTOS: Kevin Kunstadt (p. 27 middle), Robert Bredvad (p. 26 left top, bottom, p. 27 left bottom, right bottom), Christian Harder (p. 27 right top)

HOCHBURG

hochburg.net; Germany

> pp. 80–81: **Kitz Hotel**
> CLIENT: Kitz Hotel
> CLIENT WEBSITE: hotelkitz.de
> PHOTOS: Courtesy of Hochbu

I

IMPULSO STUDIO

instagram.com/impulso.studio; France

> pp. 50–51: **GF–LIMA**
> CLIENT: GF–LIMA
> PHOTOS: Courtesy of Impulso Studio

J

JENS NILSSON

jens-nilsson.com; Sweden

> pp. 82–83: **Maldini Studios**
> CLIENT: Maldini Studios
> CLIENT WEBSITE: maldinistudios.se
> PHOTOS: Courtesy of Jens Nilsson

K

KARLA HEREDIA MARTINEZ

behance.net/karlachic; Mexico

> pp. 18–19: **Alba Suarez**
> CLIENT: Alba Suarez
> CLIENT WEBSITE: albasuarez.mx
> PHOTOS: Courtesy of Karla Heredia Martinez

KIKU OBATA & COMPANY

kikuobata.com; United Kingdom

> pp. 104–105: **Velvet Coat**
> CLIENT: Velvet Coat
> CLIENT WEBSITE: velvetcoat.us
> DESIGN: Kiku Obata & Company
> PHOTOS: Courtesy of Kiku Obata & Company

KUUDES

kuudes.com; Finland, Sweden

> pp. 52–53: **Kolme Perunaa**
> CLIENT: Kolme Perunaa
> CLIENT WEBSITE: kolmeperunaa.com
> DESIGN: Piëtke Vi
> PHOTOS: Katja Hagelstam

L

LAND

workbyland.com; USA

> pp. 222–231: **Madre Mezcal**
> CLIENT: Madre Mezcal
> CLIENT WEBSITE: madremezcal.com
> DESIGNER: Ryan Rhodes, Caleb Everitt
> PHOTOS: Stefan Wigand, Tony Farfalla, Clay Grier

LARSSEN & AMARAL

larssenamaral.no; Norway

> pp. 66–67: **Formbar**
> CLIENT: Formbar Glassverksted
> CLIENT WEBSITE: formbar.no
> PHOTOS: Courtesy of Larssen & Amaral and Formbar

LETA SOBIERAJSKI

letasobierajski.com; USA

> pp. 46–49: **Le Turtle**
> CLIENT: Le Turtle
> CLIENT WEBSITE: leturtle.fr
> GRAPHIC DESIGN, ART DIRECTION: Wade Jeffree and Leta Sobierajski
> TYPE DEVELOPMENT: The Designer's Foundry
> PHOTOS (INTERIOR): Scottie Cameron

> pp. 118–119: **RŪH Collective**
CLIENT: RŪH Collective
CLIENT WEBSITE: ruhcollective.com
GRAPHIC DESIGN: Leta Sobierajski
PHOTOS: Courtesy of Leta Sobierajski

LOBBY DESIGN

lobbydesign.se; Sweden

> pp. 114–115: **Vinköket**
CLIENT: Bockholmengruppen
CLIENT WEBSITE: vinkoket.com
DESIGN: Filip Callas
PHOTOS: Sanna Dahlén

LOTTA NIEMINEN STUDIO

lottanieminen.com; United States

> pp. 84–85: **Rent The Runway**
CLIENT: Rent The Runway
CLIENT WEBSITE: renttherunway.com
PHOTOGRAPHER: Lotta Nieminen (portfolio), Marko Macpherson (campaign)
PRINTED IMPLEMENTATIONS: René Graham-Bastien

LUNDGREN+LINDQVIST

lundgrenlindqvist.se; Norway

> pp. 60–63: **Markus Form**
CLIENT: Markus Form
CLIENT WEBSITE: markusform.se
PHOTOS: Kalle Sanner

M

MADISON TIERNEY

instagram.com/madisontierney; Australia

> pp. 116–117: **Graze**
CLIENT: Graze
PHOTOS: Courtesy of Madison Tierney

MARTA VELUDO

martaveludo.com; Netherlands

> pp. 108–109: **Airdate**
CLIENT: Men at Work
CLIENT WEBSITE: menatwork.nl
PHOTOS: Courtesy of Marta Veludo
CAMPAIGN PHOTOS: Jeroen Mantel
COPY: Claudia Kopardi

MENTA

estudiomenta.mx; Mexico

> pp. 236–237: **Era Ceramics**
CLIENT: Era Ceramics
CLIENT WEBSITE: eraceramics.com
PHOTOS: Courtesy of Menta

MILCH+HONIG DESIGNKULTUR

milchundhonig-dk.de; Germany

> pp. 178–179: **Salome**
CLIENT: Laura Langgärtner/Salome
CLIENT WEBSITE: salome-goldschmiede.de
CREATIVE DIRECTOR: Christina John
PHOTOS: Philipp Altheimer
MODEL: Anna Meier

MILDRED & DUCK

mildredandduck.com
Australia

> pp. 134–135: **Sister**
CLIENT: Sister
CLIENT WEBSITE: sister.melbourne
PHOTOS: Shelley Horan
STYLING: Sigiriya Brown

> pp. 168–169: **Souk**
CLIENT: Souk
CLIENT WEBSITE: soukmelbourne.com.au
PHOTOS: Shelley Horan
STYLING: Sigiriya Brown

MOODLEY BRAND IDENTITY

moodley.at; Austria

> pp. 76–79: **Hannes Reeh**
CLIENT: Hannes Reeh
CLIENT WEBSITE: hannesreeh.at
DESIGNER: Volkmar Weiss
PHOTOS: Daniel Gebhart de Koekoek

MOTHER DESIGN

motherdesign.com;
United Kingdom and USA

> pp. 180–181: **Callen-Lorde**
CLIENT: Callen-Lorde Community Health Center
CLIENT WEBSITE: callen-lorde.org
DESIGNER: Mother Design New York
PHOTOS: Courtesy of Mother Design

O

ODDDS

oddds.com; Singapore

> pp. 94–95: **Informal Anymade Cafe**
CLIENT: Self-initiated, Oddds
PHOTOS: Courtesy of Oddds

OLSSON BARBIERI

olssonbarbieri.com; Norway

> pp. 126–127: **Territoriet**
CLIENT: Territoriet Wine Bar
CLIENT WEBSITE: territoriet.no
DESIGNER: Henrik Olsson and Erika Barbieri
PHOTOS: Sigve Aspelund (Tinagent) (p. 126 left top, p. 126 bottom, p. 127 left and right middle, middle bottom), Lars Myhren Holand (p. 126 right top, p. 127 left bottom, right bottom) Marie Thorsen (p. 127 left top)
SOUND MACHINE: build by Stian Korntvedt Ruud

> pp. 158–159: **Balholm Handverkcider**
CLIENT: Balholm
CLIENT WEBSITE: balholm.no
DESIGNER: Henrik Olsson and Erika Barbieri
PHOTOS: Sigve Aspelund (Tinagent)

OMFGCO

omfgco.com; United States

> pp. 30–37: **Serra**
CLIENT: Groundworks
CLIENT WEBSITE: shopserra.com
DESIGNER: OMFGCO + JHL Design
PHOTOS: Courtesy of OMFGCO; Half Court Studio

> pp. 162–163: **The Laylow**
CLIENT: Rockbridge Capital
CLIENT WEBSITE: laylowwaikiki.com
PHOTOS: Courtesy of OMFGCO; Andrew Rizer
ARCHITECT: DLR Group

OSCAR MAIA

oscarmaia.com; Portugal

> pp. 242–245: **Barbearia Porto**
CLIENT: Barber Shop Barbearia Porto
CLIENT WEBSITE: instagram.com/barbeariaporto
PHOTOS: Courtesy of Oscar Maia

P

PARÁMETRO

parametro.studio; Mexico

> pp. 4–5: **Hula del Hawaii**
CLIENT: Hula del Hawaii
CLIENT WEBSITE: instagram.com/huladelhawaii
PHOTOS: Ana Hinojosa

PARASOL

parasol-projects.com; Sweden

> pp. 8–9: **Savoir Joaillerie**
CLIENT: Savoir Joaillerie
PHOTOS: Courtesy of Savoir Joaillerie, Fredrik Altinell and Trevor Good (Campaign), Alexander Crispin (Other)

PARIS+HENDZEL CO.

parishendzelstudio.com; Poland

> pp. 186–187: **Ministerstwo Dobrego Mydła**
CLIENT: Ministerstwo Dobrego Mydła
CLIENT WEBSITE: ministerstwodobregomydla.pl
DESIGNER: Łukasz Hendzel
PHOTOS: Agnieszka Pattynowicz
PROCESS PHOTOS: Borys Roswadowski

PASSPORT

wearepassport.com; United Kingdom

> pp. 164–165: **The Faversham**
CLIENT: The Faversham
CLIENT WEBSITE: thefaversham.com
PHOTOS: Courtesy of Passport
INTERIOR/WEDDING PHOTOS: The Faversham

PENTAGRAM

pentagram.com; United States

> pp. 120–121: **Van Leeuwen**
CLIENT: Van Leeuwen
CLIENT WEBSITE: vanleeuwenicecream.com
DESIGNER: Natasha Jen, Joseph Han
PHOTOS: Courtesy of Pentagram

> pp. 182–183: **On Rye**
CLIENT: On Rye
DESIGNER: Michael Bierut, Jesse Reed
PHOTOS: Bobby Doherty

> pp. 188–189: **The Wing**
CLIENT: The Wing
CLIENT WEBSITE: the-wing.com
DESIGNER: Emily Oberman, Christina Hogan, Alex Stikeleather, Deva Pardue
PHOTOS: Claudia Mandlik

PERKY BROS.

perkybros.com; United States

> pp. 184–185: **Little Wolf**
> **CLIENT:** Little Wolf Coffee
> **CLIENT WEBSITE:** littlewolf.coffee
> **PHOTOS:** Brett Warren, Mark Spooner

> pp. 238–239: **Common Lot**
> **CLIENT:** Common Lot
> **CLIENT WEBSITE:** commonlot.com
> **PHOTOS:** Brett Warren, Daniel Krieger

PINKEYE CROSSOVER STUDIO

pinkeye.be; Belgium

> pp. 198–199: **Umamido**
> **CLIENT:** Umamido
> **CLIENT WEBSITE:** umamido.be
> **DESIGNER:** Pinkeye Designstudio
> **PHOTOS:** Courtesy of Pinkeye Designstudio

S

SAVVY STUDIO

savvy-studio.net; Mexico

> pp. 22–23: **Gowanus Inn & Yard**
> **CLIENT:** Gowanus Inn & Yard
> **CLIENT WEBSITE:** gowanusinn.com
> **PHOTOS:** Courtesy of Savvy Studio

> pp. 24–25: **Hüngry Beast**
> **CLIENT:** Hüngry Beast
> **CLIENT WEBSITE:** thehungrybeasts.com
> **PHOTOS:** Courtesy of Savvy Studio

SEBASTIAN HAUS

hausgemacht.es; Germany

> pp. 10–11: **Feiner Herr**
> **CLIENT:** Yannick Pfeiffer—Feiner Herr, Berlin
> **CLIENT WEBSITE:** feinerherr.net
> **DESIGNER:** Hojin Kang, Sebastian Haus
> **PHOTOS:** Johannes Hoeller

SHAUN HILL

shaunhill.co.za; South Africa

> pp. 190–193: **Baba G**
> **CLIENT:** Baba G/Rotisserie and Deli
> **CLIENT WEBSITE:** babag.co.za
> **DESIGNER:** Shaun Hill + Candice Bondi
> **PHOTOS:** Candice Bondi
> **STYLING:** Candice Bondi + Shaun Hill
> **ILLUSTRATION:** Shaun Hill

SKINN BRANDING AGENCY

skinn.be; Belgium

> pp. 196–197: **Group Monument**
> **CLIENT:** Group Monument
> **CLIENT WEBSITE:** monument.be
> **CREATIVE DIRECTOR:** Kurt De Vileghere
> **DESIGNER:** Sophie Bossuyt
> **PHOTOS:** Bob Janssens

SNASK

snask.com; Sweden

> pp. 110–113: **Kaibosh**
> **CLIENT:** Kaibosh
> **CLIENT WEBSITE:** kaibosh.com
> **PHOTOS:** Courtesy of SNASK

SONIA CASTILLO STUDIO

soniacastillo.com; Spain

> pp. 54–55: **IGC Art Conservation & Restoration**
> **CLIENT:** IGC Art Conservation & Restoratio
> **PHOTOS:** Courtesy of Sonia Castillo Studio

SP-GD

sp-gd.com; Australia

> pp. 64–65: **Andrew Burns Architecture**
> **CLIENT:** Andrew Burns Architecture
> **CLIENT WEBSITE:** andrewburns.net.au
> **PHOTOS:** Courtesy of SP-GD

STUDIO ROUND

round.com.au; Australia

> pp. 68–75: **Meatsmith**
> **CLIENT:** Meatsmith
> **CLIENT WEBSITE:** meatsmith.com.au
> **PHOTOGRAPHER:** Tom Blackford for Studio Round
> **INTERIOR DESIGN:** Herbert & Mason

> pp. 86–87: **The Big Group**
> **CLIENT:** The Big Group
> **CLIENT WEBSITE:** thebiggroup.com.au
> **PHOTOS:** Courtesy of Studio Round

> pp. 240–241: **Ricky & Pinky**
> **CLIENT:** Ricky & Pinky
> **CLIENT WEBSITE:** buildersarmshotel.com.au
> **PHOTOS:** Courtesy of Studio Round

STUDIO&

studioand.nl; Spain

> pp. 208–209: **RENS**
> **CLIENT:** RENS
> **CLIENT WEBSITE:** madebyrens.com
> **PHOTOS:** Courtesy of Studio&
> **COLLABORATION WITH:** Mariëlle van Genderen

T

TRACTORBEAM

tractorbeam.com; United States

> pp. 92–93: **44 Build & Tradesmith**
> **CLIENT:** 44 Build & Tradesmith
> **CLIENT WEBSITE:** 44build.com
> **PHOTOS:** Courtesy of Tractorbeam

> pp. 98–103: **Belmont Hotel**
> **CLIENT:** Belmont Hotel
> **CLIENT WEBSITE:** belmontdallas.com
> **PHOTOS:** Courtesy of Tractorbeam

> pp. 220–221: **Blind Butcher**
> **CLIENT:** Blind Butcher
> **CLIENT WEBSITE:** theblindbutcher.com
> **PHOTOS:** Courtesy of Tractorbeam

> pp. 248–251: **Heritage Pizza**
> **CLIENT:** 33 Restaurant Brands
> **CLIENT WEBSITE:** heritagepizza.com
> **PHOTOS:** Courtesy of Tractorbeam

TWO TIMES ELLIOTT

2xelliott.co.uk
United Kingdom

> pp. 160–161: **The Dayrooms Café**
> **CLIENT:** The Dayrooms Café
> **CLIENT WEBSITE:** thedayroomscafe.com
> **PHOTOS:** Courtesy of Two Times Elliot

V

VIOLAINE & JÉRÉMY

violaineetjeremy.fr; France

> pp. 204–207: **Big Fernand**
> **CLIENT:** Big Fernand
> **CLIENT WEBSITE:** bigfernand.com
> **DESIGNER:** Jérémy Schneider, Violaine Orsoni
> **PHOTOS:** Courtesy of Studio Violaine & Jérémy
> **ILLUSTRATION AND FONT CREATION:** Jérémy Schneider

VRINTS-KOLSTEREN

vrints-kolsteren.com; Belgium

> pp. 214–215: **Shana Teugels**
> **CLIENT:** Shana Teugels
> **CLIENT WEBSITE:** shanateugels.com
> **PHOTOS:** Courtesy of Vrints-Kolsteren

Z

ZÉ STUDIO

ze-studio.com; Australia

> pp. 194–195: **Fatking**
> **CLIENT:** Fatking
> **CLIENT WEBSITE:** fatkingfilms.com
> **PHOTOS:** Courtesy of Zé Studio
> **WEB DEVELOPMENT:** Lundgren+Lindqvist

> pp. 234–235: **Cake Wines Cellar Door**
> **CLIENT:** Cake Wines
> **CLIENT WEBSITE:** cakewines.com
> **PHOTOS:** Traianos Pakioufakis

UPSTART!
VISUAL IDENTITIES FOR START-UPS AND NEW BUSINESSES

This book was conceived, edited, and designed by GESTALTEN.

Edited by ROBERT KLANTEN, ANNA SINOFZIK, and ANJA KOUZNETSOVA

Preface and case studies by ANNA SINOFZIK
Project texts written by REBECCA SILUS

Project Management by BRITTA GIMMINI, LARS PIETZSCHMANN

Design and layout by ANNA SINOFZIK
Cover design by JAN BLESSING

Typeface: Futura PT by ISABELLA CHAEVA and VLADIMIR YEFIMOV, based on the original Futura design by PAUL RENNER

Cover photography: Courtesy of F61 WORK ROOM, image by ANATOLY VASILIEV
Back cover photography (from top to bottom): COURTESY OF ANJE JAGER, ANA HINOJOSA, DAN BLACKMAN, KIKU OBATA & COMPANY, and SAVVY STUDIO

Printed by NINO DRUCK GMBH, Neustadt/Weinstrasse
Made in Germany

Published by Gestalten, Berlin 2018
ISBN 978-3-89955-954-5

© Die Gestalten Verlag GmbH & Co. KG, Berlin 2018

All rights reserved. No part of this publication may be reproduced or transmitted in any form or by any means, electronic or mechanical, including photocopy or any storage and retrieval system, without permission in writing from the publisher.

Respect copyrights, encourage creativity!

For more information, and to order books, please visit gestalten.com.

Bibliographic information published by the Deutsche Nationalbibliothek. The Deutsche Nationalbibliothek lists this publication in the Deutsche Nationalbibliografie; detailed bibliographic data are available online at dnb.d-nb.de.

None of the content in this book was published in exchange for payment by commercial parties or designers; Gestalten selected all included work based solely on its artistic merit.

This book was printed on paper certified according to the standards of the FSC®.